THE DARK SIDE OF TRANSLATION

We tend to consider translation as something good, virtuous and bright, but it can also function as an instrument of concealment, silencing and misdirection—as something that darkens and obscures. Propaganda, misinformation, narratives of trauma and imagery of the enemy—to mention just a few of the negative phenomena that shape our lives—show patterns of communication in which translation either functions as a weapon or constitutes a space of conflict. But what does this dark side of translation look like? How does it work?

Ground-breaking in its theoretical conception and pioneering in its thematic approach, this book unites international scholars from a range of disciplines including philosophy, translation studies, literary theory, ecocriticism, game studies, history and political science. With examples that illustrate complex theoretical and philosophical issues, this book also has a major focus on the translational dimension of ecology and climate change.

Transdisciplinary and topical, this book is key reading for researchers, scholars and advanced students of translation studies, literature and related areas.

Federico Italiano is Senior Researcher at the Institute of Culture Studies and Theatre History, part of the Austrian Academy of Sciences in Vienna; University Lecturer in Comparative Literature at LMU Munich and at the University of Innsbruck; and Visiting Professor of Translation Studies at the University of Graz. His recent publications include *Translation and Geography* (2016) and an anthology of young European poetry, *Grand Tour* (with Jan Wagner, 2019). An Italian poet and translator, Federico Italiano has published five poetry collections.

THE DARK SIDE OF TRANSLATION

Edited by Federico Italiano

LONDON AND NEW YORK

First published 2020
by Routledge
2 Park Square, Milton Park, Abingdon, Oxon OX14 4RN

and by Routledge
52 Vanderbilt Avenue, New York, NY 10017

Routledge is an imprint of the Taylor & Francis Group, an informa business

© 2020 selection and editorial matter, Federico Italiano; individual chapters, the contributors

The right of Federico Italiano to be identified as the author of the editorial material, and of the authors for their individual chapters, has been asserted in accordance with sections 77 and 78 of the Copyright, Designs and Patents Act 1988.

All rights reserved. No part of this book may be reprinted or reproduced or utilised in any form or by any electronic, mechanical, or other means, now known or hereafter invented, including photocopying and recording, or in any information storage or retrieval system, without permission in writing from the publishers.

Trademark notice: Product or corporate names may be trademarks or registered trademarks, and are used only for identification and explanation without intent to infringe.

British Library Cataloguing-in-Publication Data
A catalogue record for this book is available from the British Library

Library of Congress Cataloging-in-Publication Data
Names: Italiano, Federico, 1976- editor.
Title: The dark side of translation / edited by Federico Italiano.
Description: 1. | New York : Taylor and Francis, 2020. | Includes bibliographical references and index.
Identifiers: LCCN 2019045967 | ISBN 9780367337278 (hardback) | ISBN 9780367337285 (paperback) | ISBN 9780429321528 (ebook)
Subjects: LCSH: Translating and interpreting–Political aspects. | Translating and interpreting–Errors.
Classification: LCC P306.97.P65 D37 2020 | DDC 418/.02–dc23
LC record available at https://lccn.loc.gov/2019045967

ISBN: 978-0-367-33727-8 (hbk)
ISBN: 978-0-367-33728-5 (pbk)
ISBN: 978-0-429-32152-8 (ebk)

Typeset in Bembo
by Swales & Willis, Exeter, Devon, UK

CONTENTS

List of contributors vii
Acknowledgements x

The dark side: an introduction 1
Federico Italiano

PART I
(Post-)colonial translations and hegemonic practices 17

1 Beyond a taste for the dark side: the apparatus of area and the modern regime of translation under *Pax Americana* 19
 Jon Solomon

2 The language of the hegemon: migration and the violence of translation 38
 Monika Mokre

PART II
The Holocaust and the translator's ambiguity 57

3 Primo Levi's *grey zone* and the ambiguity of translation in Nazi concentration camps 59
 Michaela Wolf

| 4 | Translating the uncanny, uncanny translation
Christoph Leitgeb | 75 |

PART III
The translation of climate change discourses and the ecology of knowledge   93

5	Shady dealings: translation, climate and knowledge *Michael Cronin*	95
6	Climate change and the dark side of translating science into popular culture *Alexa Weik von Mossner*	111
7	Darkness, obscurity, opacity: ecology in translation *Daniel Graziadei*	126

PART IV
Translation as zombification   143

| 8 | Zombie history: the undead in translation
Gudrun Rath | 145 |
| 9 | 'MmmRRRrr UrrRrRRrr!!': translating political anxieties into zombie language in digital games
Eugen Pfister | 161 |

Index   *176*

CONTRIBUTORS

Michael Cronin is 1776 Professor of French (Chair) in the Department of French at Trinity College, Dublin, and Director of the Trinity Centre for Literary and Cultural Translation. He is the author of many works on translation, language and culture, and his work has been translated into more than sixteen languages. He is an elected Member of the Royal Irish Academy, the Academia Europeae/Academy of Europe and is an Officer of the Ordre des Palmes Académiques. He is an Honorary Member of the Irish Translators' and Interpreters' Association.

Daniel Graziadei is Head of the Writing Centre and Assistant Professor at the Institute of Romance Philology at LMU Munich, Germany. He is currently working on a research project for his Habilitation, on intercultural misunderstandings in literature. His doctoral thesis (*Insel(n) im Archipel*), on the nissopoietical construction of islands and archipelagos in contemporary Caribbean literatures, was published in 2017, and his MA thesis on literary neoavantgarde groups in Latin America and the USA in 2008. When he isn't reading or researching, Daniel is translating poetry from Italian and Spanish to German, or writing and performing his own poetry (danielgraziadei.de).

Federico Italiano is Senior Researcher at the Institute of Culture Studies and Theatre History of the Austrian Academy of Sciences in Vienna, University Lecturer in Comparative Literature at LMU Munich and at the University of Innsbruck, and Visiting Professor of Translation Studies at the University of Graz. His recent publications include *Translation and Geography* (2016) and an anthology of young European poetry, *Grand Tour* (with Jan Wagner, 2019). An Italian poet and translator, Federico Italiano has published five poetry collections.

Christoph Leitgeb is a researcher in modern German literary studies at the Institute for Cultural Studies and Theatre History of the Austrian Academy of Science in Vienna. He publishes the scholarly magazine *Sprachkunst* and teaches at the universities of Salzburg and Vienna. Previously, he was a literary critic for the Austrian newspaper *Der Standard*, a university lecturer in Sheffield, Osaka and Olomouc, and a visiting professor at Leiden.

Monika Mokre is Senior Researcher at the Institute of Culture Studies and Theatre History of the Austrian Academy of Sciences in Vienna. She is a political scientist and political activist in the field of asylum and migration. Her research fields include democratic theory, asylum and migration politics, cultural politics, gender studies. She is the author of *Solidarität als Übersetzung. Überlegungen zum Refugee Protest Camp Vienna* (2015) and, jointly with Cornelia Bruell, of *Postmarxistisches Staatsverständnis* (2018).

Eugen Pfister is project manager of the SNF-Ambizione research project 'Horror—Game—Politics' at the Hochschule der Künste Bern (HKB). Born in 1980 in Vienna, he studied History and Political Sciences at the University of Vienna and the Université Paris-Sorbonne (Paris IV). From 2008 to 2013, he held a fellowship at the international research training group 'The History of Political Communication from the Antiquities to the 20th Century' at the Johann-Wolfgang-Goethe-Universität, Frankfurt am Main. He completed his PhD in co-tutelle at the Università degli Studi di Trento and the Johann-Wolfgang-Goethe-Universität. He is a founding member of the research group *Geschichtswissenschaft und Digitale Spiele* (gespielt.hypotheses.org).

Gudrun Rath is Professor of Cultural Studies at the University of Art and Design, Linz, Austria. She is a member of the Young Academy (Austrian Academy of Sciences, ÖAW) and holds a PhD from the University of Vienna. Her publications include *Zwischenzonen. Theorien und Fiktionen des Übersetzens* ('Interstices of Translation', 2013) and the edited volume *Zombies* (2014). At present, she is working on her second monograph on narratives of zombification from a historical and transatlantic perspective.

In a professional career covering Europe, East Asia and North America, **Jon Solomon** has concentrated his research activities on the biopolitics of translation, focusing on the specificity of translational and linguistic labour in the context of East Asia and East Asian studies. The modern regime of translation that governs this crucial form of social labour is a privileged place for understanding the relations among anthropological difference, geo-cultural area, areal divisions in the humanities and the abstractions of capitalist accumulation. His recent publications include, 'Logistical Species and Translational Process: A Critique of the Colonial-Imperial Modernity', *Intermédialités* 29 (2016).

Alexa Weik von Mossner is Associate Professor of American Studies at the University of Klagenfurt in Austria. Her research explores the theoretical intersections of cognitive science, affective narratology and environmental literature and film. She is the author of *Cosmopolitan Minds: Literature, Emotion, and the Transnational Imagination* (2014) and *Affective Ecologies: Empathy, Emotion, and Environmental Narrative* (2017).

Michaela Wolf is Associate Professor at the Department of Translation Studies, University of Graz. She is the author of *The Habsburg Monarchy's Many-Languaged Soul: Translating and Interpreting, 1848–1918* (2015), and the editor of *Interpreting in Nazi Concentration Camps* (2016). Her areas of teaching and research interest include translation sociology, cultural studies and translation, translation history, and translation and visual anthropology. Her present research focus is on communication among the Interbrigades of the Spanish Civil War.

ACKNOWLEDGEMENTS

The essays collected in this book stem from the papers, discussions and considerations that animated the international conference *The Dark Side of Translation*, which I organised in Vienna in 2017 on behalf of the Institute of Culture Studies and Theatre History of the Austrian Academy of Sciences. I am deeply thankful to the director of this institute, Michael Rössner, who not only approved and supported the realisation of said conference and made it possible, but also enriched our discussions with his profound knowledge, helping to lay the foundations for the conception of this book. I am very grateful to all the authors for their wonderful commitment to this project and their willingness to rework, revise and refine their chapters. A special thank goes to Routledge and its staff, in particular to Louisa Semlyen for firmly believing in this book and to Eleni Steck for her valuable support during production. Finally, I am most sincerely grateful, especially as a non-native English speaker, to Kirsty Jane Falconer for her meticulous, indispensable, spotless (I would go on with adjectives, but she would erase them) copy-editing of the book.

Federico Italiano
Vienna, Austria
September 2019

THE DARK SIDE

An introduction

Federico Italiano

We tend to consider translation as a cultural activity that enables communication and, in this sense, as something useful, good, virtuous and bright. Translation, however, be it a simple linguistic undertaking or a broader cross-cultural negotiation, can also function as an instrument of concealment, silencing and misdirection—as something that darkens and obscures. Post-colonial scholars have broadly demonstrated this already, but the dark side of translation is not limited to imperialism. Propaganda, misinformation, narratives of trauma and imagery of the enemy—to mention just a few of the gloomy phenomena that shape our lives—show patterns of communication in which translation either functions as a weapon or constitutes a space of conflict.

So what does this dark side of translation look like? How does it function? What are the shades and nuances that we can identify and study? What does the 'dark' colonial practice of translation have in common, for example, with the obscurity that pervades the uncanny dimension of translation? By operating a sort of 'dark adaptation'—as ophthalmologists call the adaptation of the sensitivity of the eye when the brightness of the environment decreases—this book explores these issues, uniting international scholars from a range of disciplines including philosophy, translation studies, literary theory, ecocriticism, game studies, history and political science. If we want to understand the forces that steer and shape communication, it is also crucial to try to fathom translation in its most unpleasant and murky configurations.

Dark practices

In the first English synonym dictionary ever written, *The Difference Between Words Esteemed Synonymous* (1766), the eclectic (if not eccentric) author, Reverend John Trusler, distinguishes between *darkness* and *obscurity* as follows: 'Darkneſs, ſeems to signify, something real, in opposition to light: Obscurity, is, a mere privation of brightness [...] darkness, implies, a state of life' (Trusler, 1766: I 66). If he is right, then darkness is something real. It exists on the ontological level in opposition to light. And as does light, so darkness too generates things, mostly dark things: '[W]hat will not a fearful man conceive in the dark? What strange forms of bugbears, devils, witches, goblins?' wrote Robert Burton (1961 [1621]: I 254). Etymologically, 'dark' (which comes from Middle English *deork*, from Old English *deorc*) is cognate to Old High German *tarchanjan*, meaning 'to hide, conceal', to Middle High German *terken*, 'to make dark, soil' and to Lithuanian *dárga*, which means 'dull, rainy weather' (cf. Partridge, 1966: 140). Usually, the adjective 'dark' denotes something destitute, or partially destitute, of light, such as colours or objects that do not reflect much light or approach shades of black—something as concrete, as real, in fact, as bad weather; however, like its Old German cognate *tarchanjan*, 'dark' stands for something hidden from knowledge, mysterious, inconspicuous. In this last acceptation, 'dark' is very close to one of its most proximate, Latinate synonyms: 'obscure'.

The title of this book, however, makes quite overt reference to two popular usages of the locution 'dark side'. The first one comes from the epic space opera and science-fiction saga *Star Wars*, created by George Lucas in 1977 and still running, supported by an almost planetary success. The second acceptation comes from the title of one of the greatest concept albums of rock history, *The Dark Side of the Moon*, released by British band Pink Floyd in 1973. The double allusion of the title also mirrors this twofold (if not manifold) meaning of dark side of translation.

One of the central narrative elements of *Star Wars* is the all-encompassing, all-driving Force, which creator George Lucas describes as 'a giant mass of energy in the universe that has a good side and a bad side' (Bouzereau, 1997: 181). The dark side of the Force is nourished by emotions such as resentment, aggression, fear and fury, and is used primarily by the Sith Lords, former Jedi seduced by the strength and the power that the dark side gives them. The light side of the Force, on the contrary, aligns with altruistic, positive attitudes such as mercy, selflessness, rectitude and empathy. Cultivated primarily by the Jedi, the light side can be defined as a distributive, participative, inclusive energy, whereas the dark side of the Force behaves as an exclusive drive that concentrates power in the hands of the few. Alluding to this acceptation of 'dark side' as defined by *Star Wars*, one of the meanings of the dark side of translation we must consider has to do with 'dark practices' such as colonisation, domination, manipulation, tyranny, war and so forth.

Of course, ours is not the first attempt to associate Star Wars with postcolonial practices. Ground-breaking, in this sense, was Salman Rushdie's article 'The Empire Writes Back with a Vengeance' (1982), in which he underlines the importance of post-colonial literatures ('writers from nations which have recently gained independence') as a challenge to the essentialist, homogenising logic of the British imperial system (Rushdie, 1982: 8). This article, in turn, inspired the no-less famous and influential book *The Empire Writes Back: Theory and Practice in Post-Colonial Literature* by Ashcroft, Griffiths and Tiffin, which is generally considered the first book to name and examine post-colonial writing as a field of cultural and literary study (1989). Interestingly enough, however, neither in Rushdie's article nor in *The Empire Writes Back* does translation play a paramount role. The concept of translation was simply not yet on the radar; or, at least, not to the extent it would be following the publication in 1994 of *Location of Culture* by of Homi K. Bhabha. In this true milestone of post-colonial criticism, Bhabha defines (cultural) translation as a negotiation between 'differential identities', as a 'staging of cultural difference' (Bhabha, 2005: 325). However, Bhabha is not as interested as we are, in this book, in the murky, shady corners of translation. For him, translations are the 'in-between spaces' that create 'the terrain for elaborating strategies of selfhood—singular or communal—that initiate new signs of identity, and innovative sites of collaboration, and contestation, in the act of defining the idea of society itself' (ibid.: 2).

Though he does not refer explicitly to *Star Wars*, Walter D. Mignolo, an Argentine semiotician and decolonial theorist, introduces the concept of dark, gloomy cultural practices in his *The Darker Side of the Renaissance: Literacy, Territoriality, Colonization* (1995). He uses the concept of 'darker side' in relation to the Renaissance to underline the rebirth of the classical tradition as a justification of colonial expansion.

> While the concept of *Renaissance* refers to a rebirth of classical legacies and the constitution of humanistic scholarship for human emancipation and *early modern period* emphasizes the emergence of a genealogy that announces the modern and the postmodern, the darker side of the Renaissance underlines, instead, the rebirth of the classical tradition as a justification of colonial expansion and the emergence of a genealogy (the early colonial period) that announces the colonial and the postcolonial
> *(Mignolo, 1995: vii, italics in the original)*

With the 'darker side' of the Renaissance, then, Mignolo singles out the relationship between humanism, literacy and racism. Arguing from an inter-semiotic and translational perspective, he describes the colonisation of languages, memories, and space that took place when the New World began to emerge in the European consciousness.

In another important work from the golden age of post-colonial theory-making, *The Poetics of Imperialism* (1997), Eric Cheyfitz explores how foreign and domestic policies are the translation of one another. 'Within its history', he argues, 'Anglo-American imperialism has alienated the world outside the West in the form of the other, so that it could dream the other's redemption in the form of the self' (ibid.: xiv). This 'dynamic of domination', as he argues, eradicates 'all the nuances of translation' to such an extent that 'the imperialist finds himself lost in the figurative, which he necessarily mistakes for the literal' (ibid.).

In his implacable analysis of the history of Anglo-American policy, Cheyfitz gives us an illuminating example of the dark, devious side of translation. Given the 'impossibility of translating the English notion of "selling land" into the [native] languages, which did not contain the concept of land as property, that is, as an alienable commodity' (Cheyfitz, 1997: 8), the English translated the natives into their civil code by forcibly designating Powhatan, the Chief of the Algonquians, as 'Emperor' of the Algonquians. In a ceremony held in 1608 at Powhatan's village of Werowocomoco, the new Emperor became automatically a legal subject of the English Crown, and his land part of the Crown (ibid). As civilised Europeans, in fact, the English could not simply steal the land from the natives as common thieves would do: they had to own it rightfully as property. Law has quite a few dark sides of its own, as history has proven.

Providing an intersection between cultural, post-colonial and translation studies, works produced in the 1990s by translation scholars such as André Lefevere and Susan Bassnett (Bassnett and Lefevere, 1990; Bassnet and Trivedi, 1998; Lefevere, 1992) investigated the relationship between translation and ideologies, focusing on power relations and the strategies of manipulation employed by translators in the service of power. In their editors' preface to *Translation, History & Culture* (1990), Bassnett and Lefevere point out that every translation is the 'rewriting of an original text' and 'all rewritings, whatever their intention, reflect a certain ideology and a poetics and as such manipulate literature to function in a given society in a given way' (ibid.: ix). In this sense, every translation is manipulation, 'undertaken in the service of power'. Understood in this way, translation displays many 'positive' facets, since it introduces 'new concepts, new genres, new devices', helping literature and society to evolve (ibid.).

> But rewriting [that is, translation] can also repress innovation, distort and contain, and in an age of ever increasing manipulation of all kinds, the study of the manipulation processes of literature are exemplified by translation can help us towards a greater awareness of the world in which we live.
>
> *(ibid.: ix)*

Another significant acceptation of 'dark', referring to translation within the *Star Wars* paradigm, is what Dipesh Chakrabarty calls 'rough'. In his highly influential book *Provincializing Europe*, he argues that the 'problem of capitalist modernity cannot any longer be seen simply as a sociological problem of historical transition [...] but as a problem of translation, as well'. Taking the example of the 'English-language monograph in area studies' and its 'standard, mechanically put together and least-read feature[s]', the glossaries, he argues that

> [n]o reader was ever seriously expected to interrupt their pleasure of reading by having to turn pages frequently to consult the glossary. The glossary reproduced a series of 'rough translations' of native terms, often borrowed from the colonialists themselves. These colonial translations were rough

not only in being approximate (and thereby inaccurate) but also in that they were meant to fit the rough-and-ready methods of colonial rule.

(Chakrabarty, 2000: 18)

However, even in their 'roughness', those translations were sharp, complex examples of cultural translation. Therefore, 'to challenge that model of "rough translation" is to pay critical and unrelenting attention to the very process of translation' (ibid.: 18). In his book, Chakrabarty claims that we should take translation in all seriousness, since what 'translation produces out of seeming "incommensurabilities" is neither an absence of relationship between dominant and dominating forms of knowledge nor equivalents that successfully mediate between differences, but precisely the partly opaque relationship we call "difference"' (ibid.).

In *The Translation Zone* (2006), Emily Apter emphasises another kind of dark side of translation in the *Star Wars* sense: the relationship between translation and war. Published a dozen years ago, when academic text production dealing with 9/11 discourse was at its peak, Apter's book rethinks translation studies within a broad theoretical framework that 'emphasizes the role played by mistranslation in war' (Apter, 2006: 3).

> Mistranslation in the way I have conceived it is a concrete particular of the art of war, crucial to strategy and tactics, part and parcel of the way in which images of bodies are read, and constitutive of *matériel*—in its extended sense as the hard- and software of intelligence. It is also the name of diplomatic breakdown and paranoid misreading.
>
> *(ibid.: 15)*

Paraphrasing Clausewitz's dictum that 'war is a mere continuation of policy by other means', Apter maintains that war is 'continuation of extreme mistranslation or disagreement by other means'. 'War', she continues, 'is, in other words, a condition of nontranslatability or translation failure at its most violent peak' (ibid.: 16).

The same year *The Translation Zone* came out, Mona Baker published a book on a similar subject—the relationship between translation and armed conflict—though from a very different perspective. Drawing on Paul Chilton's reflections on the role of language in human conflict (Chilton, 1997), Baker argues that 'translation and interpreting are part of the *institution of war* and hence play a major role in the management of conflict—by all parties, from warmongers to peace activists' (Baker, 2006: 1–2). From the declaration of war, which is a genuinely 'linguistic act', to the mobilisation of both military power and civilians, on whose support every war relies, 'translation participates in shaping the way in which conflict unfolds in a number of ways' (ibid.). Returning to the issue in a 2010 article, 'Interpreters and Translators in the War Zone', Baker argues that translators and interpreters, 'however they are narrated, and however they wish to narrate themselves and the ongoing conflict', are an integral part of the 'violence of war', which they cannot escape (Baker, 2010).

> They are made to fit into the dominant accounts of the war irrespective of what they themselves believe and how they wish to interpret the events in which they are embedded. They find themselves being defined in terms of their ethnicity or religious affiliation. They have to perform tasks that strain their loyalties and disrupt their sense of identity.
>
> *(ibid.)*

Within this tendency, we can pinpoint further excellent publications such as *Globalization, Political Violence and Translation*, edited by Esperança Bielsa and Christopher W. Hughes (2009); *Translation under Fascism*, edited by Christopher Rundle and Kate Sturge (2010); the special issue of *The Translator* edited by Moira Inghilleri and Sue-Ann Harding under the title *Translation and Violent Conflict* (2010); and the work of many other important translation scholars, such as Zrinka Stahuljak (2009, 2010), Sherry Simon (2012, 2019) and Michael Rössner (2015, 2016). In particular, we can locate the work of the South Asian historian Vicente L. Rafael as bringing us to a further, more radical step, explicitly claiming structural proximity between war and translation: 'Translation *at* war and *as* war [...] If translation is like war, is it possible that war is also like translation? It is possible I think if we consider that the time of war is like the movement of translation' (Rafael, 2009: 18). Arguing that translation increases the experience of untranslatability in time of war, he asserts that it is precisely the disarranging effect of war on our notions of space and time that makes the association between war and translation, not only plausible, but unavoidable. Similarly to war, in fact, translation 'scatters meaning, displaces origins, and exposes the radical undecidability of references, names and addresses [...] Put differently, translation in wartime intensifies the experience of untranslatability and thus defies the demands of imperial assimilation' (ibid.). In his last book, *Motherless Tongues* (2016), Rafael discusses the relationship between language and history with a focus on the weaponisation of speech and linguistic militarisation (see in particular ibid.: 124–148), viewed from the perspective of translation practices in the Philippines and the United States. As he argues, translation is based on the 'inevitability of mistranslation', spawning 'undecidability, ambivalence, and, at times, violent misinterpretations'. In this sense, 'translation tends to become a kind of war and, in the context of revolution and military occupation, to instigate and intensify conflict' (Rafael, 2016: 15).

This rough overview shows us what we more or less know about the dark side of translation within the frame of the *Star Wars* paradigm; that is, approximately within the frame of a Foucauldian post-colonial, power-knowledge argument. None of the books and scholars named here as dealing with translation as a 'dark practice' has explicitly called out and investigated the 'dark side' of translation; nevertheless, they provide us with strong premises on which to develop and elaborate our perspective.

Retrieving the dark side

What we want to do in this book, however, is not only further develop this kind of approach but also introduce another meaning of 'dark side', where 'dark' stands for invisible, latent, hidden, concealed; thereby touching on various phenomena and processes that post-colonial theories, for example, still tend to overlook. This would be, so to speak, the Pink Floyd paradigm.

Astronomically, the far side—or dark side—of the moon is the hemisphere of our satellite that we cannot see from Earth, since it faces away from any possible observational standpoint on Earth. The reason why we see only one hemisphere of the Moon is 'tidal locking', a process that stops the moon from rotating more than once on its own axis during its orbit of the Earth. In this sense, the 'dark side of translation' indicates what translation hides and conceals beyond an ethical or political ratio. As in the case of the moon—the dark side of which is only dark to us, here on Earth, since the sun does in fact shine on it—darkness, within the Pink Floyd paradigm, is due not so much to an absence of light as it is to the quality of being invisible, covert or opaque or, to put it another way, unfathomable.

Within the frame of the *Star Wars* paradigm, we are dealing with a sort of 'darkness visible', in Milton's words: with dark practices, dark issues, something that is murky and gloomy but visible—if you are willing to face it and see it. Within the frame of the Pink Floyd paradigm, on the other hand, we address darkness as obscurity, invisibility, latency, repression: something that enshrouds and covers, that consciously or unconsciously prevents us from seeing. What I refer to here is therefore not—or only peripherally—the 'invisibility' issue thoroughly explored by Lawrence Venuti in his *Translator's Invisibility* (1995)— and even less the controversial ethics of translation he pursues in his later works (1998, 2013). Embedded in a long hermeneutical tradition that runs from Schleiermacher to Antoine Berman, Venuti's concept of invisibility, based on the domesticating/foreignising polarity of literary translation, remains within the research furrow marked out by André Lefevere, which we mentioned above.

Rather, the dark, invisible side of translation we highlight here is what we might call the hidden *translandum*: the concealed, buried bundle of verbal or non-verbal meaning and symbols that wait to be unearthed, retrieved, revealed and re-located. To retrieve something invisible, something covered, is an operation that is closer to the word 'translation' than we may at first be inclined to think. One of the meanings of the Latin term *translatio*, before it entered the linguistic scene with the contribution of Leonardo Bruni's *De interpretatione recta* at the beginning of the fifteenth century (probably 1426) (cf. Italiano, 2016), indicates in Christianity the solemn transmission of relics (body, clothes and utensils of saints) from one place to another. As Heinzelmann has shown, from the Carolingian period onwards, reports on such 'translations' (*translationes*) became a literary genre in its own right, which shaped the reliquary cult of the Middle Ages (Heinzelmann, 1979). *Translatio* was the central part of a ritual process that started with *inventio* ('discovery'), *revelatio* ('revelation') and *elevatio* ('uplift') of the relics and was followed by their *advectio* ('transport'), *illatio* ('carry-in'), *processio* ('solemn procession') *receptio* ('reception', in the sense of 'acceptance'), *adventus* ('solemn arrival') and, finally, *depositio* ('deposit') (ibid.). In this translation of the saints' relics—or in this ritualised translation of ghosts, if you will—we find a process of retrieval and relocation of meaning, of de- and re-contextualisation, which resurfaces in every cultural activity we would call 'translation'.

Today the word 'translation' is frequently used in trauma studies to mean the retrieval and exposure of something hidden, concealed and repressed. In particular, we find it adopted in numerous studies on trauma in literature, film and the arts inspired, among others, by the works of Felman and Laub (1992), Cathy Caruth (1995, 1996) and Dominick LaCapra (2001). Important books such as *Trauma Culture: The Politics of Terror and Loss in Media and Literature* by E. Ann Kaplan (2005), *Translating Holocaust Literature*, edited by Peter Arnds (2015), *Translating Holocaust Lives*, edited by Jean Boase-Beier, Peter Davies, Andrea Hammel, Marion Winters (2017) and, more recently, *Witness Between Languages: The Translation of Holocaust Testimonies in Context*, by Peter Davies (2018), are centred on the concept of the possibility of translating a traumatic experience into words and/or images, between texts and across media.

As Bettina Stumm explains, the concept of trauma translation as deployed in trauma studies and psychoanalysis has usually been formulated in two primary ways, 'in terms of the survivor's challenge to *retrieve* repressed traumatic memories or to *represent* those traumatic memories in language and narrative form' (Stumm, 2015: 46). Drawing on 'Repression, Accessibility, and the Translation of Private Experience' (1990), by George A. Bonanno, Stumm describes the translation of trauma 'as a practice of retrieval (what can be remembered) and representation (what can be told) within a dialogic context' (Stumm, 2015: 47). In this framework, translation should be understood as a collaborative practice of 'piecing together various non-verbal, non-cognitive fragments and rendering them into verbal and often narrative form,' the goal of which is 'not simply to access repressed memories, but to construct new meaning from a past traumatic event' (ibid.).

However, in the context of Holocaust trauma translation, a further layer of complexity adds to the inherent difficulty for the traumatised in accessing and communicating trauma.

> The Holocaust, as a 'limit event', has long provoked discussion not only about whether its suffering can be represented or understood but whether it should be, adding an ethical dimension to the dilemmas of transmission. In one sense, translating trauma into something knowable and speakable can loosen the hold that it has on the psyche, giving survivors a way to

begin working through their memories of suffering. But at the same time, it can simplify the complexities involved in remembering and representing trauma, glossing over the very real gaps in memory and emotional blockages that trauma produces.

(Stumm, 2015: 46)

In examining the very core of the excruciating experiential and linguistic dynamics that caused that trauma, and exploring the atrocities of the concentration camp from the perspective of translation and interpreting studies, the volume edited by Michaela Wolf, *Interpreting in Nazi Concentration Camps* (2016)—drawing on the work of Alan Rosen (2005) and Lina N. Insana (2009), among others—aims to provide a possible answer to the complexities mentioned by Stumm above. In particular, Wolf's edited collection of essays analyses to what extent the 'order of terror' (Sofsky, 1997), on which the camp was based and on which its organisation and its power relations were built, depended on language and on the mediating figure within the Babel-like incommunicability of the camp: the prisoner-translator. In Wolf's book, therefore, the dark side of translation is already considered, although not explicitly, from both of its sides in the sense of the 'darkness visible' of its murky, shadowy practice and in the sense of the invisible *translandum*, the trauma that has to be retrieved, lifted, exposed, and translated.

Dark adaptation

In this book, we will discuss these two different but complementary meanings of darkness in relation to translation and interpreting. The volume is structured thematically in four parts, each focusing on an area of study in which our paradigms of darkness, the *Star Wars* paradigm and the Pink Floyd paradigm, are noticeable, if not manifest, and significantly intermingled: (post-)colonial translations and hegemonic practices, the Holocaust and the translator's ambiguity, the translation of climate change discourses and the ecology of knowledge, and, finally, translation and ontological amphiboly—or, to put it more simply, translation as zombification.

The first section, dedicated to (post-)colonial translations and focused on translation as both a hegemonic and a counter-hegemonic practice, opens with a chapter by Jon Solomon on the apparatus of area and the modern regime of translation. In Martin Scorsese's *Silence* (2016), based on the eponymous novel by Shūsaku Endō (Endō, 1969), Solomon sees a film that involuntarily stages the dark side of the modern regime of translation operated by 'the perennial governmental technologies in the postwar *Pax Americana*': faith and conversion. The 'apparent anti-imperialism' of Father Ferreira, who renounced his faith and adopted the Japanese name of Chûan Sawano, 'turns out to serve', as he argues, 'a new kind of neo-imperial organisation, the colonial governmentality under erasure that characterises *Pax Americana*.' Reading the scene of translation in Martin Scorsese's film, he explores in the first part of his essay the vexing role of silence in relation to the modern regime of translation after colonialism and the Shoah. In the second part, Solomon explores the questions the modern regime of translation poses to area studies and comparative literature, with a particular focus on the institutional experience of postwar international China studies.

In the following chapter, 'The Language of the Hegemon', Monika Mokre investigates how the violent practice of translation shapes the lives of migrants and refugees. As she argues, the encounter of a 'community' with a 'state' is a form of translation, since the language of legal documents, with its own peculiar grammar and recondite terminology, does not correspond with everyday language. However, while *de jure* citizens are excluded *de facto* if they fail technically and linguistically to translate themselves into the mother tongue of the state, non-citizens, such as migrants and refugees, are not only excluded as political subjects but also *de jure* since they do not have any rights in their territory of residence. Drawing on Giorgio Agamben, Jean-François Lyotard and Gayatri Chakravorty Spivak, among others, and touching on varied and often acutely painful case studies, Mokre examines the translation of the refugee into the intractable language of the hegemon as a specific challenge: not only do the languages differ from one another, but the refugee's experiences are distant and incomprehensible to the officials who decide on their right to stay. One example of this is when individual or collective traumas have to be translated into and narrated in a language that is utterly incapable of expressing them. If the subaltern cannot speak, the hegemon cannot listen.

The translation of, and within, experiences of traumatisation is one of the main issues of the second section of the book. By focusing on the sensitive context of the Holocaust and its narration, both chapters of the section will explore the translator's dark side in the sense of its ambiguous, split, uncanny dimension. Drawing on Primo Levi's seminal concept of the *grey zone* (Levi, 1989) and analysing numerous examples of *Lager* translation, Michaela Wolf's essay focuses on the 'heterogeneous character of the interpreting phenomenon'. As she argues, while on one hand the camp's translators and interpreters helped many inmates to survive, at least for a while, on the other, their 'mediator' role gave them a certain power in the network of terror—and the opportunity of some marginal benefits for themselves, too. Within the context of the *Lager*, therefore, as Wolf states, the dark side of translation manifests itself in various forms, from the gloomy context of dehumanising, traumatising imprisonment to collusion with the SS, 'which shaped the labour of translation and interpreting, motivated through one of the main driving forces of the *grey zone*, survival'. In this sense, Wolf sees Primo Levi's *grey zone* as one the paradigmatic 'loci' of the dark side of translation.

In psychoanalytical praxis, the 'uncanny' is a concept normally used to elucidate how trauma and anxiety are remembered, narrated, translated. When applied to literature, however, as Christoph Leitgeb states in his chapter, it 'describes an aesthetic convention' that 'accompanies the transition from personal to cultural memory'. Ingrained in a more general investigation of the uncanny in the literary recollection of National Socialism, Leitgeb's essay explores the correlation between theories of (cultural) translation and theories of the uncanny. Rereading Wolf-Dieter Stempel's speech-act theory of irony (1976) by the light of Georg Simmel's social philosophy (Simmel, 1992), he analyses the translator as a possible embodiment of a 'figure of the third', outlining why this figure becomes uncanny when doubt arises about its implication of 'neutral transparency'. Furthermore, drawing on Emily Apter, Homi K. Bhabha and Gayatri Chaktavorty Spivak, among others, and focusing on a highly controversial case of literary treatment of the Holocaust, he explores how some leading theories of cultural translation have explained translational processes in connection with the uncanny, asking whether these perspectives imply the concept of a 'figure of the third'.

In the third and longest section of the book, we explore the dark side of translation in connection with climate change discourses, Anthropocene challenges and ecologies of knowledge. As Michael Cronin's ground-breaking book *Eco-Translation* (2017) claims, we urgently need to rethink translation not only beyond the concept of nation, but also beyond that of globalisation, bringing it literally back to Earth: to the concrete exigencies and vulnerabilities of our planet's ecology, to the endangered richness of its human and non-human voices. Michael Cronin's chapter, 'Shady dealings: Translation, climate and knowledge', explores how the 'particular Western ontological prejudice' that places substance above transformation and the subject above the process 'has cast translation into the dark side of conventional thought and how this inattentiveness to a translational dynamic is having far-reaching consequences for how we think about knowledge and human society in the era of human-induced climate change'. Inspired by process-oriented thinking about transition—implied in the Chinese word *biàntōng* ('to accommodate to circumstances'), which the French sinologist Jullien explains in terms of 'silent transformation' (Jullien 2009) —Cronin advocates a reorientation, a redress in the organisation of knowledge that sees in the process, in the phenomena of transition, the true subject of enquiry. Drawing on Braidotti's conception of the subject as a transversal entity that encompasses the human, the animals and the earth (Braidotti, 2013), he argues that the answer of translation studies to the challenges posed by climate change should be to stress what he calls the '(in)humanity of translation'. That is, its capacity to engage with questions crossing the divide between the human and the non-human and to shape 'terracentric' (as opposed to geocentric or ethnocentric) forms of knowledge organisation.

In her essay on 'Climate change and the dark side of translating science into popular culture', Alexa Weik von Mossner explores the popularisation of highly complex scientific findings as a translational process located at the junction of the humanities and natural sciences, involving transmedia and narratological issues. In recent years, Weik von Mossner argues, the efforts to translate 'dry science into emotionally moving stories' have steadily increased. However, as she points out, the 'problematic proclivity towards dark, even apocalyptic storytelling' of such translations has met with profound scepticism among scholars and journalists, who tend to consider this dystopian rendering a debilitating rather than an enlightening communication strategy. In response to this critique, this essay tries to show that the emotions induced by such 'dark translations' must not automatically cause pain, apathy or despair, but can genuinely improve the attentiveness and critical potential of their readers and viewers. Drawing on

Michael Cronin's concept of 'eco-translation' (2017) and Timothy Morton's *Dark Ecology* (2016), Weik von Mossner discusses some of the eco-critical and psychological research on the matter, relating it to cultural texts that deliberately employ 'emotional darkness' in their translations of climate science research findings.

Daniel Graziadei's essay on 'Ecology in Translation' focuses on what is being translated when darkness is translated into language, paying particular attention to three forms of darkness: that is, darkness as the absence of light, as concealment, and as opacity. Drawing on Sky Marsen's reflections on embodiment (2008) as 'a meaning-making process based on a negotiation between multisensory impressions, memory of experience, and human discourse', Graziadei argues that darkness, as a sensory limitation, does not solely provoke irritations and fears (such as the common *nyctophobia*, fear of the dark) but can also improve our mental efforts and our cognitive life, enhancing our concentration and our meditation. As Mehtonen's cultural history of obscurity has shown (2003), Western thought systems are not exclusively products of 'light', but 'seem to be built upon negotiations between clarity and obscurity, or light and darkness, rather than any absolute preference for only one aspect of the continuum'. Following this fruitful line of thought, and elucidating Éduard Glissant's claim for a right to opacity (2009), Graziadei introduces and elaborates on Singh's concept of 'translative' forms of multilingual writing (2014), in which opacity is not only a right to be claimed but also a strategy 'against the extermination of difference and the celebration of uniformity'. Furthermore, he explores the connection between opacity and 'geopoetic translations', pointing out that our ecosystem already consists, at a global level, at least since Columbus, of what Bewell calls 'natures in translation' (2017). Finally, drawing on Michael Cronin's concept of 'slow translation' as a 'form of resistance to the extractivist lockdown of toxic uniformity' (Cronin, 2017: 153), he argues that 'slow translation in darkness, obscurity, opacity and complexity is pivotal to a survival in plurality'.

The chapters of the final section focus on the dark, uncanny, amphibological figure of the zombie, which vividly (no pun intended—well, maybe a little) shows how what is being translated and the very process of translation—*translandum* and *translatio*—are interwoven and almost inseparable at many levels. As living dead, in fact, the oxymoronic, fear-evoking figure of the zombie has not only been translated across different geographies, epochs and media but is itself the product of a translation process, the 'zombification' of the living, both as a thematic trope of the narrative (e.g. the transition from living being to 'living dead' in the classic zombie plot-line) and at a discursive level (e.g. the zombification of the Other from a post-colonial perspective).

In her chapter 'Zombie history: The undead in translation', Gudrun Rath explores the zombie as a figure of violent translation. Drawing critically on Wade Davis' influential book *Passages of Darkness* on the ethnobiology of the Haitian zombie and discussing, in particular, some implications of his poison hypothesis (1988), Rath focuses on the multiple functions of historical zombie texts from the seventeenth century onward as encountered in different textual media, especially scholarly works, and traces the ways in which the zombie was used in scholarly discourse published in France and Louisiana in the eighteenth and nineteenth centuries, creating a variety of significations of the undead. Furthermore, Rath examines the use of the zombie as a figure of twentieth-century scholarly discourse, and how elements of historical zombie texts continue to live on in filmic representations. In the last part of her chapter, she discusses the zombie as a figure of multiplicity, and to what extent it can be considered a figure of translation.

In the book's final chapter, Eugen Pfister explores zombie video games as a translational moment within a political discourse. Evocatively titled 'MmmRRRrr UrrRrRRrr!!'—that is, the phrase 'political anxieties' translated into zombie language (see the author's note on this matter)—this essay maintains that zombie apocalypses in video games have their 'own perverted beauty', made of 'mesmerising dystopia[s] of gigantic collapsed skyscrapers and picturesquely crumbling government buildings'. However, as Eugen Pfister argues—touching on Jürgen Habermas, Sarah J. Lauro and Todd K. Platts, among others—zombie video games go well beyond their ludic function, contributing to global discourse by generating and spreading 'political statements through the medium of popular culture'. He describes the translational dimension of zombie video games, not as frictionless 'transfers' of 'real' political discourses into 'fiction', but rather as the adaptation of a content (e.g. the breakdown of a democratic executive power, which has become a natural trope for the zombie genre) into the very grammar and syntax of the zombie video game language. In comparison with cognate 'languages' such as post-apocalyptic fiction, Christian iconography and action video games, Eugen Pfister shows in which sense and to what extent zombie video games translate political anxieties into popular culture.

References

Apter, E. (2006) *The Translation Zone: A New Comparative Literature*, Princeton: Princeton University Press.
Arnds, P. (ed.) (2015) *Translating Holocaust Literature*, Göttingen: Vandenhoeck & Ruprecht.
Ashcroft, B., G. Griffiths & H. Tiffin (1989) *The Empire Writes Back: Theory and Practice in Post-colonial Literatures*, London and New York: Routledge.
Baker, M. (2006) *Translation and Conflict: A Narrative Account*, London and New York: Routledge.
Baker, M. (2010) 'Interpreters and Translators in the War Zone: Narrated and Narrators', *The Translator: Studies in Intercultural Communication* 16(2): 197–222.
Bassnett, S. & A. Lefevere (1990) 'Preface', S. Bassnett & A. Lefevere (eds), *Translation, History and Culture*, New York: Pinters Publishers.
Bassnet, S. & H. Trivedi (1998) *Post-colonial Translation: Theory and Practice*, London: Routledge.
Bewell, A. (2017) *Natures in Translation*, Baltimore: John Hopkins University Press.
Bhabha, H. K. (2005) *The Location of Culture* [1994], 2nd ed, London: Routledge.
Bielsa, E. & C. W. Hughes (eds) (2009) *Globalization, Political Violence and Translation*, Basingstoke: Palgrave Macmillan.
Boase-Beier, J., P. Davies, A. Hammel & M. Winters (eds) (2017), *Translating Holocaust Lives* (Bloomsbury Advances in Translation), London: Bloomsbury.
Bonanno, G. A. (1990) 'Repression, Accessibility, and the Translation of Private Experience', *Psychoanalytic Psychology* 7(4): 453–473.

Bouzereau, L. (1997) *Star Wars: The Annotated Screenplays*, New York: Ballantine Books.
Braidotti, R. (2013) *The Posthuman*, Cambridge: Polity.
Burton, R. (1961 [1621]) *The Anatomy of Melancholy*, ed. by H. Jackson, 3 vols, London: Dent/New York: Dutton.
Caruth, C. (ed.) (1995) *Trauma. Explorations in Memory*, Baltimore and London: Johns Hopkins University.
Caruth, C. (1996) *Unclaimed Experience: Trauma, Narrative, and History*, Baltimore and London: Johns Hopkins University.
Chakrabarty, D. (2000) *Provincializing Europe: Postcolonial Thought and Historical Difference*, Princeton: Princeton University Press.
Cheyfitz, E. (1997) *The Poetics of Imperialism: Translation and Colonization from The Tempest to Tarzan*, Philadelphia: University of Pennsylvania Press.
Chilton, P. A. (1997) 'The Role of Language in Human Conflict: Prolegomena to the Investigation of Language as a Factor in Conflict Causation and Resolution', *Current Issues in Language and Society* 4(3): 174–189.
Cronin, M. (2017) *Eco-Translation: Translation and Ecology in the Age of the Anthropocene*, London and New York: Routledge.
Davies, P. (2018) *Witness Between Languages: The Translation of Holocaust Testimonies in Context*, Woodbridge: Boydell & Brewer.
Davis, W. (1988) *Passages of Darkness: The Ethnobiology of the Haitian Zombie*, Chapel Hill and London: University of North Carolina Press.
Endō, S. (1969) *Silence* trans. W. Johnston, London: Peter Owen Publishers.
Felman, S. & D. Laub (1992) *Testimony: Crises of Witnessing in Literature, Psychoanalysis, and History*, London and New York: Routledge.
Glissant, É. (2009) *Philosophie de la relation: Poésie en étendue*, Paris: Gallimard.
Heinzelmann, M. (1979) *Translationsberichte und andere Quellen des Reliquienkultes* (Typologie des sources du moyen âge occidental 33), Turnhout: Brepols.
Inghilleri, M. & S.-A.Harding (eds) (2010) *Translation and Violent Conflict*, Special issue of *The Translator*, 16(2).
Insana, L. N. (2009) *Arduous Tasks: Primo Levi, Translation, and the Transmission of Holocaust Testimony*, Toronto: University of Toronto Press.
Italiano, F. (2016) *Translation and Geography* (New Perspectives in Translation and Interpreting Studies), London and New York: Routledge.
Jullien, F. (2009), *Les transformations silencieuses: Chantiers, I*, Paris: Livre de Poche.
Kaplan, A. E. (2005) *Trauma Culture: The Politics of Terror and Loss in Media and Literature*, New Brunswick: Rutgers University Press.
LaCapra, D. (2001) *Writing History, Writing Trauma*, Baltimore and London: Johns Hopkins University.
Lefevere, A. (1992) *Translation, Rewriting, and the Manipulation of Literary Fame*, London: Routledge.
Levi, P. (1989) *The Drowned and the Saved* trans. R. Rosenthal, London: Abacus.
Marsen, S. (2008) 'The Role of Meaning in Human Thinking', *Journal of Evolution and Technology* 17(1): 45–58.
Mehtonen, P. (2003) *Obscure Language, Unclear Literature: Theory and Practice from Quintilian to the Enlightenment*, Helsinki: Academia Scientiarum Fennica.
Mignolo, W. (1995) *The Darker Side of the Renaissance: Literacy, Territoriality and Colonization*, Ann Arbor: University of Michigan Press.
Morton, T. (2016) *Dark Ecology: For a Logic of Future Coexistence*, New York: Colombia University Press.

Partridge, E. (1966) *Origins: A Short Etymological Dictionary of Modern English*, London: Routledge & Kegan Paul.
Rafael, V. L. (2009) 'Translation, American English, and the National Insecurities of Empire', *Social Text* 27(4 (101)): 1–23.
Rafael, V. L. (2016) *Motherless tongues: The insurgency of language amid wars of translation*, Durham and London: Duke University Press.
Rosen, A. (2005) *Sounds of Defiance: the Holocaust, Multilingualism, and the Problem of English*, Lincoln: University of Nebraska Press.
Rössner, M. (2015) 'Translation/s of Identity-Building Narratives: The Character of *El Cid* in Spanish and Latin American Texts from the 12th to the 20th Century', in H. Blume, C. Leitgeb & M. Rössner (eds), *Narrated Communities—Narrated Realities: Narration as Cognitive Processing and Cultural Practice*, Amsterdam: Rodopi/Brill, 173–183.
Rössner, M. (2016) 'Translating War. Zur kulturellen Übersetzung des Weltkriegserlebnisses in die europäische Literatur', in B. Mazohl (ed.), *Translating War. Der Erste Weltkrieg und seine kulturelle Verarbeitung* (= Forschung und Gesellschaft 9), Wien: Österreichische Akademie der Wissenschaften, 7–18.
Rundle, C. & K. Sturge (eds) (2010), *Translation under Fascism*, Basingstoke: Palgrave Macmillan.
Rushdie, S. (1982) 'The Empire Writes Back with a Vengeance', in *The Times* (UK), 3 July 1982: 8.
Simmel, G. (1992) *Soziologie. Untersuchungen über die Formen der Vergesellschaftung*, Frankfurt a. M.: Suhrkamp.
Simon, S. (2012) *Cities in Translation: Intersections of Language and Memory* (New Perspectives in Translation and Interpreting Studies), London and New York: Routledge.
Simon, S. (2019) *Translation Sites: A Field Guide* (New Perspectives in Translation and Interpreting Studies), London and New York: Routledge.
Singh, K. A. (2014) 'Translative and Opaque: Multilingual Caribbean Writing in Derek Walcott and Monchoachi', *Small Axe* 18(3 45): 90–106.
Sofsky, W. (1997) *The Order of Terror: The Concentration Camp*, Princeton: Princeton University Press.
Stahuljak, Z. (2009) 'War, Translation, Transnationalism: Interpreters in and of the War. (Croatia, 1991–1992)', in M. Baker (ed.), *Critical Readings in Translation Studies*, London and New York: Routledge, 391–414.
Stahuljak, Z. (2010) 'Minor Empires: Translation, Conflict, and Postcolonial Critique', *Translator* 16(2): 255–274.
Stempel, W.-D. (1976) 'Ironie als Sprechhandlung', R. Warning & W. Preisendanz (eds), *Das Komische*, München: Fink, 205–235.
Stumm, B. (2015) 'Collaborative Translation: The Relational Dimensions of Translating Holocaust Trauma', in P. Arnds (ed), *Translating Holocaust Literature*, Göttingen: Vandenhoeck & Ruprecht, 45–62.
Trusler, J. (1766) *The Difference between Words Esteemed Synonymous, in the English Language; and the Proper Choice of them Determined*, Vol. 2, London, Printed, for J. Dodsley.
Venuti, L. (1995) *The Translator's Invisibility: A History of Translation*, London: Routledge.
Venuti, L. (1998) *The Scandals of Translation: Towards an Ethics of Difference*, London and New York: Routledge.
Venuti, L. (2013) *Translation Changes Everything: Theory and Practice*, London and New York: Routledge.
Wolf, M. (2016) *Interpreting in Nazi Concentration Camps*, New York: Bloomsbury Academic.

PART I
(Post-)colonial translations and hegemonic practices

1

BEYOND A TASTE FOR THE DARK SIDE

The apparatus of area and the modern regime of translation under *Pax Americana*

Jon Solomon

A different taste

In a series of lectures at Yale University in 1979–80 on the relation between the institution of comparative literature and the modern regime of translation, Jacques Derrida prefaces his lecture with an expression of prudent reserve:

> Nor is it in my intentions, in my taste {or within my means}, to organize a general and radical problematic (as my title could nonetheless lead one to believe) in order to begin with a tabula rasa and establish the basis of a new foundation, of another legitimacy.
>
> (Derrida, 2008: 23)

Endowed with far fewer means than Mr Derrida, I will admit that I count myself as one of many devoted to nothing other than *a yearning for a different taste*, a new foundation for a different kind of comparativism.

The term *taste* comes to Derrida via René Étiemble. 'I would like', intones Étiemble in a key passage cited by Derrida, 'our [ideal] comparativist to be equally a man of taste and of pleasure' (Derrida, 2008: 48). Hence, the meaning of the 'new foundation' to which Derrida refers must be understood in the context of his reading of a crucial inaugural moment in the historical trajectory of comparative literature, specifically the praise lavished in 1958 on René Wellek by Étiemble (whose identical given name, René, highlights Derrida's reflections via the proper noun on translation[1]). Étiemble's devotion to aesthetic humanism and his juxtaposition with Wellek becomes the touchstone for Derrida's critique of the essential ambivalence at the heart of the modern regime of translation and the institution of literature.

Ultimately indissociable from the rise of the modern bourgeoisie and its attempt to mediate the relation between capital and labour through the disciplines of national aesthetics, the category of *taste* is an invention of early modernity (Perullo, 2016: ix). Understood as the pinnacle of individualisation, taste is also, it must be remembered, a species-specific *faculty*. As a species faculty, it is subject to differences that go to the heart of subjectivity (a central concern for aesthetic humanism), not just in the sense of individualising experience, but also in the sense of specialisation and expertise—those elements that the bourgeoisie will utilise to legitimate new forms of class difference based on an emergent division of labour. For the modern era, the problem of subjectivity is always inextricably bound to the question of knowledge. Yet knowledge in the modern context is not associated only with the division of labour. It is also associated with the emerging discourse of species difference.

Hence, the transformation of a species trait, such as taste, into a distinguishing, or specialised, sign of intra-species difference, such as that between experts and laymen, brings us face-to-face with the two sides of *the apparatus of anthropological difference*. Externally, the face of this apparatus is characterised by the *anthropological exception*, the notion that *homo sapiens* is not only one species among many, but also an exceptional species able to intervene in its own speciation and that of other species through its unique command of tools and language. Internally, this apparatus appears under its other face, that of the *colonial difference*: the notion that certain populations or segments—or even gifted individuals—within the species approach more than others the heights of the anthropological exception by virtue of their superior knowledge of tools and language. These two faces of the apparatus of anthropological difference—which are fundamentally *comparative*—are invariably articulated to a nature that is supposed to be rooted in an area. Henceforth, area becomes the ground or basis of comparison. If the category of taste to which Étiemble refers is anthropological before being class-based, this is also a reflection of modern liberalism, which extrapolates from the apparatus of anthropological difference a series of *anthropological invariants* based on the bourgeoisie's projection of its values into the beginning and end of history as the protagonist of evolution. Equal parts biological and cultural, the hero of the story of evolution will henceforth be known as *human nature*, a fiction that will increasingly come to be identified with *homo economicus* precisely through the active involvement of the colonial novel.

Étiemble's pairing of pleasure with taste deepens the speciesist logic of imperial nationalist, class-based liberalism. Whereas taste is a species faculty appropriated by a class with universal pretensions, pleasure is a sign of the indifference of the individual to society, a proof of auto-affectivity. Adding the *affect of pleasure* to the *sense of taste* reminds us that liberalism wants us to understand *homo naturans* as a self-grounding, self-referential creation of *homo faber*. This dual aspect of man's specificity is principally aesthetic.[2] Literature, as the artistic form that corresponds most closely, particularly in the form of the modern novel, to the rise of the bourgeoisie and the creation of the modern nation-state, would thus be the art of self-referentiality (pleasure) that is devoted to giving the apparatus of anthropological difference (in its guise as an apparatus of taste) a human face. Behind the institution of literature thus lies the aesthetic articulation of capitalism, colonialism, and science in the form of an evolutionary narrative. Étiemble's ideal comparativist, composed of equal parts taste and pleasure, is not just something that belongs to the realm of literature; rather, it is the figure of evolution *par excellence*. As such, it comprises an intrinsic element of comparison, in which comparison serves to identify superiority in a taxonomic sense. Let us call this *the taste of anthropological superiority* crystallised in the comparative aesthetics of national humanism, and realised in the figure of the literary comparativist.

Just as I share in Derrida's rejection of this aesthetics, I also share what I discern to be Derrida's complementary rejection of an outright disqualification of the aesthetic category of taste. Hence, I will take the risk of speaking of, or at least evoking, a *different* taste, even if I, far more than Derrida, lack the 'means' to explain it fully. This taste, which I will call definitively common (hence neither colonial nor capitalist), not exceptional but singular in each instance, cannot be contained in the schema of the One and the Many or the logic of genus and species. To explain it via Derrida in relation to comparative literature, we might say that this taste is neither that of the generalist, who 'transcribes [...] the very object' into a scientific, 'universal metalanguage' (Derrida, 2008: 41; word order modified), thus reducing the multiplicity of tastes to the one taste, nor that of the specialist, whose obsession with a particular object, invariably anthropologically coded and stamped with a particular taste, is easily conflated with or appropriated by the conceit of nationalism. Nor is it the sexualised taste of the 'polygamist' (as opposed to that of the 'monogamist') championed by Étiemble's Japanese admirer, Sukehiro Hirakawa (Hirakawa, 2002), only several years after the appearance, in English, of an attempt by his compatriot Takayuki Yokota-Murakami to rescue the possibility of 'non-comparison' from hegemonic aesthetic humanism (Yokota-Murakami, 1998: x). The alternative taste that I have in mind is one that does not correspond to an anthropologically coded object, but is to be found, rather, in the *practice of translation* as a practice of relation to non-relation. We will have more to say about this practice in a moment.

In short, *the dark side of translation* is a brilliant formula that simultaneously captures both the various different tropes that have dominated the modern regime of translation (bridge, filter, transfer, exchange and brokerage), as well as the problematic ambivalence of translation in relation to 'Aesthetic Humanism'[3] (Redfield, 2003). How might we go beyond this configuration?

Silence and the apparatus of anthropological difference

Wherever translation serves as a bridging technology (Solomon, 2014: 175 *passim*) for the apparatus of anthropological difference, silence is appropriated and mobilised in specific ways. Gayatri Spivak's essay, 'Can the Subaltern Speak?', offers one of the classic introductions to the theoretical and political problems of this silence. In a post-colonial, post-*Khurbn*[4] world, such appropriation by silencing has never appeared more untenable. Whether seen in the figure of the subaltern described by Gayatri Spivak or in that of the concentration camp survivor narrated, first in

Yiddish then in French, by Elie Wiesel,[5] silence denotes those places where the modern, i.e. international (hence colonial-imperial) notion of sociality, based on a representational order of nativity guaranteed by the state, enters into crisis. Silence is both a witness to the historical simultaneity of the post-colonial and the post-*Khurbn* moment as well as the rem(a)inder of the unrepresentable difference between (and internal to) the two. My aim is not assimilate one to the other, much less to privilege one over the other, but rather to call attention to the way in which *the recuperation of silence by the self-referential system of anthropological difference through the modern regime of translation* continues to be a necessary moment for political projects based on the imperial aesthetics of national humanism.

Martin Scorsese's 2016 film *Silence*, based on Endō Shûsaku's 1966 novel of the same name, will help me illustrate this point. Rather than being a film about missionary universalism and the irreducible quality of cultural particularism, as it is commonly billed, it would be more accurate to qualify *Silence* as a film about the scene of translation, in which the object of *faith and conversion* (two of the perennial governmental technologies in the postwar *Pax Americana*) has been directed towards secular power relations and political faith in cultural essentialism, identity politics and national sovereignty. *Silence* recounts the story, mediated by author Endō's investment in the modern regime of translation, of Portuguese Jesuit priests in Tokugawa, Japan. The scene of translation occupies a central role in Scorsese's film, particularly through characters such as The Interpreter (played by Tadanobu Asano), working for the *Bakufu* (the conventional term for the Shogunate that ruled Japan for nearly seven centuries), and the priests' own translator (played by Ken Watanabe). Translational issues are featured in dialogues between the lead protagonist, Father Sebastião Rodrigues, played by Andrew Garfield, and The Interpreter and the priests' translator, as well as in various scenes depicting Rodrigues's encounters with members of the local ruling élite attempting to secure his apostasy (particularly governor Masashige Inoue, known in the film as The Inquisitor, played by Issey Ogata).

The crucial moment in the cinematic representation of the scene of translation occurs, however, near the end of the film, in the dialogue between Rodrigues and his mentor, Father Cristóvão Ferreira, played by Liam Neeson. Neeson's casting in this high-budget production takes advantage of what Guy Debord identified as accumulation in the image. Neeson's filmography boasts characters imbued with spiritual significance: including not only Jedi Master Qui-Gon Jinn in *Star Wars: Episode 1—The Phantom Menace* (1999), whose name and title are permeated with an Orientalist fetishisation of 'Eastern mysticism'—something that also echoes throughout Scorsese's film—but also seen in the halo around characters such as Godfrey of Ibelin in Ridley Scott's *Kingdom of Heaven* (2005) and Oskar Schindler in *Schindler's List* (1993). James Wolcott, writing for *Vanity Fair* about Neeson's career transition from a 'Much-Admired-Actor' to a 'vengeful giant', summarises the image carefully crafted in Neeson's career before the transition: 'Neeson casts the cloud of a poetic brooder [...] a wounded romantic who quotes Yeats and seems to crave soft candlelight'

(Wolcott, 2013). After the transition detected by Wolcott, Neeson's image morphs, with post-9/11 films such as *Taken* (2008), the story of a one-man rescue mission launched by a former CIA agent whose daughter has been kidnapped. ('America' always wants to believe that CIA regime-change operations happen exclusively in the past tense.) The composite image that emerges after the transition is replete with significance for patriarchal authority in an era that is itself marked by struggles associated with historical transition. Neeson's career is metonymically associated with the *Zeitgeist* of post-imperial, heterosexual, white male *ressentiment* in the wake of the disillusionment with anti-systemic, anti-patriarchal movements since the 1960s that for a brief moment seemed to challenge *Pax Americana*: his composite character is the consummate wounded wounder of the post-patriarchal return to white patriarchal normativity.

Having renounced his faith, adopted a Japanese name (Chûan Sawano), and taken a properly 'local' wife, Ferreira would seem to be the spokesman for an anti-imperialist ethics of respect for difference. Ferreira meets Rodrigues in the Buddhist temple where the former has been studying Buddhism for the past year and proceeds to tell Rodrigues that Christianity is a 'lost cause in Japan'. Tinged with bittersweet pain, Neeson's Ferreira explains to Rodrigues that the Catholic missions to the Bakufu failed precisely because the Catholic missionaries *failed to understand the limits of translation*. In a re-enactment of the mythical scene of first translation, Neeson's Ferreira explains that the subjects of the Tokugawa shogunate, assimilated to an historically fictive 'Japanese' ethnos, never understood the word 'God':

> Our religion does not take root in this country. The Japanese only believe in their distortion of our gospel, so they did not believe at all. They never believed [...] Francis Xavier came here to teach the Japanese about the son of God, but first he had to ask about how to refer to God. *Dainichi* he was told. Shall I show you their Dainichi? [Pointing at the sun] Behold! There is the son of God. God's only begotten son. [...] The Japanese cannot think of an existence beyond the realm of nature. For them nothing transcends the human. They can't conceive of our idea of the Christian God. [...] There's a saying here: Mountains and rivers can be moved, but Man's nature cannot be moved. It's very wise, like so much here. We find our original nature in Japan, Rodrigues. Perhaps it's what's meant by finding God.

Ferreira's understanding of translation is based on the primary distinction, dear to modern linguistics, between signification and indication. Yet the reality at which indication points is a nationalised reality, for which the culturalist discourse of culture and soil, typified in modern Japan by the philosophy of Watsuji Tetsurō (1889–1960; see Sakai 1997 for a convincing analysis), provides a foundational trope. Ferreira's reference to 'taking root' echoes the words, heard earlier in the film, of a Tokugawa official present on Rodrigues's hearing before The Inquisitor, speaking (after stumbling with English) in translation through The Interpreter:

> The doctrine you bring with you may be true in Spain and Portugal, but we have studied it carefully, thought about it over much time, we find it is of no use (*mueki*) and no value in Japan (*nihon-koku*). [...] I see you do not work with your hands, Father. Everyone knows that a tree which flourishes in one kind of earth may decay and die in another.

The culturalist trope plays on a metonymical association between roots, soil, and the fantastical totality of a nation. This is an example of the continuing indebtedness of the modern regime of translation to the cultural imaginary of romanticism and aesthetic humanism. It recalls Nietzsche's critique of the tropic nature of truth, between philology and philosophy, brilliantly analysed by Paul de Man in a chapter on Nietzsche, titled 'The Rhetoric of Tropes', in *Blindness and Insight*:

> The trope is not a derived, marginal, or aberrant form of language, but the linguistic paradigm par excellence. The figurative structure is not one linguistic mode among others but it characterizes language as such [...] the paradigmatic structure of language is rhetorical rather than representational or expressive of a referential, proper meaning
>
> (de Man, 1979: 105–106)

As discourse, Scorsese's *Silence* enacts the *tropic of area*. Where de Man cites Nietzsche talking about the 'linguistic event' as a form of 'translation' that occurs *within* the construction of 'inner experience' (de Man, 1979: 108), we understand that translation is an essential, integral process to the pedagogical and essentially literary figuration of the modern self-reflexive subject of international comparison.

In a somewhat mundane vein, we might observe that the only obstacle, in the end, to a de Manian critique of the tropic nature of subjective formation amounts to a clear distinction between indication and signification that can only be upheld by *faith* in the referential function of language. It takes an awfully strong dose of faith indeed for the viewers of *Silence* to ignore the curious semantic confusion, seen in Liam Neeson's Father Ferreira pointing at the sun while talking about the Son of God, that takes place between the two homophonous English words paired with the entirely aleatory coincidence that the Japanese nation is called *nihon*, the 'root of the sun', in an expression whose origins are shrouded in notions of language and community that fundamentally differed from the post-Meiji construction of the 'sentiment of nationality'. The confusion between semantic registers and linguistic difference cannot but infect that line between indication and signification that forms the basis of 'faith' in *Silence*, yet the film plods on, confident that its audience will not want to break the pact of self-referential self-evidence.

This faith in 'silence' is at the heart of the type of *conversion* envisaged by *Pax Americana*. It is the form of conversion that substitutes post-colonial national sovereignty for the decolonial transition to a non-colonial, non-capitalist world that might have occurred after the end of European and Japanese Imperialisms. While many commentators have understandably emphasised the hegemonic aspects of postwar American leadership, exemplified by the role of Hollywood cinema, it is important to stress that the basic mode of international governance envisaged by *Pax Americana* is not homogenisation, but rather the progressive codification of difference in order to facilitate and defend the geopolitics of market segmentation. Post-colonial sovereignty, based on an ideology of cultural difference assimilated to specific difference, is one of the primary tools used by *Pax Americana* to interdict the emergence of an alternative world. *Pax Americana* silences the proliferation of originary hybridity that runs rampant throughout modernity, while forcing the ventriloquism of speech devoted to national representation. Ferreira's apparent anti-imperialism turns out to serve the ideology of a different kind of neo-imperial organisation: the colonial governmentality under erasure that characterises *Pax Americana*.

As a film that enacts the scene of translation but crushes it under the weight of brute indication, Scorsese's *Silence* is imbued with *the ideology of referentiality* that forms the basis of the dialectic of identity, faith, and conversion at the heart of the postwar *Pax Americana* in east Asia. Whether the source of the film's confidence is honesty or conspiracy barely matters, since the two poles are ultimately systemically related, and integral to the operation of finance capital (cf. Solomon, 2017). That is why the Tokugawa official, who is really speaking as a mask for the post-Second World War hegemony of the Liberal Democratic Party[6] wing of *Pax Americana*, explains that the rejection of Christian faith was based on the calculus of interest. The filmic representation of the translational scene allows a bilingual audience to hear enough of the Japanese 'original' to catch the Japanese word *mueki* before cutting into English translation overdub. Translated by The Interpreter as 'no use and no value', the term *mueki* covers a semantic range that shifts from the social to the economic, all the way to the financial. Just as the modern regime of translation institutes the capitalist law of exchange value that hides behind the festishisation of the commodity and labour through use value, the compound performance of *mueki*/no use value performs an eminently *ideological* role.

This is the 'faith' that is fundamental to the co-figuration, through the modern regime of translation, between US imperial nationalism and postcolonial sovereignty for the glory of militarised capital accumulation in the postwar (but really permanent war) era known as *Pax Americana*. Although it might appear as if the celebrated director of *Taxi Driver* would like to claim artistic inspiration from Antonin Artaud's 'Theatre of Cruelty', the effect in fact is quite the opposite: rather than rudely awakening viewers from the silent slumber of quotidian *mensonge* and spectacle that compensates for labour's complicity with capitalist colonisation, Scorsese's *Silence* puts to rest entirely the possibility of revolution. The repression is axiomatic. Labour never passes through a process of commodification. The Tokugawa official, who deploys the rhetorical mode of indication when he begins his statement with the words 'I see', demonstrates that logic as he finishes his sentence by observing that Rodrigues is a man who does not 'work with [his] hands'. The official's words do not lead to a reflection about the division of labour between manual and intellectual work, but rather immediately incorporate labour into the metonymic chain connecting territory, nation, language, and referential function. Labour becomes yet another part of the economy of the tropic of area, anthropologically coded and collated into taxonomies of nation and civilisational. Just as 'man's nature' is assimilated to an essentialised national identity, labour is reduced, through a culturalist representation of translation, to the realisation of an anthropological type or figure. Deployed in this manner, the labour of translation dissimulates the commodification of labour in general, with the two serving as the basis for an operation of comparison essential to the apparatus of area and anthropological difference.

Having traced with broad strokes the outlines of the way in which the *faith in conversion* turns translation into an essential operation in the transnational ideological hegemony of the *Pax Americana*, I think that it would be an apposite moment to reflect on the fact that *Silence* was filmed not in Japan, but in Taiwan. What are the implications of filming an on-screen adaptation of a literary work thoroughly imbued with the ideology of the translational regime of *Pax Americana* (transferentially inherited from Imperial Japan) in a former Japanese colony whose population had once enjoyed the status of full Japanese nationality? Did Martin Scorsese ever reflect on the politics of this displacement? I cannot find any public indications of such reflection. Speaking to an audience in Taipei of state officials and representatives from industry, finance, and cultural institutions, Scorsese opts for a repression of historical memory:

> It [*Silence*] was brought to fruition in this extraordinary country. This is something that has been a dream of mine for so many years. I hope it would be received as a gift to Taiwan and the Taiwanese people, who made this possible.
>
> *(Smith, 2017)*

The gift, as *Time.com* journalist Nicola Smith suggests, is the funding opportunities brought by a world-famous director with the clout to buck the constraints of massive Chinese investment in Hollywood production that otherwise excludes cooperation with Taiwanese studios on account of Hollywood's own demands to capture a Chinese market with its products. (Smith cites the example of Viacom Inc's Paramount Pictures, which announced a day after Scorsese addressed his audience in Taipei that it had received a $1 billion investment from two Chinese film companies.) No wonder Scorsese aims to make his next film after *Silence* about former President Bill Clinton, the US president most emblematic of neoliberalism's strategies of global financial market penetration! Self-consciously adopting the role of the colonial missionary, Scorsese gives *the gift of conversion*—an operation that blends the ideological and the financial, typical of the *Pax Americana*.

Against Scorsese's high-decibel, neoliberal 'gift' of financialised conversion masquerading as 'silence', there is a different flavour of silence that is fractured, multiple, common and shared (Kanngieser and Bueret, 2017). Perhaps the best way to pose the problem of just what kind of silence this might be lies in returning to the apparatus of area and anthropological difference with which we began. Just as the apparatus of anthropological difference contains the two aspects of colonial difference and anthropological exception, the irreducible difference between *Di Khurbn Eyrope* and colonial violence has to be paired with that other irreducible difference that concerns species extinction induced by human action. There where *Di Khurbn Eyrope*, colonialism and the Anthropocene silently meet is in the place where the din of the machine of anthropological difference becomes deafening. Here, the role of silence(s) must be measured in relation to the immeasurable excess of extinction. Between the anthropological exception (of a species deemed superior and unique) and colonial difference (the notion that certain parts of the human species approach the ideal of the exceptional species more than others), there is a different kind of silence. How might we rethink translation in relation to that other kind of silence?

Colonial causality

Against my expectations, I could not find any evidence that Derrida's ruminations about the predicament of comparative literature and the modern regime of translation have been taken up by scholars of Chinese literature in France or among scholars of Sino-French literary and cultural relations in China. Yet the thought of narrating this lacuna according to a schema of disciplinary divisions and periodic succession is unappealing. Notions of periodisation that once served to unify the field of comparative literature are not likely, as Marc Redfield argues, to help us understand the persistence of aesthetic humanism beyond its original sell-by date in romanticism. Such periodisations ultimately reinforce the humanist's reliance on anachronistic models of causality. Left with no alternative, I will have to rely on a negative example, for which I thank the reader for their patience. This comes to me by way of an essay from 2010, generically titled 'Comparative Literature and Chinese Studies', by one of the few institutionally appointed Sino-comparativists in France, Philippe Postel.

Postel's admirable argument for a pragmatic approach to comparative literary studies is marred by assumptions about anthropological difference. Starting from the premise that translation should always observe directional propriety, conducted from the foreign into the translator's native tongue, Postel infers that comparative research should equally follow the same general rule that binds nativity, language and knowledge (Postel, 2010: 273). Postel's apparently benign proscriptions, the good intentions of which are beyond reproach, nevertheless amount to the endorsement of a division of academic labour based on national identity that views hybridity as secondary, and assimilates difference to a logical schema of diaphora or specific difference. Within that context, even the undoubtedly modest intent behind Postel's expression of admiration for his Chinese counterparts, 'what I was going to call their *natural* knowledge of Chinese literature' (Postel, 2010: 274; emphasis added), unwittingly reinforces a comparative framework based on the erasure of originary hybridity and the normalisation of a symmetrical, international schema of difference. Postel's implausible, yet socially powerful, identification of racialised nativity with innate knowledge of even abstract things like a literary canon unfortunately reminds us of the agonisingly ridiculous racist prejudice described sixty years before Postel by the black literary genius James Baldwin. Comparing himself to illiterate Swiss peasants, Baldwin facetiously expresses the racist postulate of inherent knowledge: 'The most illiterate among them is related, in a way that I am not, to Dante, Shakespeare, Michelangelo, Aeschylus, Da Vinci, Rembrandt, and Racine' (Baldwin, 1984: 165). In the context of Chinese studies, the aesthetic proscriptions of national humanism amount to yet another instance where the labour of translation dissimulates the commodification of labour and naturalises it through a scheme of symmetrical international difference modelled according to the logic of specific difference. Regardless of the author's intention, such endorsement unavoidably reverts into a form of 'racism without races' (Balibar, 2007).

Yet it is not enough for us to detect the unavowed racism hiding behind the notion of cultural difference institutionalised through literary studies; one must also attend to its methodological support. In Postel's essay, the principal form of support can be pinpointed to the insistence on a 'connection of historical or factual nature' (Postel, 2010: 272) that must serve as the basis for comparison, without which comparative work would be illegitimate or fanciful. In other words, comparative studies must limit themselves to the dictates of origin and influence that can be traced to the hard evidence of mechanistic causal relations: Author X read Author Y's work and, under the influence of Author Y, produced a work of the same genre. Indeed, much of the history done by literary studies to this day, in France as elsewhere, consists of consulting the ledger of such 'Writing Under the Influence'. This approach also occupies a central place in the 'cultural transfer' school of cultural studies that turns translation into a logistical operation of *translatio*. Michel Espagne, one of the founders of this school, holds that 'historically verifiable contacts' (Espagne, 2013: 2) form the sole, acceptable basis for research into the history of cultural individuation. Anything else belongs, he asserts, to a 'magical dimension'.

What appears to be a sound, scientific practice turns out to be a form of colonial governmentality under erasure. When the exigency of verifiable contact becomes an exclusive imperative, other forms of causality are banished to the realm of 'magic' in an operation typical of the epistemic violence of colonial science that played a crucial role in the establishment of modern Chinese studies. As Michael Dutton invites us to confront the 'relationship between science, translation, and the epistemic violence of imperialism', he concludes:

> The West, it seems, could translate anything. Through the spread of scientific method, texts, buildings, and even life itself were opened to the West's gaze. The tower of Gustave Eiffel became its Babel and the new universal message was that science could conquer all.
>
> *(Dutton, 2002: 501)*

This historical process of epistemic violence becomes institutionalised in the discipline of comparative literature whenever it is surreptitiously tied to a translational ethics of self-referential causality that reinforces a hegemonic version of modern science. We might as well dub Postel's notion of historical or factual connection a form of *colonial causality*, emblematised by the literary figure of Robinson Crusoe. Crusoe's status as 'master' derives ultimately from his command of mechanistic causality, metaphorically condensed into the power of his gun. There is little room here for alternative forms of causality and relationship that do not fit into the mechanistic epistemologies and ontologies of individualism favoured by colonial domination. This is the sort of causality that was used, as Michael Dutton chronicles, to wage epistemological violence against indigenous knowledge as 'science' began to impose its dominance upon the Manchu Qing Dynasty. Little wonder that Gayatri Spivak, in a 2009 essay titled 'Rethinking Comparativism' that might never be read by China studies comparativists in France or French studies comparativists in China, felt the need not only to remind her readers that 'comparison assumes a level playing field and the field is never level' (Spivak, 2009: 609), but also of the importance of 'those trajectories in Emmanuel Levinas [...] and, of course, the work of Jacques Derrida, whose brilliant topological slides do indeed teach us to think about relations without relations between diverse European texts' (Spivak, 2009: 611). For the critic who moves outside of the boundaries defined by civilisational transfer and does not want to buy into the modern regime of translation, these *relations without relations* are of utmost importance.

If thinking about the basis for comparativism beyond mechanistic causality escapes the international institution of comparative literature in its Chinese declination, it is not, I will wager, because the 'relations without relations' are too abstract and too *theoretical* for admission. After all, social relations mediated by the modern state are filled with such quotidian abstractions that bind people who never know each other, let alone see each other, in webs of civil society. On the contrary, *the series of operations required to create and sustain the apparatus of area through the modern regime of translation is the theoretical gesture* par excellence *of modernity*. The international institution of China studies is merely a fascinating instance of consolidation-through-denial of theory's dual role in the anthropological difference: somewhat like religion, theory is associated with innate species faculties at the heart of the anthropological exception; by the same token, accession to and mastery of theory is also what distinguishes different populations within the species according to the index of colonial difference.

I should like to make clear that my interest is anything but theoretical, if that term is restricted to a hermeneutical sphere. *To find the relation in the face of apparent unrelatedness, or again, the causality in the midst of apparent disjunction, might well be the most succinct definition of translation as a social practice.* Hence it is comforting to find that, even in Meng Hua's eulogy to aesthetic humanism associated with the proper name Étiemble, we can still detect a moment where the sociality of knowledge production-as-translation becomes visible. A Chinese specialist of

French literature, Meng cites the Confucian proverb *yi wen hui you* to describe the international bonds among comparativists. Meng translates this phrase in French as '*l'amitié se noue par la lecture des beaux textes*' (Meng, 2002: 106), a translation for which I now oblige the English reader with an English translation: *friendship is fastened through the reading of great texts*. Returning to the Chinese phrase, however, I propose a different translation, one which I hold to be superior on account of its sparse economy like the original: 'To make friends through literature (*wen*) [And, to be fair, a retranslation into French: *Se faire des amis à travers la littérature* (wen)]'. Whether *wen* is considered 'literature' or, as it was for much of Imperial China's history, a governmental technology of inscription (and whether those inscriptions should be viewed under the sign of the beautiful, the sublime, or some other category) is a moot issue in this context. The important point to take away here is that *wen*/literature is always connected, in the Confucian proverb, to the aleatory, affective encounter with the other (although there can be no doubt that the social practice of *wen* in successive empires was generally a class and gender privilege, much like 'literature'). What happens when this encounter is 'transferred' from the realm of subjective formation and confined exclusively to the prison-house of referential causality? One answer can be seen in a phrase attributed by Postel to Li Jinjia, a PhD candidate in France who asserted during her oral defence: the 'study of translations [...] obliges us to go straight to the text, the core [*noyau dur*] of literary research' (Li Jinjia, cited with approval and admiration in Postel, 2010: 279). The proliferation of metaphors is confusing, to say the least. Are we dealing with a weave, which is essentially open unless sealed by a border, or a kernel, which is essentially closed? The confusion is compounded by the semantic excess of the metaphor. Perhaps *noyau dur*, literally 'hard core', refers to a firmness of commitment, suitable for true devotees ('the converted'); or perhaps it speaks of a seminal foundation that will later grow into something much larger, like a tree—a favourite metaphorical device for the representation of linear descent and specific difference. Surely it is for that reason that Derrida reminds us that

> We must understand the structural temptation of this encyclopedic opening [associated with the difficulty of defining what is and is not literary or textual]; we must try to understand why it cannot avoid *opening*, in a way, the alleged field of the aforementioned comparative literature.
>
> (Derrida, 2008: 30)

It would seem that the obligation of which Postel and Li speak is the obligation to confine translational theory to the arborescent form of colonial causality that used to be called philology, shorn of its metaphysical preoccupations: seeds and sprouts, native species and foreign soil, origins and influences, all joined in a vast tapestry of logistical connections ...

On earth, no one can hear you scream

Undoubtedly, the problematic nature of modern causality experienced by the international institution of literature, like the repression of that experience, is intrinsically related to events that have nothing to do with the literary per se.

A significant clue comes from a detail that the normally encyclopaedic Derrida neglected to mention in the course of bringing our attention to bear on the significance of the year 1958. This is the year, Derrida helpfully reminds us, in which Étiemble was elected chair of Comparative Literature at the Sorbonne and published an article that would become a classic of the field in a collection with the significant title *Knowledge and Taste* (a title that effectively summarises the intrinsically speciesist and racialist superiority baked into the mode of comparison); it was also the year of a historical conference

> that marked the world history of comparative literature after the war: the famous Congress of Chapel Hill [...] where [...] pitched battles broke out on the subject of what was called at that time the Crisis of Comparative Literature, *Krise der Komparatistik, Crise de la littérature comparée*.
>
> *(Derrida, 2008: 45–46)*

To this highly overdetermined concatenation of historical forces converging in 1958 around comparative literature's investment in the apparatus of area and anthropological difference, we must now add a detail conspicuously omitted by Derrida that will nevertheless have enormous significance for us: 1958, the year of the Sputnik crisis, also saw the official induction and institutionalisation of 'area studies' (including China studies) into the US university system as part of the Cold War regime of knowledge production and translation under *Pax Americana*.

The challenge to causality and self-referentiality often mistakenly attributed to postmodern theory turns out, rather, to be an unavoidable result of scientific discovery. As Hannah Arendt reminded her readers in 1963, when atom bombs and space travel had already become reality:

> These ideals were lost when scientists discovered that there is nothing indivisible in matter, no *a-tomos*, that we live in an expanding, non-limited universe, and that chance seems to rule supreme wherever this 'true reality,' the physical world, has receded entirely from the range of human senses and from the range of all instruments by which their coarseness was refined. From this, it seems to follow that causality, necessity, and lawfulness are categories inherent in the human brain and applicable only to the common-sense experiences of earthbound creatures.
>
> *(Arendt, 2007: 49)*

Yet in spite of massive evidence to the contrary, the areal declination of comparative literature and the modern regime of translation on which it depends continue to remain social institutions that breed an ethics of speciesist and racialist comparison, rather than opening up an arena for the mobilisation of the common.

For Hannah Arendt, the launching of the world's first man-made satellite was an 'event, second in importance to no other' (Arendt, 1998: 1) that brought to visibility the ultimate quest of modernity: the effort to escape the bonds of earthly imprisonment through technological means. Taken as a whole, the Sputnik crisis and the institutionalisation of area studies together are emblematic of the two poles around which modernity oscillates: the imperative of area, and the dream of no area. If modernity is characterised, as we have seen, by the apparatus of anthropological difference in its two different faces of colonial difference and anthropological exception, then it is no less important to understand the operations and technologies involved in the creation of the space that ostensibly serves as the 'natural' container for the subjects produced by that apparatus. Hence, in addition to the apparatus of anthropological difference, we must also speak about the *apparatus of area* as its corollary and complement.

In modernity, the spatialised container of area is characterised by a fundamental duality, oscillating between the dream of absolute freedom and a nostalgia for complete rootedness. The problem since Sputnik, however, is that our thinking about area has been irrevocably wrested away from us by a logistical understanding of science. For Arendt's placed-based sense of ethics, this situation was deeply distressing. Yet if Sputnik represented for Arendt the destabilising initiation of the human species to a non-earthly perspective, the role of area studies as a form of response to the Sputnik Crisis of 1958 needs to be equally interrogated. While area studies would seem to have instantiated the Arendtian ethics of place-based community that could form, according to the Arendt of *The Origins of Totalitarianism*, a defence against the biopolitical horrors of the Second World War, area studies, as part of the apparatus of area and anthropological difference, in fact represents the destruction of any such ethical possibility. Michael Dutton's damning appraisal of area studies is unequivocal: fundamentally dominated by a pedagogy emphasising 'descriptive and applied translational practice' (Dutton, 2002: 504), the modern area studies born after the Second World War and instituted in the Sputnik crisis have lost any claim to place-based ethics as much as to metaphysical or ontological truths. *Applied translation* means nothing other than the reduction of aesthetic humanism, which was always a pedagogical as well as a literary practice of subjective formation, to an operation of logistics. In an unthematised gesture towards the hegemony of logistics, Dutton identifies 'extraction, translation, [and] mobility' (Dutton, 2002: 499) as integrally related operations in the production of knowledge serving the hegemonic, colonial version of science. Such analysis encourages us to recognise how translation, reduced to a logistical operation of transfer, becomes nothing but a purveyor of standardised taste-products, while area studies consolidate the apparatus of anthropological difference in the service of the logistical accumulation of capital.

The phrase, the *dark side of translation*, through its implicit reference to the topology of a spherical celestial body orbiting a single sun, reminds us of the need to distinguish translation from logistics. When it's light on one side, it's dark on the other. Although the notion of a spherical earth can apparently be traced back to early Greek astronomy, it is only with the modern era of colonial exploration that the notion of a single, spherical world, i.e., the *global* world, becomes a concrete social practice. Ferdinand Magellan's circumnavigation of the earth between 1519 and 1522 operates a similar effect to Sputnik, turning a theoretical perspective into a concrete *social practice*.

Much like translation (in the representational form that I criticise), logistics is concerned with relay and transfer across heterogeneous spaces according to quantitative benchmark standards of efficiency. Although logistics has its origins in military transport and communication, today it is a field that encompasses virtually every domain of human endeavour. The advent of information technology (IT), big data, robotisation and the various technologies of codification, recombination and repurposing at the heart of the fourth industrial revolution are essentially logistical in nature. Where translation differs noticeably from logistics, however, concerns the element of *subjective formation* at the heart of the relation between art, education and democracy characteristic of modernity.

Naoki Sakai's work on translation highlights this subjective element by theorising translation as an eminently social practice of indeterminacy and discontinuity in the social. Sakai's approach is attentive to the nature of discontinuity, and resists the attempt to turn discontinuity into continuity by capturing it within the classical logic of specific difference. He develops a theory of comparativism that resists the naturalisation of the schema of nationality, and develops a theory of translation that does not presuppose the border between languages. In a passage that summarises these themes, Sakai distinguishes the concept of *transnationality* from that of nationality:

> By transnationality, I want to designate not the systematic of location configured by the logical economy of *species* and *genus*, but instead the locale of translation that opens up the place of comparison. While internationality operates within the logical economy of *species* and *genus*, transnationality undermines and reconfigures the schemata of nationality and internationality. It is in this sense that translation deterritorializes. And this deterritorializing potential of translation has been reterritorialized by the schematism of cofiguration. Hence, transnationality indicates to us the locus of the foreign, something irreducible to the logical economy of *species* and *genus*. Precisely because translation is prior to the determination of *species difference*, can the conceptual topos of the foreign, where translation is in demand, be found not in internationality but rather in transnationality.
>
> *(Sakai, 2013)*

Sakai has connected the dots between the separate notions of globality and translation by interrogating the schema of international symmetry that constitutes one of the essential frameworks for modern sociality based in the element of the apparatus of area and anthropological difference. The modern regime of translation critiqued by Sakai is at the heart of a representational cartography that maps globality onto internationality, effacing the element of discontinuity in the common and supplanting it with the continuity of mutually co-figured national cultures that excludes originary hybridity and the indeterminacy of practical relations. From this perspective, the modern humanities are an inherently comparative enterprise, yet under the regime of translation, the dominant mode of comparison is confined to aesthetic humanism. Comparison occurs among different figures of man, according to a schema of anthropological difference bifurcated into colonial difference and the anthropological exception. This comparative mode leads from the anthropological difference to the logistical apparatus of area and the modern regime of translation that characterises the contemporary post-colonial, post-imperial world.

Advertisements for Ridley Scott's 1983 film *Alien* were accompanied by the phrase, 'In space, no one can hear you scream'. Sputnik would seem, however, to have generalised that predicament down to the very core, or *noyau dur*, of the Earth—which, by the way, is a molten mass rather than a hard kernel. Arendt's glum reflections on the meaning of space exploration after Sputnik emphasise this unprecedented reversal:

> We have come to our present capacity to 'conquer space' through our new ability to handle nature from a point in the universe outside the earth [...] Without as yet actually occupying the point where Archimedes had wished to stand, we have found a way to act on the earth as though we disposed of terrestrial nature from outside.
>
> *(Arendt, 2007: 54)*

Arendt is adamant, as she channels Heisenberg, that the 'conquest of space' will only serve to exacerbate the metaphysical conundrum of Man's essentially literary self-referentiality. 'All of this makes it more unlikely ever day that man will encounter anything in the world around him that is not man-made and hence is not, in the last analysis, he himself in a different disguise' (Arendt, 2007: 52). In the post-Sputnik world of the Anthropocene, our view of the Earth is irrevocably space-bound. Even on Earth, screams from the sixth mass extinction of species (the first engendered by human action) have been muffled by the vacuous infinity of anthropocentric self-referentiality.

One of the results of this displacement is to be found in what Frédéric Neyrat calls, in a *tour de force* survey of the philosophical errors behind recent anthropocenic discourses, the perspective of 'geo-constructivism' (Neyrat, 2016). Whereas yesterday's authors and scientists dreamt of terraforming, turning an alien planet into one habitable for the human species, today's geo-constructivists dream of re-formatting the Earth in a new kind of process, based on the integration of information technology with biotechnology, for which the most apt term might be the neologism, 'terraformatting'.[7] For Arendt, the horror is specifically dialled in on what futurologists like Ray Kurzweil would later come to call the Singularity, that post-human moment when 'the whole of technology [becomes] [...] a large-scale biological process' (Arendt, 2007: 54). If liberalism is thoroughly biopolitical, and if biopolitics is inextricably invested in and by logistical capitalism, it is no surprise that the totalisation of technology in the biological will be realised by the ideology of logistics, a.k.a. neoliberalism. For Arendt, the dread associated with this development is represented by the demise of natural language as such and its replacement by a form of logistical extremism:

> Under these circumstances, speech and everyday language would indeed be no longer a meaningful utterance that transcends behavior even if it only expresses it, and it would much better be replaced by the extreme and in itself meaningless formalism of mathematical signs.
> (Arendt, 2007: 54)

The replacement of translation by logistics would thus be complete, and the project of 'complit' (homphonous with the English word 'complete', as Derrida reminds us, when the two are pronounced with a continental accent) finally consummated in an uninhabitable totalitarian utopia (Derrida, 2008: 33).

A different taste

I began this essay with the promise of a different taste. It might be fitting, to that end, to remember a time before geo-constructivism, when the Earth was defined not in opposition to space, but rather to water. Miller, the sterile water planet in Christopher Nolan's ode to geo-constructivism, *Interstellar* (2014), epitomises the difficulty we have in the post-Sputnik era in thinking about earth in relation to water. It's as if water were simply an evolutionary dinosaur.

Perhaps water, not earth, is the element in which and from which we should reconsider the view after Sputnik. Working back from Arendt, let's think about what it would mean for language. If language is more like water than apples and oranges (Sakai, 2009), and yet nevertheless extremely difficult to taste, this does not mean that it is for that reason any less important for us to taste it, 'literally'. Isn't it rather the case that water subverts the entire anthropological category of taste? It originally requires no expertise, no knowledge, no *episteme* and no *technê* in order to appreciate it. Water is the very epitome of the common, non-knowledgeable, practical experience of translation. Its progressive privatisation today is emblematic of the Anthropocene, or Capitalocene. Cheers to water, the taste of commonism, the translation (of) the world.

Notes

1 Derrida has addressed translation in relation to the proper noun in many different texts, yet the one that will surely be remembered as central to an understanding of this relationship is 'Les Tours de Babel' (1985), in *Difference in Translation*, trans. and ed. Graham F. Joseph, Ithaca and London: Cornell University Press, 165–208.

2 While I support and militate for the use of inclusive language, the substitution of a noun like 'the human' for 'man' is equally unsatisfactory. It merely resolves one problem (gendered universalism) by introducing another (speciesism/anthropocentrism). It is precisely this kind of metonymical displacement that makes aesthetic humanism so difficult to counter.
  Following an argument brilliantly elaborated by Naoki Sakai, I hold that the kind of difference encountered in translation—hence in social practice in general—cannot be comprehended by the logical economy of genus and species. Hence, the categories of social ontology that rely on the logic of specific, or species, difference are to be rejected, with several caveats to prevent the recuperation of discourses of domination under the pretence of universalism. This rejection applies equally to specific difference between *homo sapiens* and other species, i.e. inter-species difference, as well as to specific difference between different segments of *homo sapiens*, i.e. intra-species difference. In view of the need to reject this social ontology, I find it useful to retain the term 'man', when used by authors such as Étiemble (or Michel Foucault, for example) who are blind to their own gendered, anthropocentric, or Eurocentric presuppositions. The only justification for preserving the term is, hence, to turn it into an object of criticism. The crucial caveat, however, is that the context in which such a term is deployed, even as an object of criticism, necessarily includes additional, explicit criticism of specific or species difference, minimally, and, more generally of domination that occurs under the pretext of universalism. Hence, it is necessary to attend to difference in all its forms, especially those that defy or complicate normalised schemas of representation.
3 Aesthetic humanism refers to a project that joins subjective formation to an aesthetic figuration of the human according to a biopolitical typology of anthropological difference.
4 Throughout this chapter I use the Yiddish term, *Di Khurbn Eyrope*, to refer to the destruction of European Jewry during the Second World War.
5 See Seidman, Chapter 5, 'The Holocaust in Every Tongue' (Seidman, 2006: 199 *passim*).
6 The Liberal Democratic Party (LDP) was founded in 1955 by a number of Japanese politicians, including war criminals such as Hatoyama Ichirō and Kishi Nobusuke, both of whom were former cabinet ministers in the wartime government. In terms of its composition and its interests, the LDP represented the remnants of pre-war Japanese imperialism incorporated into the formation of *Pax Americana* that extends to the current day. Kishi, an unindicted Class A war criminal, is the grandfather of the current Japanese Prime Minister Abe Shinzō. The LDP has ruled Japan continuously since 1955, but for a ten-month hiatus in 1993–94 and a brief stint out of power from 2009 to 2012.
7 The neologism is not used by Neyrat, nor can I claim to have invented it myself, yet I cannot recall where I first saw its occurrence.

References

Arendt, H. (1998) *The Human Condition*, Chicago: The University of Chicago Press.
Arendt, H. (2007) 'The Conquest of Space and the Stature of Man', *The New Atlantis* 18: 43–55.
Baldwin, J. (1984) 'Stranger in the Village', in J. Baldwin (ed.), *Notes of a Native Son*, Boston: Beacon Press, 159–175.
Balibar, É. (2007) 'Is There a "Neo-Racism"?' In T. Das Gupta, C. E. James, C. Andersen, G.-E. Galabuzi & R. C. A. Maaka (eds.), *Race and Racialization: Essential Readings*, Toronto: Canadian Scholars, 130–140.
de Man, P. (1979) *Allegories of Reading: Figural Language in Rousseau, Nietzsche, Rilke, and Proust*, New Haven & London: Yale University Press.
Derrida, J. (1985) 'Les Tours de Babel', in J. Derrida (ed.), *Difference in Translation*, trans. and ed. Graham F. Joseph, Ithaca and London: Cornell University Press, 165–208.

Derrida, J. (2008) 'Who or What Is Compared? The Concept of Comparative Literature and the Theoretical Problems of Translation', in trans. E. Prenowitz *Discourse* 30(1–2): 22–53.

Dutton, M. (2002) 'Lead Us Not into Translation: Notes toward a Theoretical Foundation for Asian Studies', *Nepantla: Views from South* 3(3): 495–537.

Espagne, M. (2013) 'La Notion De Transfert Culturel', *Revue Sciences/Lettres* 1/2013: 1–9.

Hirakawa, S. (2002) 'Étiemble ou la polygamie intellectuelle', *Révue de littérature comparée* 301: 109–114.

Kanngieser, A. & N. Bueret (2017) 'Refusing the World: Silence, Commoning, and the Anthropocene', *South Atlantic Quarterly* 116(2): 363–380.

Meng, H. (2002) 'Étiemble, maître spirituel des comparatistes chinois', *Révue de littérature comparée* 301: 103–107.

Neyrat, F. (2016) *La Part Inconstructible De La Terre: Critique Du Géo-Constructivisme*, Paris: Éditions du Seuil.

Perullo, N. (2016) *Taste as Experience: The Philosophy and Aesthetics of Food*, New York: Columbia University Press.

Postel, P. (2010) 'La littérature comparée et les études chinoises', *Études chinoises* hors-série 2010: 261–291.

Redfield, M. (2003) *The Politics of Aesthetics: Nationalism, Gender, Romanticism*, Stanford: Stanford University Press.

Sakai, N. (1997) *Translation and Subjectivity: On 'Japan' and Cultural Nationalism*, Minneapolis: University of Minnesota Press.

Sakai, N. (2009) 'How do We Count a Language? Translation and Discontinuity', *Translation Studies* 2(1): 71–88.

Sakai, N. (2013) 'The Microphysics of Comparison: Towards the Dislocation of the West': https://transversal.at/transversal/0613/sakai/en (viewed 20/08/2019).

Seidman, N. (2006) *Faithful Renderings: Jewish-Christian Difference and the Politics of Translation*, Chicago & London: The University of Chicago Press.

Smith, N. (2017) 'Martin Scorsese's *Silence* Is a Win for Taiwan but Producers Are Worried About a China Backlash', in *Time.com*, 20 January: http://time.com/4640566/taiwan-silence-scorsese-movies-china/ (viewed 05/07/2017).

Solomon, J. (2017) 'Knowledge Production in the Apparatus of Area under *Pax Americana*: the Labor of Translation, the Financialization of Knowledge, and the Work of the Common'. *Presentation at the international conference 'Paradigm Shift of the Colonial-Imperial Order and the Aporia of the Human Sciences'*, June 2–6, 2017, National Chiao Tung University, Hsinchu, Taiwan.

Solomon, Jon. (2014) 'The Postimperial Etiquette and the Affective Structure of Area', *Translation* 4: 171–201.

Spivak, G. C. (2009) 'Rethinking Comparativism', *New Literary History* 40(3): 609–626.

Wolcott, J. (2013) 'Wham! Bam! Thank You, Liam!', in *Vanity Fair*: www.vanityfair.com/culture/2013/03/taken-liam-neeson-action-star (viewed 11/09/2017).

Yokota-Murakami, T. (1998) *Don Juan East/West: On the Problematics of Comparative Literature*, Albany: State University of New York Press.

2

THE LANGUAGE OF THE HEGEMON

Migration and the violence of translation

Monika Mokre

Introduction

Abdelmalek Sayad (1999) defines the state by its specific form of discrimination—between citizens and non-citizens, between those who 'belong to the state' or 'come out of the state' and those who do not.[1] The state recognises its citizens, and recognises itself in its citizens, as the citizens recognise themselves in the state. The 'others', the 'foreigners' are only recognised by the state in a physical or instrumental way as they happen to reside on its territory. This holds true for all states, but even more so for nation states striving for complete—i.e. political, economic, social and cultural—homogeneity. Thus, every 'foreigner' is a disturbance of the 'natural' order of the nation state.

> Apart from the fact that immigration or, in other words, the presence of 'non-citizens' [...] within the nation is disturbing the national order as a whole, immigration also disarranges the separation or demarcation between the national and the non-national and, thus, also the order based on this demarcation. Immigration disturbs this order, endangers its integrity, its mythical purity or perfection and, in the end, also the completion of the logic inherent in this order.
>
> (Sayad, 1999: 5–14)

However, the homogenous nation state has always formed an idealised abstraction of really existing nation states. The nation itself is a construction; the cohesion of the national people is based on a 'fictive ethnicity' which, according to Balibar (1998: 118), should be 'understood by analogy with the *persona ficta* of the juridical tradition in the sense of an institutional effect, a "fabrication".' Language plays a crucial role in this fabrication:

> [W]hat is perceived as one single language of the sovereign, or what we might also call the mother tongue of the state, is a sort of universalist extract of the language of the community—one which has been purified and filtered of its particularities, i.e. of all the meanings that express particular interests.
>
> *(Buden, 2013)*

Thus, every encounter of the 'community' with the 'state' requires or constitutes a form of translation. This becomes evident in everyday life every time a citizen has to deal with legislation or jurisdiction, as neither the grammar nor the terminology of legal documents corresponds with everyday language. This is partly due to the universalism of the 'mother tongue of the state', and partly due to a form of exclusion inherent in the concept of 'the people', a term positioned in the tension between naked life (*zoe*) and political subjectivity (*bios*) (Agamben, 1998). Even those included *de jure* as citizens and, thus, as political subjects are frequently excluded *de facto* due to their inability to translate themselves into the mother tongue of the state. Non-citizens, however, are also excluded *de jure*, not only as political subjects, but also as holders of any rights in their territory of residence. They have to prove this right to the state and so to translate themselves into its mother tongue.

The universalism of human rights and the rights of refugees

However, in principle, every human being should enjoy human rights as a minimum, irrespective of his or her political status. While political rights depend on affiliation to a political community, human rights are defined as universal in the Universal Declaration of Human Rights (1948). In this sense, for example, protection against torture or the right to a family life apply to all human beings irrespective of citizenship. In her considerations on statelessness, Hannah Arendt asked whether rights can exist which are neither given nor defended by a state. If such a right exists, it must be fundamentally different from all rights derived from citizenship: it must be based on human dignity and constitute the right to act and speak, i.e. to be politically active (Arendt, 1958: 296). This is what Arendt calls 'the right to have rights' (Arendt, 1958: 298). Without this right to have rights, human rights are nothing more than a moral appeal. This appeal is unnecessary so long as it is commonly agreed that all human beings are free and equal in dignity. And it becomes ineffective as soon as this principle is questioned. Here, Arendt links the question of human rights to community and solidarity:

> As human rights are only endangered when they are questioned in practice, in human coexistence, the acknowledgement of human rights forms, for Arendt, rather a problem of practice and resistance against politics infringing human rights. Human rights depend on political solidarity.

> Thus, Arendt asks for the preconditions of political solidarity. [...] If one poses the problem in this way, it becomes obvious that human rights are not a steadfast property of individuals guaranteed by birth. Rather, they are the expression of a specific human relationship that has to be continuously renewed and maintained. Their validity and consideration are a constant mission of care. People have to take care that human rights appear in the world, that they attain reality and practical efficacy. [...] Referring to a term by Derrida, one can say that human rights are not given to us as a fact but as a task. We bear the responsibility for them. They are a promise we give to each other.
>
> *(Förster, 2009)*

Such a promise can only be given within a community. According to Arendt (1958: 272), from their beginning—that is, since the French Revolution—human rights were connected to national sovereignty. In a nation state, human rights form the fall-back device for minorities of another nationality; for example, refugees. The Geneva Convention on Refugees refers to these rights and defines the conditions for being recognised as a refugee. A refugee is

> [a] person who owing to a well-founded fear of being persecuted for reasons of race, religion, nationality, membership of a particular social group or political opinion, is outside the country of his nationality and is unable or, owing to such fear, is unwilling to avail himself of the protection of that country; or who, not having a nationality and being outside the country of his former habitual residence as a result of such events, is unable or, owing to such fear, is unwilling to return to it.
>
> *(UNHCR, 2010: Art. 3)*

Translating the refugee

A person asking for asylum has to translate their story in a way that qualifies them as a refugee. Peter Waterhouse describes the effort required in creating a translation that serves as proof of a well-founded fear:

> A from a place I cannot remember told me [...] that she could not sell herself. [...] 'I cannot promote myself, I cannot apply on my own behalf, I also cannot apply for asylum, present myself as higher or more fearful than others . [...] I remain silent about my fear, I do not talk about its foundations. My fear is not unfounded. I did not found it, somebody else laid the foundations for it. If I began to justify it, in front of an official whom I have never seen in my life and whom I take for a policeman, in the presence of a translator whom I do not know and with whom I do not want to speak, in presence of a secretary summarising or condensing

my fear in minutes—I would perhaps die. Fear—I also fear the policeman, who asks questions like a policeman. I fear that he will decide against me, that I will not understand the foundation of this decision, that this decision is better founded than my fear ...'

(Waterhouse, 2012)[2]

But the fear has to be well-founded according to the law. And not every fear counts as a legally well-founded fear. You can be recognised as a refugee if you have been threatened by agents of the state, the army, the police, or political enemies. You will not be recognised if you were threatened due to a family feud, or another problem in your region that is not regarded as political. And, of course, you will not be recognised if you are threatened by poverty or even starvation—then, you are a fake refugee, an economic refugee, i.e. an economic migrant. A considerable amount of translation work is thus needed in order to establish whether a refugee should be recognised. Dates, places, numbers and names have to be stated and proven or, at least, made plausible. A 2017 novel by Mascha Dabić, about the experience of a psychotherapeutic translator who has to compile reports, describes how this process works:

> This was disturbing for her. The story of a life composed like a mosaic in many intense conversations was, in the language of bureaucracy, reduced to a 'torture story' split up into its individual parts—number and function of the perpetrators, frequency of torture, methods and instruments applied, physical and psychological consequences. People on whose words she had hung for hours so as to absorb meaning and expression as completely and authentically as possible—in the forms she had to fill in, these people became 'victims' or 'survivors'.
>
> (Dabić, 2017: 35)[3]

For the hegemon, it is very important that dates, places and names are correct. For the asylum applicant, this was frequently not the most important issue during their flight. The question of an official, 'When did you leave Ghana?', was answered by the applicant: 'I don't know, I was crying.'[4] But data are needed even if they cannot be provided. This is why a surprising number of refugees have the birth date 1 January—the hegemon assigns a date if one cannot be provided. In a novel by Sophie Hardach, a perplexed Kurdish asylum seeker in Germany asks the interpreter:

> 'How do they know when I was born? *I* don't know when I was born.' They know everything', the interpreter said with conviction [...].
>
> (Hardach, 2011: 10)

Hardach also describes how the date of birth could be—approximately—determined:

> You would have to travel all the way to the mountains of Kurdistan, to the wild and remote region where Turkey knocked against Iraq and Syria, all the way to Selim's village, and talk to his mother, his father, his neighbours, to find out the most basic details such as when he was born.
>
> Even then, the question would prompt a lot of head scratching and murmuring and: 'I think it was the night after *Newroz* and before Cevim's wedding ...'
>
> No, it was long before that, after we bought the second goat but before we fixed the hole in the roof, no, not the new roof, the old roof.
>
> (Hardach, 2011: 11–13)

And so on. The date of birth is important for a translation into the language of the bureaucracy, because this language has its own rules, its grammar—and this grammar is strict and universal; exceptions are not foreseen. But the date of birth is also important due to specific provisions of the asylum law: unaccompanied minors have certain rights that adults do not. So, if the applicant is not able to translate themselves into the language of bureaucracy because they do not know their date of birth, or if the translation does not seem trustworthy, the hegemon has its own translation method: in order to determine the age of the applicant, the carpal bone is X-rayed. This method is dubious for two reasons: firstly, specialists doubt its reliability[5]; and, secondly, because X-ray examinations are a health hazard, they are usually only carried out for medical reasons and with the explicit consent of the person concerned. Thus, this form of age determination was legally prohibited in Austria until 2010, when the law was changed allowing asylum authorities and the immigration police to use this method.[6]

The body of an asylum seeker can be used to translate them into the language of the sovereign state. While carpal X-rays are only used for people claiming to be minors, all refugees have to have their fingerprints taken in order to determine if they have already applied for asylum in another EU country. There is a way to prevent this form of translation: you can burn your fingers so that the fingerprints disappear for some time, as Tina Leisch (2013) describes:

> Take a strong painkiller. Then turn the two front burners of your stove on and wait until they are red hot. Then lay the four fingers of your right hand on the right burner and the four fingers of your left hand on the left burner. [...]
>
> It could be the only way to destroy the relationship between, on the one side, you, your sacred personality, your beautiful body which enables your possibly more beautiful soul to move, to get intoxicated and to have orgasms, and, on the other side, the fingerprints, birth and registration information, police photos and further information, which allegedly refer to you, determine you and which allegedly label you. [...]

> 'The borders that exclude me from elementary human rights, from leading a good life, lay beyond barbed wire. The border which separates people from unworthy people: these are the fine lines on my fingers.' This is what you say before you put your hand on the stove.
>
> *(Tina Leisch, 2013)*

By burning one's fingers, one can transform oneself into a blank page in the eyes of the law. One can forestall translation by the hegemon and translate oneself into a person with the right to apply for asylum.

Translation can hurt.

The burden of translation

> The complainant did not manage to present the story of his flight in the way an average person would who could serve as a measurement here. He told a stereotypical, empty story outline without substantiating it or bringing it to life by providing details.
>
> *(Asylgerichtshof, 2012)*[7]

This is the English translation of part of the legal argument in favour of a negative decision on an asylum application. The translation seems clumsy; but, in fact, the German text sounds clumsy and includes words normally not used in German, such as 'Maßfigur' (here tentatively translated as 'a person who could serve as a measurement'). This is a specific feature of bureaucratic and legal texts: they are written in a language which is not used in everyday speech, and which is not easily accessible to non-lawyers and non-bureaucrats. This is partly due to the complexity of legal matters and the specific requirements for legal language:

> There are good reasons for the feeling that law should have a language of its own. Special symbol systems allow clarity and precision, as with mathematics and symbolic logic. If law is to be authoritative and controlling and yet not the tool of special interests, then its language must be freed from ambiguities and other weak spots
>
> *(Probert, 1968: 253)*

However, Probert (1968: 253) also acknowledges that 'even professionals enjoy the sense of status which comes from a non-public vocabulary.' Judges, lawyers, and state prosecutors increase and affirm their cultural capital by using this non-public vocabulary. Furthermore, and more importantly, legal speech is an excellent example of the 'mother tongue of the state' (Buden, 2013). In legal procedures, the state does not have to translate itself in order to be understood; it can require its subjects to understand its mother tongue and to translate themselves into this language.

Decisions on asylum applications show this very clearly. These are usually lengthy documents twenty to forty pages long, including the statements of the applicant, their assessment by the official, a *Länderdokumentation* (country documentation[8])—and the verdict. This verdict, from a few lines up to a page in length—the application has been accepted or rejected, which leads to the following consequences—is the only part of the document translated into the applicant's mother tongue. In this way, the state tells them whether they have the right to a life here or should prepare for their return. This is the only information the state wants to give the applicant: it does not have to give its reasons, as it has the power in this equation.

The applicant does not have power, and so must translate themselves constantly into the language of the hegemon. As with every translation, this one also comes at some cost—to those who have to frame their experiences in a new language. Cunningham (1989) describes this on the basis of his experiences as a lawyer:

> What happened is not immutably fixed in an objective reality, but is a social construction based on experience and interaction [...] The primary issue may not be what happened to the client, nor what kind of trouble the client is in, but who has the power to say what happened and to define the kind of trouble.
>
> *(Hosticka, quoted after Cunningham, 1989: 2472)*

Thus, for Cunningham (1989), a lawyer is a translator who, by translating, produces a new form of knowledge:

> '[if] language is intimately bound up with the way we think about experience, then talking about experience in a different language necessarily entails knowing that experience in a somewhat different way. [...] [The client's] inability to *speak* the language of the law prevents her from *knowing* her experience as a legal event. [...] As the lawyer attempts to "make a case" out of the client's lay narrative, there is indeed a transformation of "reality" [...]'
>
> *(Cunningham, 1989: 2482–2483)*

Asylum seekers, however, are not allowed to bring a lawyer to their first interviews. They are entitled to legal counselling before the interview, and they can be accompanied by a legal counsellor, but this legal counsellor is not allowed to speak for their client. This corresponds with the logic of these procedures, in which the asylum seeker is neither a defendant nor a complainant, but an applicant. Only after an initial negative decision does the asylum seeker become a complainant and can then be represented by a lawyer or a legal counsellor. At the same time, this rule suggests that an asylum seeker does not need a translation of their experiences into the language of the law, and will still be fairly treated by the authorities. According to recent statements by members of the Austrian government, even the possibilities for legal counselling before the interview shall be limited, as they supposedly only prolong asylum procedures.[9] Obviously, the suspicion underlying these and similar statements is that asylum seekers are usually, or frequently, lying about their reasons for fleeing. However, it seems more important for the topic of this paper that asylum seekers are not granted the same support as citizens in understanding the law and dealing with it. They have to bear the full burden of translation and of its failures.

Thus, many asylum seekers feel trapped in a bureaucratic procedure without any understanding of proceedings or the reasons for decisions. Arguably, this situation stands in conflict with Article Six of the Universal Declaration of Human Rights (1948): 'Everyone has the right to recognition everywhere as a person before the law'. According to Waldron (2011), this principle includes an individual quality. The law

> conceives of the people who live under it as bearers of reason and intelligence. They are thinkers who can grasp and grapple with the rationale of the way they are governed and relate it in complex but intelligible ways to their own view of the relation between their actions and purposes and the actions and purposes of the state.
>
> *(Waldron, 2011: 19)*

The universal right to recognition by the law has to be 'transformed into those capabilities, statuses, and powers necessary for effective participation and claim making in the legal system' (Bohman, 2009: 553, cf. Mokre, 2017). As this translation is not made possible, asylum seekers are left in a state of deep insecurity about their status and their chances. In this vein, a Syrian asylum seeker speaks of 'the lottery' according to which a legal status is provided (Mokre, 2017:151) while other people in the same situation try to figure out—sometimes far-fetched—reasons for asylum decisions:

> In the meantime, two sons have arrived in Austria. They already got asylum. But I did not, as yet. I do not know why. […] I think they take the young people, not the old people. […] The old ones are beyond the expiration date, I think.
>
> *(Mokre, 2018)*

An unsuccessful translation

Coming back to the quotation above, we see an example of failure to translate one's experiences into the language of the law. 'The complainant did not manage to present the story of his flight in the way an average person would who could serve as a measurement here.' The story the complainant told in a different way to the average person serving as a measurement was about him being tortured by the police. How would an 'average person who could serve as a measurement here' describe the experience of torture? How can any yardstick be found for the description of very individual experiences?

We encounter here a general problem of the law which brings Derrida (1992) to conclude that the law can never be just. The stabilisation of expectations, and thus of a political order, is the main function of the law in society (Derrida, 1992: 17–20). The law is therefore based on a logic of calculability and generalisation. However, justice has to be adequate to the irreducible singularity of the single case, taking into its incalculability into account. Thus, the law cannot be just, and cannot be legitimised by theories of justice. In this vein, Derrida formulates three apories of justice:

1. In order to be just with regard to the single case, the law must allow for exceptions from its general rules. However, a decision without rules is not just, either. The claim for generalisation and the claim for the validity of special circumstances lead to the impossibility of justice.
2. Every decision has to be made under conditions of indecidability. A calculation based on fixed parameters is not a free decision. However, neither a decision without rules nor a decision following strict rules (that is, a decision in *sensu stricto*) can be called just.
3. Every decision with regard to justice is urgent. Thus, a horizon of justice is of no use for the problem of justice that has to be solved immediately and with regard to the special case in question.

From a different perspective, Lyotard (1987: 9) comes to a similar understanding of the impossibility of a just law. From his perspective, antagonism constitutes the opposite of a legal dispute, because it is an absolute opposition that cannot be adjudicated: the two sides are too fundamentally different to be assessed within a common framework. The law is, therefore, a false harmonisation on the base of a hegemonic rationality and so it must be renounced, philosophically as well as politically: legal reconciliation leads to injustice. And so, for Lyotard (1987: 55–56), injustice is not to be found in the damage done by an unjust judgement, but in the fact that this damage cannot be articulated.

> Like more familiar forms of language, law creates knowledge by dividing up the spectrum of human experience into new basic categories. But this new knowledge, like all forms of knowledge, involves a loss, a reduction of the particularity of experience and the perspectives of other understandings.
> *(Cunningham, 1989: 2491)*

This general dilemma of the law becomes more problematic when experiences of lawmakers and judges differ to a high degree from the experiences of those to whom the law is applied. When the Austrian Corporate Code obliges businesses to act with 'the diligence of a prudent businessman', it can be expected that most managers understand this phrase at least approximately. But how can a judge, probably living rather a stable life in Upper Austria, assess the experience of torture?[10] There is no common rule and no common language.

Translation and voicelessness

The minutes of the interview quoted above show that, in fact, the applicant did not go into vivid detail in his description. The judge might be right that this lack of detail is due to lack of personal experience. However, it is at least equally probable that the lack of detail stems, in fact, from overwhelming personal experience, from a form of suffering which leads to voicelessness: '[T]he silence of suffering also points to very practical breakdowns of speech [...] the voicelessness of suffering often resembles the quiet retreat of people who live with chronic pain' (Morris, 1997: 28, cf. Karmal, 2018).

Therapists are well acquainted with the inability to retell a trauma due to fear of re-traumatisation; so-called avoidance symptoms form one of four symptom groups of post-traumatic stress disorder (PTSD).[11] The most usual of these symptoms are '[S]taying away from places, events, or objects that are reminders of the traumatic experience [and] [a]voiding thoughts or feelings related to the traumatic event.' Conversely, speaking about the traumatising event can lead to re-traumatisation and '[f]lashbacks—reliving the trauma over and over, including physical symptoms like a racing heart or sweating.'[12] Research results have shown that asylum interviews have a

> stressful impact [...] on traumatized refugees. They indicate that the asylum interview might decrease post-traumatic avoidance and trigger post-traumatic intrusions, thus highlight the importance of ensuring that the already vulnerable group of traumatized refugees needs to be treated with empathy during their asylum interview.
>
> *(Schock et al., 2015)*

So, an asylum interview can have a traumatising impact on already traumatised persons. This holds true for the whole asylum procedure: the entire time in which a person tries to stabilise his or her situation.

> Though there are opportunities and changes for a better life as well, when reaching the country of resettlement, refugees can be faced with several problems that can affect their mental wellbeing. First and foremost this has to do with:
>
> - Insecurity about long and enduring asylum procedures;
> - Dreadful living conditions as they are likely to live in small rooms and faced with constant relocation;

- Exposure to violence whilst living in the asylum-seeker centre;
- Post-migration stressors such as a poor social support system, a lack of employment and -education possibilities and financial insecurities […]

Often it can be seen that not only the previously experienced traumatic events, but also, and sometimes even to a greater extent, the current insecure life situation can cause emotional suffering. In addition to this, asylum-seekers and refugees can be exposed to extreme discrimination due to misrepresentation in the media and in political statements; therein asylum-seekers and refugees might be dehumanized, demonized and portrayed as 'enemies at the gate' who aim to invade Europe, US and Australia, as well as a threat to economic security […][13]

The subaltern cannot speak.

Traduttore—traditore

The refugees cannot make themselves understood to the judge. The judge cannot understand them, not only due to their own lack of experience but also because they cannot develop empathy and still act as judge. The subaltern cannot speak, and the hegemon cannot listen. A Syrian refugee told me: 'If they knew, if they really knew what happened to us on our way here, they would not reject anybody'.[14]

Refugees and judges do not speak the same language. This is mostly also true in a linguistic sense. Most asylum interviews are carried out via an interpreter. Interpretation is supposed to enable mutual understanding of interviewer and interviewee. The system seems clear: questions and answers are translated and, in the end, the German language protocol is translated into the mother tongue of the interviewee, who then signs it and thereby confirms that it is correct.

Many practical problems make this procedure less clear than it seems. When refugees in Vienna protested against their situation in 2012, their first demand was:

> The translators which are being used during the asylum cases must all be replaced with new ones. These translators have been working here for a very long time, and they are making jokes about people. They translate deliberately wrong and because of that many people got bad court procedures, negative verdicts and interviews.[15]

Perhaps the refugees had really encountered cynical interpreters who misunderstood them deliberately. But they could also have encountered overworked and overwhelmed interpreters as well as ones who were not adequately trained for this work. Interpreting is hard work, and interpreting in asylum procedures is paid even less than other interpreting work (cf. Mokre, 2015: 30). Furthermore, in spite of the fact that asylum seekers are entitled to interpretation in their mother tongue, this law is not always obeyed. Frequently, Chechens have to deal with Russian interpretation, Pashtuns with Dari or Urdu, Dari speakers with Farsi. Arabic poses a special problem, as Arabic dialects are very different from one another and so, for example, a Moroccan asylum seeker can barely understand an interpreter from the Emirates. And sometimes, ethnic conflicts from the place of origin play a role in the quality of interpretation. In this vein, a member of the Pashtun minority of Turi complained to me about continuous wrong translations by Pashtun interpreters.

On a structural level, theorists of translation know well that interpretation and translation are impossible. Above all, they are impossible in the way required of interpretation within a legal procedure: to precisely convey the sense of questions and answers in the respective other language. In the first half of the nineteenth century, Friedrich Schleiermacher already summarised the problem in one sentence: 'Either the translator leaves the author in peace as much as possible and moves the reader toward him; or he leaves the reader in peace as much as possible and moves the author toward him' (cited in Buden, 2008). The interpreter in a legal procedure has to deal with two authors and two readers (or listeners), but the problem remains the same.

Literal translation is impossible. Interpreters, however, are required to deliver just that. This can lead to anecdote-worthy confusion, as Mascha Dabić describes using the example of a psychotherapy session. At the end of the session, the therapist asked rather a normal question in this situation: 'What do you take with you from this session?' The client reacted in an aggressive-defensive way: 'I did not steal anything' (Dabić, 2017: 25).

This can also lead to problems that bring us into the philosophy of law, as in an example by Cunningham (1989: 2464–2465): A Spanish-speaking client told the interpreter, about a car accident, 'Yo soy culpable'. The statement was correctly translated as, 'I am guilty', and consequently led to a defence strategy based on mitigating circumstances. Only while developing this strategy with the client did it become obvious to the lawyers that he was probably not guilty in the meaning of the law, but had spoken about a wider and more complex understanding of guilt that he felt for the event.

In a way, the interviewee is privileged in this constellation, as they receive a written translation of the interview and can assess its correctness. The interviewer, the official, is usually absolutely dependent on the interpreter. If the interviewee does not immediately reject the translation read to him/her, this privilege is not helpful in the legal case: doubts expressed about a translation after signature of the protocol do normally not give rise to a new hearing. But when it is about finding out the truth (or, at least, the truth of what has been said), the interviewee is in a better position than the interviewer. And since lawyers do not translate the refugee's experience into the language of the law, it should come as no surprise that the only translator at hand and, in fact, frequently the only person the refugee can make themselves understood to, is also the one blamed for failure of understanding.

And perhaps rightly so. The interpreter is neither a machine transforming words from one language to another, nor a neutral person. The interpreter has sympathies and antipathies towards individual interviewers and interviewees. They probably also have a political and/or personal stance on the situation in which they are interpreting.

This has been described with rare intensity by Shumona Sinha (2011) in her novel *Assomons les pauvres!* (Slay the poor). The protagonist of this novel is an interpreter in asylum procedures who hits a migrant over the head with a wine bottle on the subway. In her conversations with the police, it becomes clear that the humiliating asylum system and the role of the interpreter in this system have led to this violent and desperate act. Some quotations from this novel may illustrate the dilemma of interpretation in asylum procedures.

> There, the men were similar. [...] The tales were similar. Always the same, except for some details. Dates, names, accents, and scars. It was as if hundreds of men were telling the same story. [...] I listened to their stories of minced, dismembered, spat-out sentences. The people learned them by heart and vomited them in front of the computer screens. Human rights do not include the right to escape misery. [...] You need a more noble reason, one that would legitimate political asylum. Thus, they had to hide the truth, to forget, to unlearn and to invent a new truth. The fairy tales of human birds of passage. With broken wings and grubby, stinking feathers. With dreams as sad as rags.
>
> *(pp. 10–11)*

> It was the year of triangular constellations. Between him and me, him and her, her and me, between us: supplicant, decision-maker, and translator. He asking for help, she making decisions, me putting the hyphen between them. [...]

> The decision-maker was speaking his language, the language of the receiving country, the language of glassed-in offices. The applicant was speaking his imploring language, the language of the illegals, the language of the ghetto. [...] [S]ometimes, I was under the impression that I had poured my words like hot water on their bewildered heads. Sometimes they attacked to find their poise. When they felt cornered by the questions, when they stammered and were ashamed of stammering, when they lied and knew that they lied—then, they shouted with pretended anger that we did not understand their language. They shouted that I did not translate what they said. They shouted that I did not know their language, that it was not my language.
>
> *(pp. 25–27)*

> I felt embarrassed for these men. And without realizing it, I felt more and more attracted to the woman officials who represented the law, honesty, authority. I had changed sides. My heavy heart was attracted to these

women exhausted by the infinite stream of asking men. Those anaemic, skinny nervous women. And my politically incorrect tenderness.

(p. 50)[16]

Thus, the narrator chooses the side of the officials. And she hits a man while on her way to see a judge with whom she has somehow fallen in love. She hits him with the bottle of wine she wanted to bring to her hostess. Another interpreter mentioned in the book chooses the opposite path; she is fiercely on the side of her Chechen countrymen. As an interpreter, she feels and acts like a lawyer.

There is no neutral position.

Rule of law and the necessity of translation

It is a truism in theories of cultural translation that translation is as necessary as it is impossible. But what does this mean for a legal system?

We have seen what the (partly, legally imposed) impossibility of translation does to individuals. If you happen to be born in the wrong country, you are obliged to translate yourself, and to accept translations inflicted on you. You are subject to political decisions without being allowed to participate in decision-making, as you do not enjoy political rights: neither the right to vote nor, for example, the right to make a demonstration; i.e. to participate in the democratic public sphere.

> [I]t is not realistic to say that in contemporary democracies the subjects of the law are also its authors. These changes in circumstances of politics make it likely that many democracies have become dominators, practicing what Walzer calls 'the oldest form of domination,' the domination of noncitizens by citizens. [...] Noncitizens only have duties but no rights and have, thus, according to Pettit a similar position as 'slaves or serfs'.
>
> *(Bohman, 2009: 540–545)*

Non-citizens also have to undergo legal procedures people with the 'correct' citizenship do not have to endure. If the hegemon decides that you are allowed to stay, you have to assimilate to society—a procedure frequently, and wrongly, dubbed 'integration'. Integration, however, is defined (even in official state documents) as a two-way process of mutual recognition in which a society alters according to demographic changes.[17] Public discourse, however, focuses exclusively on the obligation of the migrant to adapt to society here. If you as a migrant are allowed to stay at all, that is—if the hegemon decides differently, then you have to leave. '[T]here [are] only two ways to solve the problem [of migration]: repatriation or naturalization' (Arendt, 1958: 281).

But what does the impossibility of translation mean for the democratic nation state? For Hannah Arendt, the Minority Treaties of the 1920s already completed 'the transformation of the state from an instrument of the law into an instrument of the nation [...]; the nation had conquered the state, national interest had priority over the law' (Arendt, 1958: 275). And, for Arendt, this also meant the end of the nation state:

> For the nation-state cannot exist once its principle of equality before the law has broken down. Without this legal equality which originally was destined to replace the older laws and orders of the feudal society, the nation dissolves into an anarchic mass of over- and underprivileged individuals. Laws that are not equal for all revert to rights and privileges. [...] The clearer the proof of their inability to treat stateless people as legal persons and the greater the extension of arbitrary rule by police decree, the more difficult it is for states to resist the temptation to deprive all citizens of legal status and rule them with an omnipotent police.
>
> *(Arendt, 1958: 290)*

To this assessment by Arendt, one might add Balibar's observation (1998a: 271) that only universal rights are real rights. If rights are not universal, then

> all questions of social rights and civic rights are perverted to questions of privileges which have to be safeguarded or reserved for specific, 'natural' beneficiaries. [...] Rights qualitatively increase due to the increased number of those having or demanding these rights. Privileges can only be protected by defending an exclusivity as restrictive as possible.

Thus, also social cohesion or solidarity as a precondition of democracy erodes.

So, we encounter another problem of translation here: translation between the nation state, with its ideal of a common people of a common nation in a common territory, and the universal concept of democracy. This translation has likewise never been possible, and always been necessary. And this translation probably still has a chance, so long as its necessity and impossibility are accepted and the dilemma is not solved by renouncing democracy altogether; so long as the constitutional state in its present form remains contested by democracy. According to Abensour (2012: 216–222), the concept of the democratic constitutional state is an illusion. Norms substitute for human actions, and the domination of norms does not limit power, but constitutes a complete power in itself. The state must be reduced to the apparatus that protects the individual against the arbitrariness of power, instead of being the entity that constitutes the public sphere and the people. What is at stake here is freedom: the freedom to think with the law and with the political. The political is not a solution but a continuing question. Democracy marks the limits of the state.

These limits have to be negotiated—with everybody concerned. Those who are muted must be given a voice and a vote. The burden of translation has to be shared in order to 'space borderlines' (Raunig, 2002) to a third space (1994).

Notes

1. Quite aptly, we start this chapter with a problem of translation: The French term 'ressortissant' for a citizens (the one coming out of the state) or the German term 'Staatsangehörige_r' (the one belonging to a state) convey Sayad's meaning much more clearly than the term 'citizen'.
2. 'A aus ich weiß nicht woher sagte mir […] dass sie nicht für sich werben könne […] Ich kann mich nicht bewerben. Ich kann mich auch nicht bewerben um das Asyl, mich höher stellen oder ängstlicher als andere […] Über meine Angst schweige ich und ich begründe sie nicht. Sie ist nicht grundlos. Ich begründe sie nicht, jemand anderer hat sie begründet. Würde ich beginnen, sie zu begründen, vor einem Beamten, den ich für einen Polizeibeamten halte und nie zuvor in meinem Leben gesehen habe, in Anwesenheit einer Übersetzerin, die ich nicht kenne und mit der ich nicht sprechen möchte, in Anwesenheit eines fremden Protokollführers, der meine Angst im Protokoll zusammenfasst oder verkürzt, ich würde vielleicht sterben. Angst; Angst habe ich auch vor dem Polizeibeamten, der Fragen stellt wie ein Polizeibeamter, davor […] dass er eine Entscheidung treffen wird gegen mich, dass ich die Begründung dieser Entscheidung nicht verstehen werde, dass diese Entscheidung wohlbegründeter sein wird als meine Furcht' (Translation MM).
3. 'Sie fand es verstörend, wie sich eine Lebensgeschichte, die sich in vielen intensiven Gesprächen wie ein Mosaik allmählich zusammenzusetzen begann, in der Sprache der Bürokratie auf eine ‚Foltergeschichte' reduzieren ließ, die wiederum in ihre Einzelteile zergliedert wurde—Anzahl und Funktion der Täter, Häufigkeit der Folterung, angewandte Methoden und Werkzeuge, physische und psychische Folgeerscheinungen. Aus dem Menschen, an dessen Lippen sie Stunde um Stunde gehangen war, um Sinn und Ausdruck so vollständig und unverfälscht wie möglich aufzunehmen, wurde im Formular ein "Opfer" oder ein "Überlebender"' (Translation MM).
4. Wann haben Sie Ghana verlassen? Ich weiß es nicht, ich habe geweint. Extract of an asylum interview, quoted after Mokre 2015: 40.
5. The standard deviation according to experts is 14.5 months for men and 11.2 months for women. www.asyl.at/de/themen/umf/altersfeststellung/[viewed 11/08/2019].
6. See for example: https://derstandard.at/1289609127655/Rezension-Feindbild-Kinder fluechtling [viewed 11/08/2019].
7. 'Es sei dem Beschwerdeführer nicht gelungen, seine Fluchtgeschichte dergestalt zu präsentieren, wie dies eine durchschnittliche Maßfigur tun würde. Er habe eine stereotype, leere Rahmengeschichte geschildert, ohne diese durch das Vorbringen von Details zu substantiieren bzw. mit Leben zu erfüllen.' (Translation MM)
8. See www.bamf.de/EN/DasBAMF/IZAsylMigration/Struktur/Laenderdokumentation/laenderdokumenation-node.html [viewed 23/09/2019].
9. See for example https://derstandard.at/2000074029949/Asyl-Kickl-dehnt-Liste-sicherer-Herkunftslaender-weiter-aus [viewed 11/08/2019].
10. I would like to thank Michael Roessner for pointing out the general dependence of the law on general measurements as well as the example of the 'diligence of a prudent businessman'.
11. See for example www.nimh.nih.gov/health/topics/post-traumatic-stress-disorder-ptsd/index.shtml [viewed 11/08/2019].
12. www.nimh.nih.gov/health/topics/post-traumatic-stress-disorder-ptsd/index.shtml [viewed 11/08/2019].

13 http://eur-human.uoc.gr/module-5-part-1-2mental-health-issues-of-refugees/[2019-08-11].
14 This conversation was broadcast in Mohamed Mouaz's film *Auf nach Europa*.
15 https://refugeecampvienna.noblogs.org/post/2012/11/26/refugee-demands-24th-nov-2012/[viewed 11/08/2019].
16 'Là-bas, les hommes se ressemblaient. [...] Les récits ressemblaient aux récits. Aucune différence. Sauf quelques détails, de date et de nom, d'accent et de cicatrice. C'était comme si une seule et unique histoire était racontée par des centaines d'hommes [...] J'écoutais leurs histoires aus phrases coupées, hachées, éjectées comme on crache. Les gens les apprenaient par coeur et les vomissaient devant l'écran de l'ordinateur. Les droits de l'homme ne signifient pas le droit de survivre la misère. ... Il fallait une raison plus noble, celle qui justifierait l'asile politique. [...] Il leur fallait donc cacher, oublier, désapprendre la vérité et en inventer une nouvelle. Les contes des peuples migrateurs. Aux ailes brisées, aux plumes crasseuses et puantes. Aux rêves tristes comme les chiffons [...]

C'était l'année des triangles tendus. Entre lui et moi, entre lui et elle, entre elle et moi, entre nous: demandeur, officier et traducteur. Lui qui quémandait, elle qui décidait, et moi qui faisais le trait d'union entre eux [...]

L'officier parlait sa langue, la langue du pays d'accueil, la langue des bureaux vitrés. Le requérant parlait sa langue de suppliant, la langue des clandestins, la langue du ghetto [...] [P]arfois j'avais l'impression d'avoir jeté l'eau chaude des mes mots sur leur tête ahurie. Quelquefois ils se ressaisissaient en nous agressant. Lorsque les questions commençaient à les mettre mal à l'aise, lorsqu'ils baffouillaient et qu'ils avaient honte de bafouiller, lorsqu'ils mentaient et savaient qu'ils mentaient, ils piquaient alors une colère sournoise et hurlaient qu'on ne comprenait pas leur langue. Ils hurlaient que moi je ne traduisais pas ce qu'ils disaient. Ils hurlaient que je ne connaissais pas leur langue, que ce n'était pas ma langue [...]

Tous ces hommes me faisaient honte. Et sans le savoir je m'inclinais de plus en plus vers ces officiers femmes qui représentaient la loi, la droiture, l'autorité. J'étais passée del'autre côté. J'étais penchée avec mon coeur alourdi vers ces femmes que le défilé incessant des hommes en demande avait épuisées. Anémiques, amaigries et nerveuses, ces femmes. Et ma tendresse politiquement incorrecte' (Translation MM).
17 BMEIA n.d.: *Nationaler Aktionsplan für Integration*. (www.bmeia.gv.at/fileadmin/user_up load/Zentrale/Integration/NAP/Bericht_zum_Nationalen_Aktionsplan.pdf) [viewed 11/08/2019].

References

Abensour, M. (2012) *Demokratie gegen den Staat. Marx und das machiavellische Moment*, Frankfurt a.M.: Suhrkamp.

Agamben, G. (1998) *Homo Sacer: Sovereign Power and Bare Life*, Stanford: Stanford University Press.

Arendt, H. (1958) 'The Decline of the Nation State and the End of the Rights of Man' in H. Arendt, *The Origins of Totalitarianism*, Cleveland and New York: Meridian Books, 26–302.

Asylgerichtshof (2012), Spruch E2 428.470-1/2012/4E: www.ris.bka.gv.at/Dokumente/AsylGH/ASYLGHT_20120914_E2_428_470_1_2012_00/ASYLGHT_20120914_E2_428_470_1_2012_00.html (viewed 02/05/2018).

Balibar, É. (1998) 'Die Nation-Form: Geschichte und Ideologie' in É. Balibar & I. Wallerstein, *Rasse, Klasse, Nation*, Hamburg: Argument Verlag, 107–130.

Balibar, É. (1998a) 'Rassismus und Krise' in É. Balibar & I. Wallerstein, *Rasse, Klasse, Nation*, Hamburg: Argument Verlag, 261–272.

Bohman, J. (2009) 'Living without Freedom: Cosmopolitanism at Home and the Rule of Law', in *Political Theory* 37(4) (August 2009): 539–561.
Buden, B. (2008) 'A Tangent that Betrayed the Circle. On the Limits of Fidelity in Translation', in *Borders, Nations, Translations, Transversal Webjournal* 06 2008: http://transversal.at/transversal/0608/buden/en (viewed 02/05/2018).
Buden, B. (2013) 'Translating Beyond Europe', in *A Communality that Cannot Speak: Europe in Translation, Transversal Webjournal* 06 2013: http://transversal.at/transversal/0613/Buden/en (viewed 02/05/2018).
Cunningham, C. D. (1989) 'A Tale of Two Clients: Thinking about Law as Language', in *Michigan Law Review* 87(8) Legal Storytelling: 2459–2494.
Dabić, M. (2017) *Reibungsverluste*, Wien: Edition Atelier.
Derrida, J. (1992) 'Force of Law: The "Mystical Foundation of Authority"', in D. Cornell, M., Rosenfeld & D. G. Carlson eds, *Deconstruction and the Possibility of Justice*, New York and London: Routledge, 3–67.
Förster, J. (2009) 'Das Recht auf Rechte und das Engagement für eine gemeinsame Welt. Hannah Arendts Reflexionen über die Menschenrechte', in *HannahArendt.net. Zeitschrift für politisches Denken* 1(5) (November 2009): www.hannaharendt.net/index.php/han/article/view/146 s(viewed 02/05/2018).
Hardach, S. (2011) *The Registrar's Manual for Detecting Forced Marriages*, London: Simon & Schuster.
Karmal, N. (2018), 'Narratives of Asylum Seekers: Between Coping and Integration', in *ROR-blog*, 24/04/2018: www.ror-n.org/-blog/narratives-of-asylum-seekers-between-coping-and-integration (viewed 02/05/2018).
Leisch, T. (2013) 'Burning Fingers', in *transversal webjournal: flee erase territorialize* 03/2013, http://transversal.at/transversal/0313/leisch/en (viewed 02/05/2018).
Lyotard, J.-F. (1987) *Der Widerstreit*, München: Wilhelm-Fink-Verlag.
Mokre, M. (2015) *Solidarität als Übersetzung*, Wien: transversal.
Mokre, M. (2017) 'Arrival in Austria. Heteronomy and Autonomy in the Experiences of Refugees', in J. Kohlbacher & L., Schiocchet eds, *From Destination to Integration – Afghan, Syrian and Iraqi Refugees in Vienna*, Wien: Verlag der Österreichischen Akademie der Wissenschaften, 145–166.
Mokre, M. (2018) 'Arrival in Austria. Heteronomy and Autonomy in the Experiences of Refugees', in *ROR-n blog*, 20/02/2018: www.ror-n.org/-blog/arrival-in-austria-heteronomy-and-autonomy-in-the-experiences-of-refugees (viewed 02/05/2018).
Morris, D. (1997) 'About Suffering: Voice, Genre, and Moral Community', in A. Kleinman, V. Das & M. Lock (eds.), *Social Suffering*, Berkeley: University of California Press, 25–45.
Probert, W. (1968) 'Law through the Looking Glass of Language and Communicative Behavior', in *Journal of Legal Education* 20(3): 253–277.
Raunig, G. (2002) 'Exkurs: Vom Grenz-Wall zum Intervall' in S. Asadi & M., Mokre *URBANe Kulturen. Kunst und Kultur in der Stadtentwicklung am Beispiel von URBAN Wien Gürtel Plus*, Innsbruck: Studienverlag, 79–87.
Sayad, A. (1999) 'Immigration et "pensée d'État"', in *Actes de la recherche en sciences sociales* 129 Septembre, Délits d'immigration: 5–14.
Schock, K., R. Rosner & C. Knaevelsrud (2015) 'Impact of Asylum Interviews on the Mental Health of Traumatized Asylum Seekers', in *European Journal of Psychotraumatalogy* 2015, 6: www.ncbi.nlm.nih.gov/pmc/articles/PMC4558273/ (viewed 02/05/2018).
Sinha, Shumona (2011) *Assommons les pauvres!*, Paris: Éditions de l'Olivier.

UNHCR (2010) *Convention and Protocol Relating to the Status of Refugees*, Geneva: UNHCR. www.unhcr.org/3b66c2aa10 (viewed 02/05/2018).
United Nations (1948) *Universal Declaration of Human Rights*, Paris: United Nations General Assembly. www.ohchr.org/EN/UDHR/Documents/UDHR_Translations/eng.pdf (11.11.2019).
Waldron, J. (2011) 'The Rule of Law and the Importance of Procedure', in *Nomos* 50 Getting to the Rule of Law: 3–31.
Waterhouse, P. (2012) 'Fügungen. Versuch über Flucht und Recht und Sprache', in *flee erase territorialize, transversal webjournal* 03 2013: http://eipcp.net/transversal/0313/waterhouse/de (02.05.2018).

PART II
The Holocaust and the translator's ambiguity

3
PRIMO LEVI'S *GREY ZONE* AND THE AMBIGUITY OF TRANSLATION IN NAZI CONCENTRATION CAMPS

Michaela Wolf

In the last few decades, the discussion of translation as an ambiguous activity has frequently appeared on the research agenda. In particular, the cultural turn in translation studies has sharpened our perception of the powerful implications of translation in many settings: the postcolonial context, to take just one example, or the cluster of activities relating to translation and conflict, especially in war zones. One field that is definitely under-researched in this respect is the role of translation in the system of death and concentration camps established under the National Socialist regime. As a strategy of survival in inhuman circumstances, it goes without saying that interpreting in these camps as a specific form of mediation can be viewed as perhaps the most violent of non-professional communication practices. In this specific context, the practice of translation is markedly distinguished by its 'dark side'.

In my paper, I will discuss the ambiguous dimension of interpreting and translation in the *Lager*. On one hand, it was a vital survival strategy for the inmates in the network of terror; on the other, it presented translators and interpreters with the possibility of acting as helpers to the SS staff, not least in the hope of receiving some reward, however tiny, in return. Primo Levi's concept of the *grey zone*, which he elaborated in his last book *I sommersi e i salvati* (1986, *The Drowned and the Saved*, 1988), will help us to conceptually position the interpreting activity within the concentration camp society. In discussing the moments which activate and drive the ambiguous dimension of interpreting, we will ask whether Levi's *grey zone* can be seen as a locus of 'the dark side of translation'. Hopefully, this will help us to enhance our understanding of the ambiguous role of translation and interpreting in more general terms.

Primo Levi: language and translation as 'survival'

Today, Primo Levi is viewed not only as one of the most important survivor-writers of the Holocaust, but also as a key literary figure of the twentieth century: an ethical thinker, a scientist, an educator, and a political philosopher (Vuohelainen, 2016: 1). He was born in Turin into a liberal Jewish family in 1919, and graduated with a degree in chemistry in 1941. In 1943, he and a number of comrades joined the Italian anti-Fascist resistance, but were soon arrested by the occupying German army. When it was discovered that Levi was Jewish, he was deported to Auschwitz in 1944, and spent 11 months there before the camp was 'liberated' by the Red Army. Of the 650 Italian Jews in his 'transport', Levi was one of the 20 who survived Auschwitz (Anissimov, 1999: 134–139).

On returning to Italy, Levi became an industrial chemist at the SIVA chemical factory in Turin. He soon began to write about his experiences in the camp and his subsequent return home through Eastern Europe in what would become his two classic memoirs: *Se questo è un uomo* (1947, *If This Is a Man*, 1959) and *La tregua* (1963, *The Truce*, 1965). However, Levi only became famous in later years, especially with his book *Se non ora, quando?* (1982, *If Not Now, When?*, 1985), which won the distinguished Viareggio and Campiello prizes. In 1977, Levi retired from his position as a manager at SIVA to devote himself full time to writing. The most important of his later works was his final book, *The Drowned and the Saved*, where he once again draws on his personal experience as an inmate of Auschwitz. Whereas *If This is a Man* is autobiographical, *The Drowned and the Saved* is an attempt at an analytical approach. The problem of the fragility of memory, the strategies adopted by the Nazis to break the will of prisoners, the use of language in the camps and the nature of violence are all treated here. Levi fell to his death, apparently by suicide, on 11 April 1987.

Primo Levi is certainly one of the most important witnesses to Nazi barbarism, but he was ambivalent about having that role attributed to him. He wished to be judged not only as a writer of autobiographical works about his experiences in Auschwitz, but also as an author who wrote poetry and novels, and published critical essays in newspapers on a range of topics. He says:

> I always thought that [building] bridges is the best job there is because roads go over bridges, and without roads we'd still be like savages. In short, bridges are like the opposite of borders, and borders are where wars start.
>
> *(Levi, 1986: 78)*

This quotation from *La chiave a stella* (1978, *The Wrench* 1986) might be seen as one of the key formulations which drove his writing. Often called 'a man with many identities—chemist, industrial manager and writer' (Cicioni, 1995: cover), he tried to build bridges between different cultures and fields of enquiry through his writing. In this way, language and, consequently, translation took centre stage in his work.

In the *Lager*, daily life was reduced to a permanent struggle for survival. Primo Levi never tired of emphasising that the knowledge of German was vital in this struggle for survival, and that a total lack of communication, if it arose, was a deadly danger:

> It could happen, above all for those who did not understand German, that the prisoners did not even know in what part of Europe the Lager in which they were was situated ... They did not know about the existence of other Lagers ... They did not know for whom they worked. They did not understand the significance of certain sudden changes in conditions, and of the mass transfers.
>
> *(Levi, 1989: 6)*

In fact, any kind of communication decisively shaped the inmates' life in the *Lager*. This was no surprise, as the societies of the camps grew more and more international: in many camps there were prisoners of up to forty different nationalities. As a consequence, more differentiated mechanisms of communication were required. In response, a camp *lingua franca* emerged, often called *lagerszpracha, lagerjargon* or, with bitter irony, *crematorium Esperanto* (Jagoda Kłodziński & Masłowski, 1987). The *lagerszpracha* was a kind of communicative code, based on German vocabulary adapted to the rules of mostly Polish grammar. Moreover, nonverbal signs designated basic activities and events in the camp's daily life. A passage from a memoir of Auschwitz written by Adolf Gawalewicz (1916–1987)[1] sheds light on the importance and also the simplicity of the *lagerszpracha*. He wrote:

> Shortly after the liberation of the concentration camp of Bergen-Belsen, so towards the end of April 1945, I was in an infirmary organised by the British. In the hall where I stayed we were a truly international group: a Greek, an Azerbaijani, a Spaniard, an ethnic German from Łódź, and yet another Pole besides myself. Remembering these days in that hall, I am still amazed by the fact that we had no troubles at all in communicating with one another, and not only about matters concerning the most basic needs, such as eating and our respective states of health. We were all using the Lagerszpracha.
>
> *(Gawalewicz, qtd. in Wesołowska, 1998: 34)*

Generally, however, the *lagerszpracha*'s vocabulary was rudimentary, brutal, and bare of any abstraction. The language conventions of the prisoners were a phenomenon *sui generis*, an integral form of speech that simultaneously served as a language of conspiratorial camouflage, a factually oriented technical language, and a jargon integrating various groups. How deeply rooted the usage of the *lagerszpracha* became in those who were compelled to use it is proven by the fact that some survivors said that they repeatedly lapsed into camp jargon, particularly in encounters with former comrades in suffering (Oschlies, 1997). In contrast, Levi consciously resisted 'normalising' the *lagerjargon*: he narrates an episode in which, after returning to his professional life, he sometimes had to deal with German businessmen when negotiating purchases. On such occasions he often used terms from *lagerszpracha*, and also adopted the pertinent pronunciation. When the Germans were stunned at this, Levi reacted as follows:

> I explained to them that I had not learned German at school but rather in a Lager called Auschwitz; this gave rise to a certain embarrassment, but since I was in the role of buyer they continued to treat me with courtesy
> *(Levi, 1989: 77–78)*[2]

In *If This is a Man*, Levi even goes so far as to say: 'If the Lagers had lasted longer a new, harsh language would have been born' (Levi, 1987: 129). In fact, common words took on new meanings in the *Lager*, and words with one connotation in the civilian world were radically deformed (see, for instance, *organisieren, Prominenter, Zugang*[3]) (Sodi, 2007: 60). Translation doubtless contributed considerably to the creation of this 'new harsh language', because, by its very nature, the *lagerszpracha* can be seen as the result of continuous translation processes: translation between different languages in order to create terms that would fully correspond to its harsh meaning; translation between different social layers (education had no significance in the concentration camp: consequently, after 'translating' themselves, all spoke the same 'language'); translation between the inner world of the *Lager* and the world outside.[4]

For Levi, translation is another key concept in building a bridge to understanding. He developed a translation concept which aimed to elucidate and represent both the language transfer and its metaphorical variant (Arnds, 2012). Despite his rather conventional ideas on translation and translating in the narrower sense, Levi recognised the strengths of the translated dimension as a means of understanding. He also had more concrete knowledge of translation as a cultural practice, having published a number of translations throughout his life, including parts of a four-volume chemistry textbook in the 1950s, anthropological works by Mary Douglas and Claude Lévi-Strauss, Holocaust narratives, poetry by Heinrich Heine and Rudyard Kipling and *The Trial* by Franz Kafka.[5] It was perhaps because of his rather prolific activity as a translator that he dedicated a whole essay to the topic of translation. In 1980 (*La Stampa*, later again in 1985) Levi published an essay called 'Tradurre ed essere tradotti' ('On Translating and Being Translated'; Levi, 2015). The essay contains few original insights into the practice of translation, but it offers a succinct description of several concerns expressed by translators and theorists of translation. What makes this essay particularly revealing, however, is that Levi views his own testimonial writing through the lens of translation. For Levi, translation becomes a fundamental component in deciphering the world in which he was compelled to live. He firmly believes in the power of communication, which he considers to be not a choice, but a moral obligation (Alexander, 2007: 158, 161). He says that 'whoever practices the craft of translation or acts as an interpreter ought to be honored for striving to limit the damage caused by the curse of Babel' (Levi, 2016: 87). Consequently, translation is closely connected to Levi's persistent quest to communicate experiences many deemed untranslatable.

Opening up a *grey zone*[6]

In the chapter 'The Grey Zone' of his book *The Drowned and the Saved*, Levi particularly refers to the inmate hierarchy that developed in the camps, and writes that the concentrationary system triggered what he refers to as a 'moral collapse',[7] which resulted in obscuring the dividing line between 'us' and 'them'. He delineates the powerful conditions that cause people to become so demoralised that they will harm each other in order to survive. One outcome of the ensuing struggle for survival was the emergence of a 'grey zone', incorporating those 'prisoners who in some measure, perhaps with good intentions, collaborated with the authority' (1989: 9). Thus, the *grey zone* can be seen as a symbol of the moral compromise many prisoners were forced to make in order to buy themselves more time (Baird, 2005: 193). Consequently, by drawing on his experiences in Auschwitz, Levi is chiefly concerned in his essay with those Jewish prisoners who obtained 'privileged' positions, including the *Kapos*, the members of the *Sonderkommandos* (special squads) forced to work in the crematoria, the prisoners working in the *Schreibstube*, in the *Sanitätsbaracke*—and (at least some of) the interpreters, among many others.

The 'zone' is described as an area with 'ill-defined outlines which both separate and join the two camps of masters and servants' (ibid.: 27). Levi further distinguishes between the 'saved' and the 'drowned' when he says: 'Preferably, the worst survived, the selfish, the violent, the insensitive, the collaborators of the "grey zone", the spies'; and, he adds, 'the best all died' (ibid.: 63). The *grey zone* is precisely the place where the two groups of 'masters' (the SS authorities) and 'slaves' (the prisoners) converge and diverge. According to Levi, this zone of collaboration and *protekcja* (protection) springs from multiple roots: the *grey zone* as a site of alleged shelter is shaped by motives of guilt, torture, terror and desire for power (ibid.: 27). Therefore, one of the strongest unifying features in the Lager is the desire to obtain and maintain some sort of privilege. In the *grey zone*, internal collaboration and corruption between inmates and Nazis gradually becomes the only way to survive.[8]

In describing the *grey zone*, Levi distinguishes between the various positions of its inhabitants, starting from a detailed analysis focusing on life and death in the Lager, where the difference between privileged and the non-privileged prisoners dominated (Bravo, 2002: 2). Levi provides us with an upsetting description of some of the protagonists of the *grey zone*. Besides the *Kapos* and other prisoner-functionaries who occupied commanding positions to guarantee the camp's ongoing administration, Levi identifies the 'low-ranking functionaries':

> They formed a picturesque fauna: sweepers, kettle washers, night-watchmen, bed smoothers … checkers of lice and scabies, messengers, interpreters, assistants' assistants. In general, they were poor devils like ourselves, who worked full time like everyone else, but who, for an extra half-litre of soup, were willing to carry out these and other 'tertiary' functions: innocuous, sometimes useful, often invented out of nothing.
>
> *(Levi, 1989: 29)*

So, among the prisoners operating in this *grey zone* were interpreters, embodying most of the characteristics described above. This is particularly revealed in the fact that Levi's paradigmatic concept of the *grey zone* focuses on the moral ambiguity in human behaviour, one of the characteristic traits traditionally and historically assigned to the interpreter or translator. As inhabitants of the *grey zone*, the interpreters thus imitated, collaborated with, or assisted the Nazis in return for marginally better treatment for themselves or others (Luban, 2001: 162), being continuously located in a position between life and death.

The ambivalence of interpreting in the *grey zone*

As we know, not understanding German meant being completely cut off from what was happening in the *Lager*, including the intrigues of the SS staff or the *Kapos*; which, at any moment, could give rise to life-endangering situations. Levi understood from the moment he entered the camp that not knowing German meant death, or, the other way around:

> Knowing German meant life: I only had to look around me. My Italian companions did not understand it, that is, almost all with the exception of a few from Trieste were drowning one by one in the stormy sea of not-understanding: they did not know what the orders meant, they received slaps and kicks without comprehending why.
>
> *(Levi, 1989: 74)*

In view of the massive coercion and pressure under which most interpreters had to carry out their duty, it seems rather surprising that the picture of interpreting activities given in the available sources is far from homogeneous. The main sources of use to us are memoirs by survivors, followed by the huge number of interviews with camp survivors which have been conducted and archived over the past seventy years. Finally, survivor associations can deliver valuable information. The following analysis is based on about four hundred survivor accounts in nine languages: Catalan, Czech, English, French, German, Italian, Polish, Russian and Spanish. Drawing on monographs, articles and other textual material, consulted both in concentration camp archives and in libraries, it is possible to trace a great variety of interpreting situations that testify to the multiple attempts to tackle communication problems in the camp. From the rich sources available, the examples presented here are categorised according both to the type of interpreter and the interpreting situation. In most Nazi *Lagers*, we can discern three groups of persons acting as interpreters. The first and smallest group consisted of SS staff, often *Volksdeutsche* fluent in Polish or Czech, or other staff members with a knowledge of languages. A separate group were the *ex officio* interpreters (*Lagerdolmetscher*). These were so-called prisoner-functionaries, whose tasks often included policing duties. The large majority of 'interpreters' were self-proclaimed *ad hoc* language mediators, who facilitated communication between their fellow prisoners (Tryuk and Wolf, 2015). In the examples, the focus will be on the second and third groups.

In his survivor account *L'espèce humaine*, Robert Antelme (1917–1990) discusses various types of interpreters in broad terms. Antelme was deported to Buchenwald, then to Gandersheim, and finally reached Dachau with a death march, where he was 'liberated' in April 1945. Subsequently, he was an editor at Gallimard for thirty years, publishing the *Encyclopédie de la Pléiade*. In the following example, Antelme portrays the two antagonistic interpreter figures Lucien and Gilbert:

> There were two types of interpreters. For Lucien, the interpreter's task meant translating the orders of the SS and the Kapos, which gradually he adopted as his own ... He skilfully positioned himself as the French-speaking auxiliary of those who gave orders in German. He was only the interpreter of the SS and the Kapos, never of the prisoners. ... Gilbert ... was the prisoners' interpreter, meaning that he only used the German language in order to try to neutralise the SS, the Kapos and the foremen. He was, incidentally, quite skilful in resolving numerous conflicts between us and the foremen, and he was brave enough to defend or excuse some comrades before the SS. He exercised his duty as political prisoner: he warned and shielded his comrades ... [By] acting in this way, Gilbert became an enemy of the Kapos.
>
> *(Antelme, 2010/1957: 139–140, my translation)*

Lucien, the interpreter who easily adapts to the role ascribed to him by the SS staff, fully corresponds to the interpreter figure whom Levi positions in the *grey zone*: he not only gradually identifies with the universe of the SS, but is also most proficient in doing so, and climbs the social ladder in the camp rung-by-rung. He behaves decisively as if he belonged to the Lager staff, or rather to the camp's 'aristocracy', confirming and helping to stabilise the order of terror imposed on the group of prisoners to which he originally belonged. On the other hand, his counterpart Gilbert seems far from collaborating with authority, and clearly takes sides in favour of his fellow prisoners, not least as his political views demand. Yet the moral ambiguity represented in this passage testifies to the double role of the camp interpreter's task: both trust and mistrust are present on the part of the prisoners, demonstrating the ethically ambiguous and potentially powerful role ascribed to the interpreter. As Heidi Aschenberg says, we do not know if the two *dolmetscher* described in *L'espèce humaine* correspond to real people whom Antelme met at the Gandersheim camp, or if they only represent types of people and their behaviour. But other survivor accounts certainly offer analogous statements about interpreters (Aschenberg, 2016: 76).

Jean-François Steiner's *Treblinka* (1966), which deals with the revolt in the extermination camp, is another case in point.[9] The interpreter in the example is Marceli Galewski, *Lagerältester* (camp-elder) at Treblinka, to which he was deported from Łódź. As Yoram Lubling (2007) reports in his book on the Treblinka revolt, Galewski seems to have been quite an ambivalent person. Some surviving eyewitnesses accused him of cruelty and even murder of prisoners, while others described him as committed leader of the revolt's organising committee and an observant Jew (ibid.: 12). Reportedly, he had become 'the aristocratic speaker for the slaves of Treblinka' (ibid.: 98), while others claim in their testimonies that Galewski was a 'respectable man' (ibid.: 122). Galewski did not survive Treblinka: he escaped during the revolt, and apparently took poison while fleeing.

In the following example, the first revolt has just failed, and Galewski is addressed by the deputy camp commander Kurt Franz[10]:

> When they reported at the ramp, Kurt Franz ordered Galewski to approach him. 'There are some bandits among you, and you didn't tell me.' With all his strength, he dealt him two blows to the face. 'This is really the last time I will beat you. If I have to complain about you once again, you will be shot.' Then a small, pudgy SS officer came and asked Galewski politely to translate his words into Yiddish, then gave a stupid speech.
>
> *(Steiner, 1966: 130, my translation)*

Galewski's situation is highly dubious: immediately after being beaten by the commander, he is asked to act as official interpreter. Thus, trust and suspicion appear almost indistinguishably merged, which highlights the morally equivocal function attributed to the mediation activity, in which Galewski apparently does not have a choice. The total loss of any kind of human right is counteracted by the SS officer's desire to have his message interpreted by Galewski, a request that implicitly assumes Galewski's loyalty to his remarks—an assumption of an undoubtedly moral nature. But as we have seen, due to his multiple and, to some extent, distinguished functions in the Lager, Galewski is also one of the 'privileged', who, according to Levi, 'were a minority within the Lager population, but they represent a potent majority among survivors' (Levi, 1989: 26). Thus, interpreting certainly contributed to being positioned on the safe side:

that of survival. This raises a question of paramount importance: is the trope of 'interpreting as survival' a constitutive feature of the 'dark side of translation'? Is the interpreter's position at the borderline of moral and immoral, of ambiguous and unambiguous behaviour one of the driving forces for classifying the activity of translation or interpreting as 'dark', or 'bleak'?

The following example from Levi's *If This is a Man* illustrates the fluidity of the borderlines between victim and perpetrator, friend and enemy, life and death:

> The door is opened and an SS man enters, smoking. He looks at us slowly and asks, '*Wer kann Deutsch?*' One of us whom I have never seen, named Flesch, moves forward; he will be our interpreter ... [W]hat about our documents, the few things we have in our pockets, our watches? We all look at the interpreter, and the interpreter asks the German, and the German smokes and looks him through and through as if he were transparent, as if no one had spoken ... [The officer] speaks briefly, the interpreter translates. 'The officer says you must be quiet, because this is not a rabbinical school'. One sees the words which are not his, the bad words, twist his mouth as they come out, as if he was spitting out a foul taste ... This Flesch, who is most unwilling to translate into Italian the hard cold German phrases and refuses to turn into German our questions because he knows that it is useless, is a German Jew of about fifty, who has a large scar on this face from a wound received fighting the Italians on the Piave. He is a closed, taciturn man, for whom I feel an instinctive respect as I feel that he has begun to suffer before us.
>
> *(Levi, 1987: 28–30)*

Flesch is affiliated to the group of inmates, and at the same time acts as a spokesman for the SS. Hence, he is positioned on the borderline between the drowned and the saved, the powerless and those who are in power. He understands, not least through mastering both languages, that communication can be one-way only, and that asking questions in the camp constitutes a tragic misunderstanding, simply because *Hier ist kein Warum*: here there is no 'why' (Cicioni, 2016: 40). Language competence thus makes the interpreter aware of the useless, futile and ineffective dimension of translation, an awareness he also transmits to his fellow prisoners; and, at the same time, language competence turns the perpetrator's gaze away from those who speak another language: their language knowledge makes them invisible to him. As a consequence, the only way the interpreter can demonstrate ethical distance between himself and the perpetrator's language and its effects is his body language, inconspicuous by nature, and noticeable through swallowing and grimacing (ibid.: 41).

However, numerous authors of survivor accounts insist on depicting the interpreters' performance in the *Lager* as highly ethical, supportive and caring, as a mouthpiece for humanity, and perhaps as a better aspect of the concentrationary system, one potentially capable of softening the daily atrocities and ensuing suffering. In the following example, the author Shlomo Venezia (1923–2012) arrives with his Italian fellow prisoners, all from Thessaloniki, at the ramp of Auschwitz-Birkenau. Venezia was one of the very few who survived the *Sonderkommandos*, and the only Italian among those who did. The scene is drawn from his book *Sonderkommando: dans l'enfer des chambres à gaz* (2007), in which he depicts in detail the 'work' of members of these 'special squads' in disposing of and cremating the prisoners killed in the gas chambers. The example explicitly depicts the help of a fellow inmate who gives the newcomers a series of valuable pieces of advice:

> We had to wait for an officer and his instructions. For quite a long time we were not allowed to move. Before the officer showed up, a Greek interpreter from Thessaloniki, whom I knew, approached to warn us that the German would ask us some specific questions. He recommended us to answer immediately and without thinking that we were healthy, that we had no lice and that we were ready to work.
>
> *(Venezia, 2008: 68, my translation)*

The Greek prisoner obviously has some experience in dealing with newcomers at the entrance gate of the *Lager*, and takes the opportunity to mingle with the inmates and help them find their way in the crucial moments of their arrival; through his help, some of the newcomers might have been saved from certain death. In this as in many other examples, the interpreter conveys to his comrades the centrality of the struggle for survival when operating in the *grey zone*, and offers them—at least, temporarily—a place of shelter. However, although his support is undoubtedly crucial, we do not know whether and to what extent the interpreter offered this help to newcomers who were not Greek. We can assume that his behaviour here is at least ambiguous.

Our final example displays most of the features discussed so far, and once again demonstrates the highly ambiguous effect of the camp's structure. The author is Anita Lasker-Wallfisch (born 1925), who was deported to Auschwitz in 1943 with her sister. As she was a cello player, she became a member of the Women's Orchestra of Auschwitz, which certainly saved her life. After liberation by the British army, Anita and her sister Renate, both of whom spoke English, became interpreters for the British liberators. In her account *Inherit the Truth* (1996, *Ihr sollt die Wahrheit erben. Die Cellistin von Auschwitz* 1997) she describes the ethically valuable interpreting activities of her comrade Mala Zimetbaum (1918–1944). Because of her language skills—she knew Dutch, French, German, Italian and Polish—Mala was assigned work as an interpreter and courier. She was killed after trying to flee. At many points in her narrative, Lasker-Wallfisch praises her comrade:

> The abuse of this power [by some of the Kapos or the block-elders] was legendary. But there were also exceptions, and one was a Belgian girl

called Mala Zimetbaum. Mala was an interpreter, and she had a lot of influence. Despite everything she kept her integrity. Everyone respected her, and everyone admired her

(Lasker-Wallfisch, 1997: 137, my translation)[11]

Levi stresses that those who were saved owed their lives most of all to chance, but also to any form of privilege, however minimal. As we have seen, privilege as one of the main characteristics of those located in the *grey zone* is closely connected to the activity of interpreter. Mala Zimetbaum knew about the privileges she could obtain as an interpreter, and she obviously also knew about the equivocal impact of these privileges. Yet she clearly opted in favour of humanity, and is consequently depicted as a highly respectable person in Auschwitz. Thus, this passage shows how interpreters could counteract the *grey zone* when a liminal space is opened up in which support and solidarity are negotiated through multilingualism.

Rethinking translation in the *grey zone*

What does the dark side of translation look like in the context of communication in Nazi concentration camps? What are its main characteristics, and what is its surplus value for our understanding of translation in epistemological terms? And, more specifically, how does it correlate with Primo Levi's *grey zone*, particularly regarding interpreting in the *Lager*?

Researching the activity of interpretation with reference to Levi's concept of the *grey zone* has shown the tremendous ambiguity that characterises mediation in the *Lager*. The integral features which make up the *grey zone* include, among others: collaboration with the authorities; dwelling at the border between the two fields of 'master' and 'servant'; the aim of survival, which is closely linked to that of obtaining privilege; the alleged invisibility of the language mediator; and the search for shelter, for whatever reason. All these features are directly connected with the dark side of the mediation activity, revealing the urge to find protection and privilege in order to survive at the expense of the other, to be saved and not to drown. However, as Holocaust researcher Anna Bravo has emphasised, 'rather than fence individuals inside the borders of right and wrong, we should evaluate their behaviors in all their contradictions and unforeseeable features while their positive and negative features are intertwining and alternating' (Bravo, 2002: 18).

Indeed, most of the examples discussed here also reveal the heterogeneous character of the interpreting phenomenon: the so-called—and often self-proclaimed—interpreters were strongly involved in social coexistence in the camp, and could not avoid the obscure and equivocal process of contamination and collaboration gradually taking hold of them as mediation figures, and of their interpreting activity. The friend-enemy distinction collapses in the *Lager* because, as Uri Cohen states, 'it is trivialized by survival, which determines that everybody is an enemy, leaving an ultimate distinction between Muselman and survivor, the drowned and the saved, in its place' (Cohen, 2016).

At this point it must be stressed that the representation of the mediating activity is, as with any other phenomenon connected to the Shoah, highly contingent. Representation is often seen as a deformation, a rupture, and an act of violence (see Wolf, 2016: 14–15), opening up a field which reaches beyond the paradigm of the 'untranslatability' both of the Holocaust experience per se and of the text written to describe it. Primo Levi is certainly one of the central thinkers in this field. As outlined, his translation concept embraces both language transfer and the metaphor of mediating. For him, 'language is the gold he [Levi] mines to counter the helplessness of meaningful communication between prisoners and guards', as Toni Morrison appropriately says (Morrison, 2015)—'language' being easily interchanged with 'translation' in this quote. Levi is convinced that experiences of translation—both in the wider and the narrower sense—can be conveyed, even if these experiences are considered untranslatable by other scholars. Indeed, Zaia Alexander reminds us that 'as many survivors aver, if we can understand what happened, they failed to convey the true horror' (2007: 161).

Consequently, in the concentration camps, the dark side of translation is manifest in various forms, whether in its grim context, in the activity per se, or in the impact of the mediation process. Regarding the context, one of the central characteristics of interpreting activity in the Lager is the exceptional situation of excessive terror: extreme fear and anxiety result from the arduous climate, in which the prisoners interpreted under enormous psychical and physical pressure, often traumatised by their camp experiences. To this dark context is added the aspect of collusion which shaped the work of translation and interpreting, motivated by one of the main driving forces of the *grey zone*: survival. The distinction between the drowned and the saved is obscured by this drive for survival and, in this process of obscuring, translation gains momentum: 'saving' through enabling communication—and thus potentially contributing to survival—works to the cost of those 'drowning'. In Levi's already quoted words: 'almost all ... were drowning one by one in the stormy sea of not-understanding' (Levi, 1989: 74). Thus, one of the darkest sides of translation in the camp was its direct intervention in the existential dimension of survival.

Similarly and closely connected to this intervention is the function of translation in transcending the dichotomy of friend (the victim) and enemy (the Nazi), of victim and perpetrator. Interpreters could not easily escape positioning themselves in these 'zones of indistinction' (Agamben, 1998: 8). In these circumstances, there was little space left to enact either lasting subversion or lasting solidarity during the performance of interpreting. Moreover, the emotional element was incumbent in most situations, and not only in cases where the mode of interpreting could be decisive for a prisoner's life or death. As a result, the blurring of the difference between 'us' and 'them' through translation, the effort to establish communication, at the same time conceals the complicity

(Cohen, 2016) operating in any kind of mediation, and especially in the daily life of the *Lager*. Levi was particularly struck by 'the ways in which the German organization of the camp led Jews, however reluctantly, to become *complicit* in the destruction of their own people' (Petropoulos and Roth, 2005: xvii, emphasis added). A case in point is the way in which the SS used the members of the *Sonderkommandos* for their 'games', when, for instance, the SS forced them to play football, which they would have never played against other prisoners. But they viewed the members of the *Sonderkommandos* as colleagues, as 'accomplices' in their horrific crimes, as fellow murderers (Lee, 2016: 280). The *grey zone* is at its worst in such situations, the ultimate threshold being transcended. The dark side of translation resides exactly in this 'complicity'.

Thus, interpreters could not easily escape being positioned, or positioning themselves, in the *grey zone*. Yet we cannot generalise about the interpreters' behaviour. As some of the examples have shown, a number of inmate-interpreters opted for solidarity, often placing themselves in mortal danger. The strong tension resulting from the encounter of an ambiguous translation concept entailing both danger and relief on the one hand, and the turmoil in the process of shaping and re-shaping the *grey zone* on the other, presages a glimpse into the unimaginable, and at the same time reveals the epistemological force of the concept of dark translation.

Notes

1 Gawalewicz was a Polish jurist and writer. He participated in the underground resistance and was deported to Auschwitz and other concentration camps.
2 See Klein (1999) for further details on the usage of *lagerszpracha* in the context of Levi's work.
3 *Organisieren*: something you cannot buy, you 'organise' in order to get it; *Zugang*: ingress; *Prominenter*: came to mean a prominent or privileged person (Sodi, 2007: 61).
4 As David Gramling has pointed out, Robert Antelme, in his survivor account *L'espèce humaine*, articulated the distinction between camp life and life outside in the following terms: 'In the camps, the "silence" of the detainee is not the silence of one who should not speak, but of one who cannot speak' (qtd. in Gramling, 2012: 178).
5 Levi also translated Giacomo Leopardi's poem 'Il sogno' into English, but without ever publishing it (Rudolf, 2016: 224).
6 The book *Gray Zones: Ambiguity and Compromise in the Holocaust and its Aftermath*, edited by Jonathan Petropoulos and John K. Roth (2005), explores multiple grey zones of the Holocaust, considerably widening our view on the significance of Levi's concept. However, they cannot directly be applied to the present context of translation and interpreting.
7 Catherine Mooney discusses in detail the question of ethics in the *grey zone* with reference to the fragility of human character (Mooney, 2016).
8 Levi's analysis of the area of collaboration between victims and perpetrators has been at the centre of heated debates. Richard Rubinstein, among others, reports that Levi's concern for discerning a continuum of good and evil extending from victims to perpetrators elicited a reaction from Elie Wiesel, who argued that, by speaking of the 'relativity' of the victims' innocence (referring to the *Sonderkommandos*), Levi was attenuating the guilt of the killers. Others, like Massimo Giuliani, insisted that Levi did not 'discharge guilt', in Rubinstein's words, but rather sought to explore the

truth of human beings in desperate situations (Rubinstein, 2005: 300). Rubinstein himself maintains that Levi saw all people in the *Lager* as 'centaurs', 'a hybrid mixture of the rational and moral and amoral animalism' (ibid.: 299). See also the insightful response of Sander H. Lee to this claim (Lee, 2016: 281–283).

9 In his 'non-fiction novel' the French writer Steiner (*1938) blames members of the *Sonderkommando* for assisting German SS in the genocide. This triggered a furious debate between a number of academics, which resulted in the republishing of the book as a fictional account (see Moyn, 2005 for this controversy).

10 Kurt Hubert Franz (1914–1998) was an SS officer and one of the commanders of Treblinka. In the Treblinka Trials he was sentenced to life imprisonment (1965) and was released in 1993 for health reasons.

11 The quoted passage is a back-translation from the German translation: the book was originally written in English (1996), and then translated into German (1997) by the author herself. Here is the English original, which shows the high degree of interference in the self-translation:

> The abuse of power by some of [the Kapos or the block-elders] was legendary. There were notable exceptions. One was a Belgian girl called Mala, whom everyone admired. She was the chief interpreter in the camp and had great integrity.
> *(Lasker-Wallfisch, 1996: 82)*

In the German version, Lasker-Wallfisch depicts Mala as an even stronger figure, foregrounding her honesty and reliability, as opposed to what she could have done otherwise ('*despite everything* she kept her integrity', emphasis added).

References

Agamben, G. (1998), *Homo Sacer*, trans. D. Heller-Roazen Stanford: Stanford University Press.

Alexander, Z. (2007) 'Primo Levi and Translation', In R. S. Gordon (ed), *The Cambridge Companion to Primo Levi*, Cambridge: Cambridge University Press, 155–169.

Anissimov, M. (1999), *Primo Levi. Die Tragödie eines Optimisten. Eine Biographie*, Darmstadt: Wissenschaftliche Buchgesellschaft.

Antelme, R. (2010/1957), *L'espèce humaine*, Paris: Gallimard.

Arnds, P. (2012) 'Translating Survival, Translation as Survival in Primo Levi's *Se questo è un uomo*', *Translation and Literature*, 21: 162–174.

Aschenberg, H. (2016) 'Linguistic Terror in Nazi Concentration Camps: *Lucien* and *Gilbert* – Portraits of Two "Interpreters"', in M. Wolf (ed), *Interpreting in Nazi Concentration Camps. With an Essay by Primo Levi*, New York: Bloomsbury, 63–78.

Baird, M. L. (2005) '"The Gray Zone" as a Complex of Tensions. Primo Levi on Holocaust Survival', In Stanislao G. Pugliese (ed), *The Legacy of Primo Levi*, New York: Palgrave Macmillan, 193–206.

Bravo, A. (2002) 'On the Gray Zone', in *Centro Internazionale di Studi Primo Levi*: www.primolevi.it/@api/deki/files/810/=MAUSC_E00002.pdf (viewed 28/ 02/2018).

Cicioni, M. (1995), *Primo Levi: Bridges of Knowledge*, Oxford: Berg.

Cicioni, M. (2016) 'Labour of Civilization and Peace', In M. Vuohelainen & A. Chapman (eds), *Interpreting Primo Levi: Interdisciplinary Perspectives*, New York: Palgrave Macmillan, 37–49.

Cohen, U. S. (2016) 'Lagersprache: Primo Levi and the Language of Survival', *Dibur*, 1: http://arcade.stanford.edu/dibur/lagersprache-primo-levi-and-language-survival (viewed 28/ 02/2018).

Gramling, D. (2012) 'An Other Unspeakability: Levi and *Lagerszpracha*', *New German Critique*, 39(3): 165–187.
Jagoda, Z., S. Kłodziński & J. Masłowski (1987) '"bauernfuss, goldzupa, himmelautostrada". Zum "Krematoriumsesperanto" der Sprache polnischer KZ-Häftlinge', trans. Jochen August *Die Auschwitz-Hefte*, 2: 241–260.
Klein, J. (1999) '"Quelle violenze fatte al linguaggio ... ". Primo Levi und die deutsche Sprache', *Italienisch*, 42: 14–21.
Lasker-Wallfisch, A. (1996), *Inherit the Truth 1939–1945: The Documented Experiences of a Survivor of Auschwitz and Belsen*, London: dlm.
Lasker-Wallfisch, A. (1997), *Ihr sollt die Wahrheit erben. Die Cellistin von Auschwitz. Erinnerungen*, trans. A. Lakser-Wallfisch Reinbek bei Hamburg: Rowohlt.
Lee, S. H. (2016) 'Primo Levi's *Gray Zone*: Implications for Post-Holocaust Ethics', *Holocaust and Genocide Studies*, 30(2): 276–297.
Levi, P. (1985) 'Tradurre ed essere tradotti', In P. Levi *L'altrui mestiere*, Torino: Einaudi, 109–114.
Levi, P. (1986), *The Wrench*, trans. W. Weaver London: Joseph.
Levi, P. (1987), *If This is a Man. The Truce*, trans. S. Woolf London: Abacus.
Levi, P. (1989), *The Drowned and the Saved*, trans. R. Rosenthal London: Abacus.
Levi, P. (2015) 'To Translate and Be Translated', trans. A. Shugaar *Yale Review*, 103(3): 1–6.
Levi, P. (2016) 'On Translating and Being Translated', trans. Z. AlexanderIn M. Wolf (ed), *Interpreting in Nazi Concentration Camps. With an Essay by Primo Levi*, New York: Bloomsbury, 87–91.
Luban, D. (2001) 'A Man Lost in the Gray Zone', *Law and History Review*, 19(1): 161–176.
Lubling, Y. (2007), *Twice-dead: Moshe Y. Lubling, the Ethics of Memory, and the Treblinka Revolt*, New York: Lang.
Mooney, C. (2016) 'The Ethics of the Gray Zone', In M. Vuohelainen & A. Chapman (eds), *Interpreting Primo Levi: Interdisciplinary Perspectives*, New York: Palgrave Macmillan, 21–35.
Morrison, T. (2015) 'Toni Morrison on Primo Levi's Defiant Humanism', *The Guardian*, 5 September 2015: www.theguardian.com/books/2015/sep/05/primo-levi-holocaust-survivor-the-complete-works (viewed 28/ 02/2018).
Moyn, S. (2005), *A Holocaust Controversy: The Treblinka Affair in Postwar France*, Waltham: Brandeis University Press.
Oschlies, W. (1997) 'The Thesaurus of Hell: Twenty-Six Years of the Periodical Przeglad Lekarski-Oswiecim', trans. M. Humphreys, in *Museum of Tolerance*: http://motlc.wiesenthal.com/site/pp.asp?c=gvKVLcMVIuG&b=395139 (viewed 28/ 02/2018).
Petropoulos, J. & J. K. Roth (2005), *Gray Zones: Ambiguity and Compromise in the Holocaust and Its Aftermath*, New York: Berghahn Books.
Rubinstein, R. L. (2005) 'Gray into Black: the Case of Mordecai Chaim Rumkowski', In J. Petropoulos & J. K. Roth (eds), *Gray Zones: Ambiguity and Compromise in the Holocaust and Its Aftermath*, New York: Berghahn Books, 299–310.
Rudolf, A. (2016) '"Best Regards from Home to Home": Primo Levi's Letters to a UK-Friend and Publisher', In M. Vuohelainen & A. Chapman (eds), *Interpreting Primo Levi: Interdisciplinary Perspectives*, New York: Palgrave Macmillan, 219–236.
Sodi, R. (2007), *Narrative & Imperative: The First Fifty Years of Italian Holocaust Writing (1944–1994)*, New York: Lang.
Steiner, J.-F. (1966), *Treblinka. Die Revolte eines Vernichtungslagers*, trans. M. Lipcowitz, M. Lepron-Buger, I. Michael & L. Thilenius Oldenbourg: Gerhard Stalling Verlag.

Tryuk, M. & M. Wolf (2015) 'Concentration Camps', In F. Pöchhacker, N. Grbić, P. Mead & R. Sutton (eds), *Routledge Encyclopedia of Interpreting Studies*, London: Routledge, 77–78.

Venezia, Sh. (2008), *Meine Arbeit im Sonderkommando Auschwitz. Das erste umfassende Zeugnis eines Überlebenden*, trans. D. Mallett München: Blessing.

Vuohelainen, M. (2016) 'Introduction', In M. Vuohelainen & A. Chapman (eds), *Interpreting Primo Levi: Interdisciplinary Perspectives*, New York: Palgrave Macmillan, 1–4.

Wesołowska, D. (1998), *Wörter aus der Hölle. Die "lagerszpracha" der Häftlinge von Auschwitz*, trans. J. August, Impuls, Kraków, Cracow: Kraków.

Wolf, M. (2016) 'Introduction: Interpreting in Nazi Concentration Camps – Challenging the "Order of Terror"?', in M. Wolf (ed), *Interpreting in Nazi Concentration Camps. With an Essay by Primo Levi*, New York: Bloomsbury, 1–21.

4

TRANSLATING THE UNCANNY, UNCANNY TRANSLATION

Christoph Leitgeb

This essay is rooted in more general research into the functions of the uncanny in the literary recollection of National Socialism. As a matter of fact, the psychoanalytical concept of the uncanny is essential to explaining how the experience of traumatisation and anxiety is remembered. However, applied to literature, the concept of the uncanny also describes an aesthetic convention; it is linked to certain motifs, a certain attitude towards the distinction between documentary and fiction. The aesthetic side of the uncanny therefore accompanies the transition from personal to cultural memory.

What does all this have to do with a concept of cultural translation? Within the framework of this volume, this question will be addressed from various angles, one of which is worth highlighting right away: a methodological perspective may question whether it is a good idea to return once again to psychoanalytic concepts following the 'cultural turn' in translation studies. The purpose here will not be to advocate such a return, because the very assumption that psychoanalytical concepts have lost their influence in the first place will appear questionable. The line of reasoning will show how some influential theories of cultural translation never ceased to depend on a long tradition of psychoanalytic theory—and a tradition of thinking about the uncanny.

The uncanny and the figure of the third

(a) A speech-act theory of irony and the uncanny

> "Nun? Was siehst du? Beschreibe das Bild", sagt die Lehrerin, noch immer zu mir gewandt.

> Ich blicke entsetzt auf das Bild, auf diesen Mann, der offenbar Tell heißt, der offenbar ein Held ist, der eine merkwürdige Waffe hält und zielt. Er zielt auf ein Kind, und das Kind steht ahnungslos da!
>
> *(?: 120)*[1]

The comic is the uncanny as it appears to those not directly affected. That is how Robert Pfaller defines the tipping effect, which was also described by an older speech-act theory of irony (Pfaller, 2002, 261–269; cf. Stempel, 1976; Stierle, 1976). According to this theory, the ironic speech-act implies communication between three people. People who use irony as a means to communicate are looking for an accomplice. Together with this accomplice, they team up against a victim who only understands the literal meaning of the ironic statement.

A change of perspective within this scene illustrates its bearings on a theory of the uncanny. Slowly, the victim of the ironic plot may become aware of his or her part in that communication. This participant in communication believed that he was being addressed directly; but now the presence of a ghostly third person makes itself felt. The laughter of her or his interlocutor is plotting with this third person against him.

Perhaps readers knowledgeable about Wilhelm Tell will detect signals of irony in the quotation above. They will laugh with the teacher about the child's naïveté. But let us pretend for a moment that the child in the anonymous quote really serves as a target for shooting practice. In this case, compassion might compel readers to identify with the child's perspective. The perception of the situation will then tilt, and the readers will suddenly see the irony of it directed against themselves and the child. The irony tilts into the uncanny; it becomes haunting.[2]

(b) The Figure of the Third Person in Social Philosophy

> "Nein, nein, ich will nicht!" begann ich verzweifelt und mit aller Kraft zu brüllen.
> "Nein, nein! Ich will nicht weg! Ich gehöre hierher! Ich bin hier zuhause!"
> Ich tobte. Aber zu meinem maßlosen Erstaunen blieb es still. Mitten in die Stille hörte ich ruhig und fest eine Stimme sagen:
> "Ja; ich komme mit."
> Diese fremde Stimme! Oder war das doch meine Stimme? Fuhr es mir durch den Kopf."
>
> *(?: 16)*[3]

Linguists have not only designed this speech-act notion of irony; they have also criticised it. In ironic speech acts the third person hardly ever truly appears, and yet their complicity is held to be decisive for the communicative success of these acts. Nonetheless, the figure of the third person has recently become prominent outside linguistics, in theoretical works by Joachim Fischer (2000, 2010) and Albrecht Koschorke (2010). Their approach also conceives of the 'figure of the third' as somehow originating from the realm of the imaginary and ending up as real: 'What was a ghost has become a key figure, which its teammates somehow feel uneasy about, but still acknowledge in an almost respectful manner' (Koschorke, 2010: 9).[4]

The rehabilitation of this figure is mainly due to Georg Simmel and his tradition in social philosophy. Simmel's *Soziologie* (1908) illustrates the various functions and constellations in which a 'figure of the third' is enunciated and personalised. Simmel suggests an independent agency for this figure in every social interaction, without discussing the theoretical possibility of its exclusion or passivity (cf. Fischer, 2000: 121). Starting from this assumption, he distinguishes between mediating (the arbitrator), laughing and dominant figures of the third (the politician in the 'divide et impera!') (cf. Bedorf, 2010: 128, 129; Fischer, 2010: 200; Hessinger, 2010: 66).

> The main point here implies that the figure of the third appears where conflict is prevailing, where a distinction is made for profit, or where a conflict is sown. The typology of the third serves to analyze how conflict imposes the categories of society on people
>
> *(Bedorf, 2010: 130)*[5]

Simmel's analysis schematically points out the various alliances speakers can forge within such a constellation of three. Any argument communicated by a first person (I) to a second person (you) may address a third person (he/she) at the same time. According to Simmel, this figure of the third may keep an impartial distance from the first and second persons, but need not necessarily do so.

> The figure of the third reflects the fundamental ambivalence of the social realm: On one hand, the figure of the third appears as a potential source of irritation and conflict; on the other, as a possible mediator of integration and reconciliation.
>
> *(Hessinger, 2010: 79)*[6]

If I am plotting with a third person against the person I am talking to, one possible rhetorical strategy of our common attitude is irony,[7] just as irony might designate a plot between you and me against somebody else.[8] A third person may also plot with my interlocutor behind my back. The uncanny is born in the moment in which the existence of this rhetorical alliance begins slowly to dawn on the person plotted against.

(c) The translator as a figure of the third

> The figure of the third has [...] a 'revelatory' function, so to speak: it brings to light what is possible between the other two—it 'objectivises' their relationship while at the same time placing it into question. Accordingly, the third party may act as an intermediary or an arbitrator, as a beneficiary or an

> injured third party, as a witness or an observer, as a scapegoat or a schemer, as a translator or an advocate, as an intruder or a parasite.
>
> (Lüdemann, 2010: 85)[9]

It is no accident that this list includes the figure of the translator. The translator has already been identified as one of the paradigmatic incarnations of the figure of the third (cf. Lange, 2015). As such, in this type of analysis, the translator is ideally positioned impartially and equidistantly in between speaker and addressee, a necessary medium of their communication. The translator emerges here as a figure, like the messenger, communicating not across a purely spatial and temporal divide, but a cultural one, too. Within an abstract typology of the figure of the third, this very position distinguishes the translator, for example, from the witness—who is actually involved in the event—the partisan advocate, or the parasitic beneficiary.

The abstract ideal of the translator excludes self-interest in the choice of alliances. The ideal translator will not ironically plot with the addressee of the translation against the text's original author; he will also not uncannily plot with the original author against the addressee of the translation. In broad terms, Simmel combines an abstract typology of the figure of the third with an analysis of this figure's embodiment within society. The designation of an ideal translator can also be confronted with this figure's empirical embodiments. In real speech acts, translators can assume roles other than that of a neutral mediator. In these cases, reflections on translators' specific embodiment of the figure of the third can be a vantage point to reflect on the connection between translations and the uncanny.

In his book *Writing and Rewriting the Holocaust*, James E. Young points out that many survivors and witnesses of the Holocaust deliberately took on the role of translator after the war: they chose English instead of Yiddish, Polish or German for their reports, because English was a language unburdened by their memories (Young, 1997: 248). In an essay focusing on testimony, Holocaust survivor Dori Laub (1995) implicitly describes how adopting positions of a figure of the third can give those witnesses a feeling of the uncanny. The very roles of witness and translator seem to converge, and challenge the identities of witnesses on three levels.

First, the traumatic experience itself splits the identity of the witness in a characteristic way, creating a 'doppelgänger': a child witnessing its own traumatisation seems to face the ongoing experience from the knowing viewpoint of a much older person (Laub, 1995: 61). Furthermore, as a grown-up witness, this child will later observe how other victims collect their traumatic memories and frame them in testimonies. Identification with these external testimonies poses a further danger of losing the sense of personal integrity. Finally, this same person will become a witness to his or her own testimony, thus incorporating both a speaker and a censorious listener. Remembering, witnesses once again become involved in the event through their own testimony; at the same time, they try to control their own storytelling by taking a critical stance (Laub, 1995: 62). The uncanny aspects of all these levels of giving testimony are reminiscent of the mixture of identification and distancing that exists within translation.

Connecting concepts of translation and the uncanny

How does this conceptual interchange of translation and the uncanny appear in theories of cultural translation? To answer this question, it is necessary to point out how some conceptions of cultural translation—for example, those of Emily Apter (2006, 2013), Homi Bhabha (1994) or Gayatri Chaktavorty Spivak (2008)—have explicitly addressed a theory of the uncanny in their work. All in all, the concept of the uncanny functions as a pivotal point in their theories of cultural translation, which revolve around a psychoanalytic tradition: a tradition they sometimes only implicitly cite.

Spivak (2008) actually criticises precisely this psychoanalytical reference point of previous post-colonial theories. For her, this is why theories analyse the making of the colonial subject without paying due attention to its political representation. But if Spivak (2008) chooses a suttee in India as an example for discussing political representation and the lack thereof, the question arises whether this example does not, again, imply basic presuppositions of a theory of the uncanny: namely, the implication of a space split by at least two different modes of representation.

Metaphorically, the uncanny is often situated at the boundary between two distinct spaces. These are quite different in nature, yet their contents sometimes exchange uncontrollably as if through a permeable membrane. The uncanny, then, is the feeling of running over thin ice, drifting in the ocean over unfathomable depths or sinking in a swamp—metaphors that foil the long tradition of imagining the translator as ferryman (Bauman 2006: 18 labelled those metaphors '*Titanic* syndrome'). In psychoanalytic theory, space is split into conscious and unconscious; in translation theory, into the two realms of distinct cultures across the boundaries of which meaning has to be exchanged.

Theories of translation articulate this connection with the concept of the uncanny in three arguments—arguments they do not always keep separate. These arguments are put forward from different standpoints: a standpoint of translation in a more linguistic sense, inspired, for example, by (a) the difficulties in the translation of Freud; (b) a standpoint of psychoanalysis and psychotherapy; and (c) a standpoint of post-colonial studies.

(a) A linguistic argument connecting translation and the uncanny

The 'linguistic' argument in the wider sense maintains that space is split by the existence of two languages considered 'untranslatable'; the necessary attempt at translation between them becomes uncanny. Apter expands her concept of 'untranslatables' to phenomena such as speaking in tongues, the encounter with the divine in the sublime, or with the traumatic—phenomena that have always been linked with the uncanny.

> Im ersten Moment sehe ich nur Rauch und Leere. Unmittelbar neben mir endet das Geleise, der Damm bricht abrupt ab, gleich einer Schanze. Meine Augen brennen und tränen. Ich blicke über die Kante in die Tiefe, ich blicke hinüber. Ich verstehe nicht, was ich durch die Rauchschwaden

dort sehe—und ich verstehe es doch. Aber es ist mit nichts zu verbinden, was ich kenne, weder mit Bildern noch mit Worten.

Ich fühle nur, daß dies ein Ort ist, an dem alles endet, nicht nur der Damm und das Geleise.

Es ist der Ort, wo diese Welt aufhört, diese Welt zu sein.

(?: 88, 89)[10]

The argument will have linguistic or pseudo-linguistic implications if it maintains that the untranslatability of a particular language is part of its very essence. The translator of this exotic language then becomes a voice for the figure of the third, which automatically plots with the unspeakable 'other' against a recipient who embodies the perspective of everyday language. The translation requirements themselves are uncanny when it comes to transferring concepts that do not exist in one language to the other: the translation of the English distinction between 'I' and 'me' into German is just one example.

The Jewish émigré George Arthur Goldschmidt (2006) wrote about the difficulties of translating Freud or Heidegger into French. He maintains that German tends to transform adjectives into nouns, using suffixes like '-heit' or '-keit'. This is how German can attribute agency to subjects, which are imaginary, abstractions. The word 'Unheimlichkeit' itself shows how German language, through essentialisation, succeeds in finding subjects for the 'it' in 'it haunts'. It is precisely this argument that is cited in many theories of the uncanny written in French or in English. It is difficult to translate 'das Unheimliche' into many other languages, despite its seemingly psychoanalytic and universal character—thus, the concept itself is often considered an 'unconcept' (cf. Masschelein, 2011) and 'uncanny'.

Apter (2006) sets out similar approaches to Turkish and Arabic, each of which, for its own reasons, might be considered an 'uncanny' language. Arabic, as she recalls an American publisher remarking, promotes a 'haunting' crossfading of tenses:

This confusion of tenses—which a hasty observer will ascribe to a love of a genius for synthesis—corresponds to so constant a feature of Arab character, so natural an orientation of Arab thought, that Arab grammar itself is marked by it.

(Apter, 2006: 103, 104)

Apter also refers to a conversation between Edward Said and another publisher seeking advice. When asked why he did not want to include a translation of Naguib Mahfouz in his catalogue, this publisher replied that Arabic was 'a controversial language'. Edward Said later wondered about his acquiescence: 'What exactly, the publisher meant is still a little vague to me—but that Arabs and their language were somehow not respectable, and so dangerous, louche, unapproachable, was perfectly evident to me then, alas, now' (Apter, 2006: 103, 104).

As far as Turkish is concerned, Apter portrays the viewpoint of Jewish émigrés, who founded the subject of modern comparative literature in Istanbul during the war. In his essay 'Learning Turkish', Leo Spitzer was haunted by the emotionality and spirituality that prevailed in the Turkish language, and recommended the influence of Romance languages as a cure. A little later, in a letter to Walter Benjamin, his colleague Erich Auerbach described how the Europeanisation of Turkey turned uncanny: 'Here they have thrown all tradition overboard, and they want to build a thoroughly rationalized, extreme Turkish-nationalist, state of the European sort. It has quickly gone fantastical and ghostly: [...]' (Apter, 2013: 194).

(b) A 'Psychoanalytical' Argument connecting Translation and the Uncanny

A psychoanalytic stance repeats some of the linguistic arguments about why theories of translation and theories of the uncanny are connected. The 'psychoanalytic' argument assumes that the transition from the unconscious and repressed to the conscious is due to an act of translation. The unconscious is thus organised like a language that is 'difficult to translate' or 'untranslatable' altogether. In the conclusion of her book *Unclaimed Experience: Trauma, Narrative and History*, Cathy Caruth (2016) conceives of trauma as an 'address' that cannot be identified 'with a single voice, nor articulated in a single language'. Sometimes we speak with a voice that precedes us, a voice that is not ours but whose only opening is through the language that cries out from our wounds. And sometimes our language must find its way through the language of others we will never understand (Caruth, 2016: 139).

> Sie begannen Fragen zu stellen, viele Fragen, aber ich erinnere mich nicht mehr. Ich erinnere mich nur, daß ich, ohne zu wissen wie, plötzlich zu reden begann, wie ich noch nie geredet hatte. Ich hörte mich reden, als ob jemand anderer in mir redete. Ich redete wie ein Wasserfall, aber ich weiß nicht mehr, was ich redete. Doch irgendwann war es genug, nur ein Würgen war noch in meinem Hals, ich schwieg—und es war wieder still in mir wie vorher.
>
> *(?: 107)*[11]

The experience of the difficulty of translating the unconscious into the 'native' languages of consciousness gives rise to the uncanny. Freud has located the uncanny precisely in the transition, in the revocation of the repressed: if the translation of the previously unconscious into the conscious is successful, the uncanny comes to an end. The psychoanalyst as a figure of the third becomes uncanny at the very moment in which he, a translator of his own kind, helps the unconscious to break through into utterance. In analogy, translating into foreign cultural contexts becomes uncanny if it reveals something 'repressed' in one's own culture.

In her book *Translation Zone* (2006), Apter sets out twenty assumptions for translation, which emphatically expose her orientation towards the analogy with psychoanalysis and the uncanny: 'Translation is an oedipal assault on the mother tongue. Translation is the traumatic loss of native language. Translation is Babel, a universal language that is universally unintelligible. Translation is the language of planets and monsters' (Apter, 2006: xi, xii).

Apter's approach to this analogy is both bold and often implicit. In her chapter about the war in the Balkans, for example, she alludes to the psychoanalytical context, maintaining that 'War has the structure of a language' (Apter, 2006: 135). This is a variation on Jacques Lacan's famous verdict: 'The unconscious has the structure of a language' (Lacan, 1987: 26). She even draws the conclusion that a sort of psychoanalytical approach to war might be possible: the analogy of translation theory and psychoanalysis raises her hopes that ruptures within the 'translation zone' could be healed by a 'talking cure'.

On the other hand, Apter believes that there is no hope of bridging these divides within a binding universalism. In her chapter 'Paranoid Globalism' (2013: 70–98), she also develops this thought by way of a psychoanalytic concept. For Apter, paranoia—the persecution delusion—is the other side of a global 'world culture'. This is the notion of a 'single world' not subdivided by the rupture of cultures (because it is completely 'Americanised', for example). This kind of globalism, which in principle holds everything to be translated and translatable, creates paranoia with what it represses into the unconscious. 'Paranoia' is just another term to describe a persistent haunting by the uncanny.

> Sie versuchten, dem Wort „Transport"andere Namen zu geben, aber ich ließ mich nicht beirren. Ich kannte ja das Wort aus eigener Erfahrung und aus den Erzählungen vieler Kinder. Auf die Frage nach Eltern oder Geschwister, hatte ich immer wieder die Antwort bekommen:
> Sie sind auf Transport!
> Und stets hieß das: Sie waren weg—für immer. Kaum einer kam zurück, der auf Transport war.
> *(?: 113)*[12]

(c) A 'post-colonial' argument connecting translation and the uncanny

A 'post-colonial' argument about a connection between translation and the uncanny stresses the fact that the act of translation becomes uncanny when a knowledge-based, 'disinterested' communication (Habermas) secretly serves the purpose of enforcing interests in the colonial context. The post-colonial author then makes the colonial subjects appear uncanny, inasmuch as they exhibit a 'desire' that is 'repressed' by the ruling discourse. Within this context, Homi Bhabha makes a direct reference to Freud's interpretation of the puppet Olympia: 'Culture is Heimlich [...] But cultural authority is also unheimlich, for to be distinctive, significatory, influential and identifiable, it has to be translated, disseminated, differentiated, interdisciplinary, intertextual, international, interracial' (Bhabha, 1994: 136, 137). Seemingly a neutral figure of the third like the analyst in psychoanalysis, the post-colonial author plots with the 'repressed' against a reader who unconsciously shares the colonising perspective.

In his book *The Location of Culture*, Bhabha (1994) introduces his reference to Freud with a chapter entitled 'Unhomely Lives: The Literature of Recognition', a self-contained text that explicitly quotes Freud's essay on the uncanny. Bhabha mediates between psychoanalytic and translational perspective in at least three respects: (1) he repeats Freud's etymological derivation of the uncanny, the implied metaphor of space in general and the house in particular; (2) he refers to the specificity of the negation that Freud points out in the 'un' of the 'uncanny'; by doing so, he emphasises that the contradictions of the colonial situation cannot be mediated in the sense of a Hegelian dialectic; (3) he questions whether, within the colonial situation, one can even speak of a 'subject' in the conventional sense: in this context, he uses the psychoanalytic concepts of the 'unconscious', 'desire' and 'repression', which are at the core of Freud's theory of the uncanny.

In general, Bhabha's famous concept of a 'third space' functions as an example of a divide that runs through spaces of the uncanny. The colonial space turns uncanny because it destroys a 'mirror of representation, in which cultural knowledge is customarily revealed as an integrated, open, expanding code' (Bhabha, 1994: 37). Bhabha (like Lacan) maintains that this 'third space' is a space of reflection 'unrepresentable in itself' (Bhabha, 1994: 37); the disorder of linguistic representation within it cannot be corrected by means of logic. In addition to his semiotic framing, Bhabha maintains a psychoanalytic terminology of the 'conscious' and the 'unconscious' (cf. Bhabha, 1994: 36), which he reshapes to fit post-colonial culture.

Bhabha's interpretative and translatory quotations, however, ultimately displace not only particular concepts, but the entire Freudian system. The 'madness' of culture within the 'third space', which results from constant processes of translation, becomes uncanny. The 'colonial compulsion to truth' (Bhabha, 1994: 135) subjugates the field of culture to a dichotomy of 'actual' and 'not actual', which Bhabha highlights by quoting Jacques Derrida: 'Translation becomes law, duty and debt, but the debt one can no longer discharge' (Bhabha, 1994: 136 quotes Derrida, 1985: 174). The uncanny division of space reproduces a division of the subject, which Bhabha spells out in his concept of mimicry.[13]

> Ich habe keine Muttersprache, auch keine Vatersprache. [...] Der Wortschatz war klein; er reduzierte sich auf das Notwendigste, um das auszudrücken und zu verstehen, was zum Überleben notwendig war. Irgendwann in dieser Zeit hatte es mir ohnehin die Sprache verschlagen, und es dauerte lange, bis ich sie wieder fand. So war es mir kein großer Verlust, dass ich dies Kauderwelsch, nirgendwo brauchbar nach dem Kriege, zu einem großen Teil vergessen habe. Die Sprachen, die ich später lernte, wurden aber nie ganz meine eigenen, waren im Grunde immer nur bewußte Nachahmungen der Sprachen anderer.
>
> (?: 7)[14]

Mimicry produces the traditionally uncanny figure of the double, which embodies the cultural split between the colonial and the colonised. The colonial subjects are no longer capable of controlling the rhetorical effects of their own translation practices. No matter their position within the power network of the colony, people react to the emergence of mimicry with fear. 'Without the doubleness that I described in the post-colonial play of the "a", it would be difficult to understand the anxiety provoked by the hybridizing of language, activated in the anguish associated with vacillating boundaries—psychic, cultural, territorial [...]'(Bhabha, 1994: 59). At the end of his book, Bhabha picks up this Lacanian approach to anxiety again by quoting Samuel Weber: 'For anxiety is the affective address of a world [that] reveals itself as caught up in the space between frames; a doubled frame or one that is split' (Bhabha, 1994: 214, cf. Weber, 1991: 161).

Bhabha's concept of mimicry thus also illustrates the connection between irony and the uncanny that is suggested here from the beginning. The 'high ideals of the colonial imagination' turn 'comic'. Colonialism can often exercise its authority only through 'figures of farce'; post-colonial texts therefore draw 'from the traditions of the trompe l'œil, irony, mimicry and repetition' (Bhabha, 1994: 85). It is also in these terms that Bhabha describes the impossibility of establishing a simple identity within the colonial situation: 'The desire to become authentic through mimicry—through a process of writing and repetition—is the final irony of partial representation' (Bhabha, 1994: 88).

Implicitly, the affinity of 'mimicry' and 'irony' suggests itself whenever Bhabha writes about mimicry's illusionary play on similarity and difference. As in the following sentences, Bhabha's text often allows us directly to replace the post-colonial concept of mimicry with the rhetorical concept of irony. 'The menace of mimicry [irony] is its double vision which in disclosing [the] ambivalence [of colonial discourse] also disrupts its authority [...]' (Bhabha, 1994: 88).

> [T]he visibility of mimicry [irony] is always produced at the site of interdiction. It is a form of colonial discourse that is uttered inter dicta: a discourse at the crossroads of what is known and permissible and that which though known must be kept concealed; a discourse uttered between the lines.
> *(Bhabha, 1994: 89)*

'In mimicry [irony], the representation of identity and meaning is rearticulated along the axis of metonymy' (Bhabha, 1994: 90).

As a matter of fact, the uncanny subversiveness of mimicry has also been proposed implicitly within a theory of irony. In his Frankfurt lectures, Martin Walser suggested that ironic literature is characterised by 'two varieties of identity': the first of these identities is much too self-assured, only playfully jumping into various crises to enjoy the excitement of a bit of eccentricity. Walser suggested Thomas Mann as an example of this, and Robert Walser as an example of the opposite, precariously insecure type of identity, which adopts everything that power holds against it. These say 'yes' to the very 'no' that circumstances express against them (Walser, 1996: 178).[15] Here, Martin Walser could certainly quote post-colonial mimicry to prove his point.

Schau, jetzt habe ich eine sprache gefunden, jetzt kann ich es übersetzen[16]

Perhaps readers of this essay are by now feeling uneasy about the quotations interspersed in German, which have so far been cited without giving the name of the author.[17] But, then, perhaps they already have an idea of the trap into which these lead: these quotations are from the fabricated autobiographical report of a child who supposedly survived the concentration camps. Their author, Binjamin Wilkomirski, alias Bruno Dössekker, triggered a major scandal that was widely debated in the feuilletons in the late 1990s, before Suhrkamp banned the book from their renowned Jewish Series. Before the scandal broke, Wilkomirski had explained to psychiatrists at a scientific congress how, as an adult, he remembered his childhood trauma. In the aftermath of the scandal, psychiatrists tried to explain how it was that they did not see through the scam from the outset, even though they should have (cf. Stoffel and Ernst 2002).

Wilkomirski's text is the result of a wide variety of translation processes, as Stefan Mächler's investigation of the case points out. Precisely the act of forgery 'represses' any conscious awareness of these processes: it 'denies' the translations. The denial of effort and purpose of these translations is not 'repression' in a psychoanalytical sense; at least not superficially. Nonetheless, the cancellation of this 'repression' creates the uncanny.

Firstly, Wilkomirski translates a psychoanalytic doctrine: he converts the 'return of the repressed' and the presuppositions of the 'speaking cure' into a poetic agenda that obscures his work of fiction. Wilkomirski's lectures on the memory of victimised children, in particular, emphasise the difficulty of reconstructing the factual content of their experience: he claims that only psychotherapeutic support and methods enabled him to remember images from the concentration camp as if a camera had captured them. Before psychoanalytical treatment, those very images were inaccessible to him because of repression, denial, and fractured and overlapping recollections (cf. Wilkomirski and Bernstein, 1999). 'Just as his therapist viewed the book as a result of this exceedingly painful and depleting process, Wilkomirski described his memories as a product of mental exercise' (Mächler, 2000: 271).[18] On the other hand, Wilkomirski forcefully defended himself against increasing doubts about the factuality of his report. He denied suspicions that a repetitive 'working through' had 'produced' his 'memory' rather than 'restored'[19] it—a suspicion that turned out to be literally accurate. 'I had NOTHING TO RECOVER! Some of the memories were—and still are—present every single day!!' (cf. Gourevitch, 1999: 54, capitalisation in the original).

Secondly, Wilkomirski does not only translate historians' depictions of the Holocaust, he also translates a specific literary text. He reports that 'scarcely anything unsettled him as much as Jerzy Kosinski's *The Painted Bird*, which he read in the sixties' (Mächler, 2000: 226). 'For the very reason it is a chronicle "The Painted Bird" … reaches its unusual intensity', Elie Wiesel wrote about this text, which he read as an authentic testimony to the Holocaust (Mächler, 2000:

226). This text, too, was allegedly autobiographical and depicted war from a traumatised child's perspective; it also told of a Polish orphanage after the war and disintegrated into episodic descriptions of sometimes extreme violence. Unlike Wilkomirski, however, Kosinski did not strictly emphasise its documentary character in what he said about the book (Mächler, 2000: 230). Yet, in the 1980s, the degree to which the book was fictional became apparent, and the excessive undeclared involvement of translators and editors destroyed the credibility of the author. Kosinski took his own life in 1991 (Mächler, 2000: 229).

Thirdly, Wilkomirski translates extracts from victims' testimonies into his own narrative to stress its authenticity. 'His memory was mine, he took possession of it.' This is how Karola described how Wilkomirski made use of her biographical life and its settings: Lviv, a concentration camp, Cracow, Dhiga, Augustiariska (Mächler, 2000: 214). An even more spectacular case of this kind of appropriation is the story of Yakov Morocco, an ultra-orthodox Gure Hasid and survivor of the Holocaust, who saw Wilkomirski in the movie *Wanda's List* and believed that he recognised his long-lost son (Mächler, 2000: 230, 231). 'To me it is not so important what the scientific blood and tissue tests reveal [...] You were also in Majdanek. [...] Also, some things that you have told [...] correspond with my own memories!' This is what Wilkomirski wrote in his first letter to this newly found 'father' (Mächler, 2000: 234). The story of father and son unfolds as a double adoption, in which Mächler emphasises the devaluation of facts against the feeling of belonging, the construction of belonging by means of the invention of a common past and the bridging of gaps in this construction by the mythical reference to the story of the 'lost son'. 'One could interpret Wilkomirski's tales as a permanent attempt to transform the story of his birth into that of an arrival, to belong elsewhere and to find a coherent story' (Mächler, 2000: 237).[20]

As in his reference to Kosinski's novel, the counterfeiting quality of Wilkomirski's text is again uncannily mirrored from the outside. While many child victims of National Socialist crimes discovered their own history in his 'Fragments' and thus translated forgery back into the authentic, Wilkomirski himself unknowingly fell prey to a forger. In Los Angeles, he met Laura Grabowski, whom he soon claimed to know since childhood from Birkenau concentration camp and a Krakow children's home (Mächler, 2000: 237). But when Wilkomirski referred to her as a witness to authenticate his own story, 'Laura Grabowski' turned out to be an alias for Laurel Rose Wilson, a.k.a. the author Lauren Stratford. Like Wilkomirski an adopted child, she first claimed in a fake autobiography to be the victim of Satanism and excessive child abuse. Under her new name, she then became an alleged Holocaust victim (cf. Mächler, 2000: 222–224).

The challenge here is not knowing better as a reader in hindsight. However, an essay on translation and the uncanny should point out how forgery seems charged with authenticity in this case, and should be interested in that author's hauntingly perfect mimicry. Wilkomirski adopted his alleged Jewish heritage so perfectly that, even after the scandal broke, he dared to visit his new-found 'father' in Israel. But if it is convincing to associate Bhabha's concept of mimicry with this case, what will this prove about Bhabha's 'post-colonial' theory frame? Is it a 'colonial' cultural trait in German-speaking countries to challenge its participants to compassionately identify with the victims of the Holocaust against all obstacles? And is someone a 'liar' or a 'counterfeiter' who believes in the truth of his forged memories, even after his deception is revealed and all the facts are publicly visible?

These are some of the haunting questions in the case of Wilkomirski, and some of the investigations into the scandal tried to soothe their uncanniness. Some of them were more about the author than his text. The case became interesting in terms of identity formation: authentic memory can be substituted with a falsification, thus creating a 'doppelgänger'. In hindsight, the text was no longer simply a scam, because real survivors of the Holocaust accepted its depiction of life in the concentration camps as authentic and accurate, proving that truth was a matter of testimony and not an act of attestation (cf. Assmann, 2006). Other arguments attacked the book's labelling as 'autobiography', assuming that labelling it as a 'novel' would have created no problem at all (cf. Klüger, 1998). And finally there was the argument that, for lack of experience, a fictive autobiographical book on this topic necessarily referred to nothing but the most well-known Holocaust motifs, thus aesthetically degrading into (Holocaust) kitsch (cf. Klüger, 1998).

So how do reflections on theories of the uncanny and cultural translation bear on this case? The idea of the concentration camp, like none other, splits our imaginary space: into a space in which culture seems to be suspended, and a space of culture that represents its consoling antithesis; into a space of perpetrators and one of victims; into a past and a present which are seemingly unconnected. The radicalism of this divide becomes visible in the demands on those figures of the third, who can still appear as mediators between the two spaces. Besides the imminent death of 'actual' witnesses, this split complicates the communicative remembrance of the crimes of National Socialism. At the same time, this split fuels the codification of memory in institutions that both conceal and suspend the communicative roles of testifying.

The demand on witnesses to speak nothing but 'facts' has been so strictly interpreted that it might seem narration and testimony are inherently contradictory. It's no accident that the silent Muselmann has been suggested as the most authentic witness (Agamben, 2003: 38), a figure in which the conceptions of 'witness' and 'translator' do not have to be mediated. Not in vain did Wilkomirski choose a child as his narrator, and mental images rather than narrations as his medium. With the knowledge of the forgery, figures of the third multiply when reading Wilkomirski's book. The implicit author splits into various doubles, and speech acts like 'translating', 'testifying', 'reporting' or 'writing fiction' and 'lying' can no longer be distinguished. The blurring of speech acts hence renders the text uncanny. This uncanny aspect is why quotes from Wilkomirski appeared to blend naturally into the theoretical reasoning of this essay. But this uncanniness also essentially sets Wilkomirski's book apart from kitsch.

> Ich sah wieder die lachenden und erleichterten Gesichter der Befreiten aus dem Dokumentarfilm:

> Gesetzt den Fall, der Film hat nicht gelogen, gesetzt den Fall, diese Gesichter haben nicht gelogen, wo war ich dann? Was hat man mir verheimlicht? Warum war ich nicht dabei? Ist wirklich etwas geschehen, von dem ich nichts wußte?
>
> *(Wilkomirski, 1997b: 141)*[21]

In this scene, the documentary film turns uncanny for the first-person narrator. Viewers seem to plot with the 'laughing and relieved faces of the people liberated' against what this narrator personally experienced as 'authentic'. Perhaps readers will identify with and share the feelings of the narrator in this scene. However, what if he only fabricated the memory of his 'authentic feelings'? What if he was not really 'there'? Then the scene turns into a trap, and the readers have been naïve enough to identify with the counterfeiting of an actor. Taking this possibility as a given, they will suddenly experience themselves as part of an uncanny fabrication. Their uncanny feeling will then be very different from the first one, produced by the identification with the narrator's state of mind: they themselves have turned out to be the victims of some 'higher' irony. From a standpoint high above the scene, with a gaze knowing all about theatrical conventions and witnessing a performance, those same readers might even laugh about themselves. They will again change sides and plot with the 'laughing and relieved faces' against this actor of authenticity and all those readers who identified with him.

Notes

1 The focus here is entirely on the accuracy of how the German-language citations fit into the theoretical framework. The author of the quotations in German will be revealed in the third chapter. Translation: '"So—what do you see? Describe the picture," says the teacher, who's still turned toward me. I stare in horror at the picture, at this man called Tell, who's obviously a hero, and he's holding a strange weapon and aiming it, and he's aiming it at a child, and the child's just standing there, not knowing what's coming' (?E: 128, 129).
2 Cf. the indefinite subject in German 'Es spukt'.
3 '"No, no, I don't want to!" I started to scream hopelessly as loud as I could. "No, no! I don't want to go away! I belong here! This is where I live!" I yelled and struggled. But to my complete astonishment, there wasn't a sound. And in the middle of the silence, I heard a voice saying quietly and clearly: "Yes, I'll come too." This unknown voice! Or was it my voice? I heard myself wondering.' (?E: 13)
4 'Aus dem einstigen Spukwesen ist eine Schlüsselfigur geworden, die zwar ihren Mitspielern nicht ganz geheuer ist, aber von ihnen nichtsdestoweniger auf fast ehrerbietige Weise anerkannt wird.'
5 'Zentral ist dabei, dass der Dritte da ist, wo Streit herrscht, aus einer Dichotomie Profit gezogen wird oder wo ein Konflikt gesät wird. Die Typologie des Dritten dient dazu, die vergesellschaftende Funktion des Streits analysierbar zu machen.'
6 'Die Figur des Dritten spiegelt dabei die grundlegende Ambivalenz des Sozialen: Zum einen erscheint der Dritte als potentielle Quelle von Irritation und Konflikt, zum anderen als möglicher Mittler von Integration und Versöhnung.'
7 … in the exact sense that Deleuze (1980) gives to the concept of irony: that it emphasises the inadequacy of empirical reality over one's own claim and idea.

8 This is Deleuze's definition of the comic (1980), which emphasises that the power of ideas is not enough to deal with reality.
9 'Der Dritte hat [...] sozusagen eine >revelatorische< Funktion: Er bringt ans Licht, was zwischen den beiden anderen möglich ist—er >objektiviert< ihre Beziehung und stellt sie zugleich infrage. Entsprechend kann der Dritte als Vermittler oder als Schiedsrichter auftreten, als begünstigter oder geschädigter Dritter, als Zeuge oder als Beobachter, als Sündenbock oder als Intrigant, als Übersetzer oder als Fürsprecher, als Eindringling oder als Parasit.'
10 'At first all I see is smoke and empty space. The tracks end right next to where I am, the embankment stops abruptly, like the end of a military fortification. My eyes are burning and watering. I look over the edge into the bottom of the trench, then out over it. I can't understand what I'm seeing through the billows of smoke, and at the same time I do understand, but it doesn't connect up with anything I know, either with pictures or in words. I just feel that this is a place where everything ends, not just the embankment and the rails. This is where this world stops being a world at all' (?E: 94).
11 'They began to ask questions, lots of questions, but I don't know what they were anymore. All I do know is that, without knowing how, I suddenly began to talk in a way I'd never talked before. I heard myself talking, as if it was someone else inside me. I talked like a waterfall, but I have no idea anymore what I said. But at some point it was enough, there was only a sick feeling in my throat, I stopped talking and everything inside me was quiet again, the way it was before.' (?E: 114).
12 'They tried to give the word "transport" other names, but I did not let myself be fooled. After all, I knew the word from personal experience and from what lots of children had told me. Whenever I asked them about their parents or brothers or sisters, it was always the same: "They were put on the transport!" And that always meant they'd gone forever. Almost nobody ever came back who'd been on a "transport".' (?E: 120).
13 For a critical assessment of how 'mimicry' appropriates a biological concept, cf. Rath (2010: 139).
14 'I have no mother tongue, nor a father tongue either. [...] It was a small vocabulary; it reduced itself to the bare essentials required to say and to understand whatever would endure survival. At some point during this time, speech left me altogether and it was a long time before I found it again. So it was no great loss that I more or less forgot this gibberish which lost its usefulness with the end of the war. But the languages I learned later on were never mine, at bottom. They were only imitations of other people's speech.' (?E:.3). Cf. Mächler (2000: 58–59): 'Und so habe ich mir gesagt: Gut, noch seid ihr die Stärkeren. Ich werde mich anpassen, ich werde eure Spielregeln lernen, ich werde eure Spiele spielen—aber ich werde sie nur spielen—ich will nie so sein wie ihr! Ihr predigt Ehrlichkeit und ihr lügt, ihr predigt Offenheit und ihr verschweigt mir die Wahrheit [...] Das gute Leben ist nur eine Falle.' ('And so I said to myself: Good, you are still stronger. I will adapt, I will learn your rules, I will play your games—but I will only play them—I never want to be like you! You preach honesty and you lie, you preach openness and you keep the truth from me . [...] The good life is just a trap.' (My translation.)
15 'Ironische Literatur sei von "zwei Sorten von Identität" geprägt: Einer "überaffirmierten, die sich fast nur spielerisch in Krisen bringt, um sozusagen durch ein bisschen Exzentrik einen genießbaren Schwankungsreiz zu produzieren"—er meint damit unter anderen Thomas Mann. Und einer "unteraffimierten", die sich alles zu eigen macht, "was Herrschaft gegen sie formuliert hat. Diese Helden sagen Ja zum Nein, das die Verhältnisse zu ihnen sagen".'
16 'Look, I have found a language, now I can translate it.' This is how Wilkomirski described his achievement to his psychoanalyst. Cf. interview with Wilkomirski (1999/04/22), Video of the Holocaust memorial Museum Washington, tape 6. (quot. Mächler, 2000: 97).
17 So '(?:)' was for '(Wilkomirski, 1997a)' and '(?E:)' for its translation by Carol Brown Janeway (Wilkomirski, 1997b).

18 'So wie seine Therapeutin das Buch als ein Ergebnis dieses überaus schmerzhaften und kraftverzehrenden Prozesses betrachtet, beschreibt Wilkomirski seine Erinnerungen als Produkt von Konzentrationsübungen.'
19 In the sense of a 'recovered memory therapy', cf. Pendergrast, 1995b.
20 'Man könnte vielmehr die Erzählungen Wilkomirskis als permanenten Versuch verstehen, seine Geburt in eine Einreise zu verwandeln, um anderswo hinzugehören und eine kohärente Geschichte zu finden.'
21 'I replayed the laughing faces of the freed prisoners, their look of relief on the film. Given that the film wasn't lying, given that these faces weren't lying, where was I? What did they conceal from me? Why wasn't I there, too? Did something really happen there and I knew nothing about it?' (Wilkomirski, 1997b: 151).

References

Agamben, G. (2003) *Homo Sacer. 3. Was von Auschwitz bleibt: das Archiv und der Zeuge*, Frankfurt a.M.: S. Fischer.

Apter, E. (2006) *The Translation Zone: A New Comparative Literature*, Princeton and Oxford: Princeton University Press.

Apter, E. (2013) *Against World Literature: On the Politics of Untranslatability*, London, New York: Verso.

Assmann, A. (2006) 'Männer mit zwei Köpfen: Hans Schneider/Schwerte und Bruno Doessecker/Binjamin Wilkomirski', In Victor I. Stoichita (ed.) *Das Double*, Wiesbaden: Harrasowitz, 249–264.

Bauman, Z. (2006) *Liquid Fear*, Cambridge and Malden: Polity Press.

Bedorf, T. (2010) 'Der Dritte als Schanierfigur. Die Funktion des Dritten in sozialphilosophischer und ethischer Perspektive', in E. Eßlinger, T. Schlechtriemen, D. Schweitzer & A. Zons (eds.) *Die Figur des Dritten. Ein kulturwissenschaftliches Paradigma*, Frankfurt a.M.: Suhrkamp, 125–136.

Bhabha, H. K. (1994) *The Location of Culture*, London and New York: Routledge.

Caruth, C. (2016) *Unclaimed Experience. Trauma, Narrative and History*, Baltimore: John Hopkins University Press.

Deleuze, G. (1980) 'Sacher-Masoch und der Masochismus', In L. von Sacher-masoch *Venus im Pelz*, Frankfurt a.M.: Insel, 163–281.

Derrida, J. (1985) 'Des tours de Babel', In J. F. Graham (ed.) *Difference in Translation*, Ithaca: Cornell University Press, 165–205.

Fischer, J. (2000) 'Der Dritte. Zur Anthropologie der Intersubjektivität', In W. Eßbach (ed.) *wir/ihr/sie. Identität und Alterität in Theorie und Methode*, Würzburg: Ergon, 103–136.

Fischer, J. (2010) 'Der lachende Dritte. Schlüsselfigur der Soziologie Simmels', In E. Eßlinger, T. Schlechtriemen, D. Schweitzer & A. Zons (eds.) *Die Figur des Dritten. Ein kulturwissenschaftliches Paradigma*, Frankfurt a.M.: Suhrkamp, 193–207.

Goldschmidt, G.-A. (2006) 'Am Waldrand', In G.-A. Goldschmidt (ed.) *Freud wartet auf das Wort*, Zürich: Ammann Verlag, 201–239.

Gourevitch, P. (1999) 'The Memory Thief', *The New Yorker* 14: June 1999 48–68.

Hessinger, P. (2010) 'Das Gegenüber des Selbst und das hinzukommende Andere. Die Figur des Dritten in der soziologischen Theorie', in E. Eßlinger, T. Schlechtriemen, D. Schweitzer & A. Zons (eds.) *Die Figur des Dritten. Ein kulturwissenschaftliches Paradigma*, Frankfurt a.M.: Suhrkamp, 65–79.

Klüger, R. (1998) 'Kitsch ist immer plausibel. Was man aus den erfundenen Erinnerungen des Binjamin Wilkomirski lernen kann', *Süddeutsche Zeitung* Nr. 225, 30 September 1998 : 17.

Koschorke, A. (2010) 'Ein neues Paradigma der Kulturwissenschaften', In E. Eßlinger, T. Schlechtriemen, D. Schweitzer & A. Zons (eds.) *Die Figur des Dritten. Ein kulturwissenschaftliches Paradigma*, Frankfurt a.M.: Suhrkamp, 9–31.

Lacan, J. (1987) *Die vier Grundbegriffe der Psychoanalyse: Das Seminar, Buch XI*, Norbert Haas (ed.) Berlin: Turia + Kant: Weinheim.

Lange, S. (2015) 'Der unheimliche Dritte. Der Übersetzer zwischen Literatur und Literaturwissenschaft', In A. Buschmann (ed.) *Gutes Übersetzen: Neue Perspektiven für Theorie und Praxis des Literaturübersetzens*, Berlin and Boston: de Gruyter, 201–216.

Laub, D. (1995) 'Truth and Testimony: The Process and the Struggle', In C. Caruth (ed.) *Trauma: Explorations in memory*, Baltimore and London: Johns Hopkins University Press, 61–75.

Lüdemann, S. (2010) 'Ödipus oder ménage à trois. Die Figur des Dritten in der Psychoanalyse', in E. Eßlinger, T. Schlechtriemen, D. Schweitzer, A. Zons (eds.) *Die Figur des Dritten. Ein kulturwissenschaftliches Paradigma*, Frankfurt a.M.: Suhrkamp, 80–93.

Mächler, S. (2000) *Der Fall Wilkomirski. Über die Wahrheit einer Biographie*, Zürich: Pendo.

Masschelein, A. (2011) *The Unconcept: The Freudian Uncanny in Late-Twentieth-Century Theory*, Albany: State University of New York Press.

Pendergrast, M. (1995b) *Victims of Memory: Incest Accusations and Shattered Lives*, Hinesburg: Upper Access.

Pfaller, R. (2002) *Die Illusionen der anderen. Über das Lustprinzip in der Kultur*, Frankfurt a. M.: Suhrkamp.

Rath, G (2010) '"Hybridität" und "Dritter Raum". Displacements postkolonialer Modelle', In E. Eßlinger, T. Schlechtriemen, D. Schweitzer & A. Zons (eds.) *Die Figur des Dritten. Ein kulturwissenschaftliches Paradigma*, Frankfurt a.M.: Suhrkamp, 137–149.

Simmel, G. (1992) *Soziologie. Untersuchungen über die Formen der Vergesellschaftung. (= Gesamtausgabe in 24 Bänden – Band 11)*, Frankfurt a. M.: Suhrkamp.

Spivak, G. (2008) *Can the Subaltern Speak? Postkolonialität und subalterne Artikulation*, Wien: Turia + Kant.

Stempel, W.-D. (1976) 'Ironie als Sprechhandlung', In R. Warning und W. Preisendanz (eds.) *Das Komische*, München: Fink, 205–235.

Stierle, K. (1976) 'Komik der Handlung, Komik der Sprachhandlung, Komik der Komödie', In R. Warning und W. Preisendanz (eds.) *Das Komische*, München: Fink, 237–268.

Stoffel, H. & C. Ernst (2002) 'Erinnerung und Pseudoerinnerung. Von der Sehnsucht, Traumaopfer zu sein', *Der Nervenarzt* 5 (2002): 445–451.

Walser, M. (1996) *Selbstbewußtsein und Ironie. Frankfurter Vorlesungen*, Frankfurt a. M.: Suhrkamp.

Weber, S. (1991) *Return to Freud: Jacques Lacan's Dislocation of Psychoanalysis*, Cambridge: Cambridge University Press.

Wilkomirski, B. (1997a) *Bruchstücke. Aus einer Kindheit 1939–1948*, Frankfurt a.M.: Suhrkamp: Jüdischer Verlag.

Wilkomirski, B. (1997b) *Fragments. Memories of a Wartime Childhood*, trans. C. B. Janeway New York: Schocken Books.

Wilkomirski, B. & E. Bernstein (1999) 'Die Identitätsproblematik bei überlebenden Kindern des Holocaust. Ein Konzept zur interdisziplinären Kooperation zwischen Therapeuten und Historikern', In A. Friedmann, E. Glück, D. Vysocki (eds.) *Überleben der Shoah – und danach. Spätfolgen der Verfolgung aus wissenschaftlicher Sicht*, Wien: Picus, 45–58.

Young, J. E. (1997) *Beschreiben des Holocaust: Darstellung und Folgen der Interpretation*, Frankfurt a. M.: Suhrkamp.

PART III

The translation of climate change discourses and the ecology of knowledge

5
SHADY DEALINGS
Translation, climate and knowledge

Michael Cronin

Standing on a bank of the river Oder, the protagonist of Olga Tokarczuk's novel *Flights* wonders about the risks of standing still:

> Staring into the current, I realized that—in spite of all the risks involved—a thing in motion will always be better than a thing at rest; that change will always be a nobler thing than permanence; that that which is static will degenerate and decay, turn to ash, while that which is in motion is likely to last for all eternity.
>
> *(Tokarczuk, 2018: 9)*

If translation carries within a notion of movement, of passage across space and time, we might ask how settled societies relegate it to the dark side of established thinking. Are 'all the risks involved' too unsettling for frames of reference and understanding deeply embedded in epistemic habits which die hard and which are now coming back to haunt us in the age of the Anthropocene? In this essay, we wish to explore how a particular Western ontological prejudice has cast translation into the dark side of conventional thought and how this inattentiveness to a translational dynamic is having far-reaching consequences for how we think about knowledge and human society in the era of human-induced climate change.

Changing the event

In *Language and Conquest in Early Modern Ireland* (2001) and in *The Severed Head and the Grafted Tongue: Literature, Translation and Violence in Early Modern Ireland* (2011), Patricia Palmer details the extreme levels of state violence in the Tudor period that accompanied the eradication of the Irish language from the public sphere, and the role of translation and non-translation in the legitimation of atrocity. The Great

Famine in the mid-nineteenth century, which particularly affected the Irish-speaking population on the island, further strengthened the connection between a means of expression and a mode of extinction (Ó Tuathaigh, 2015). By the end of the nineteenth century, the translation of the population from one language to another—from Irish to English—was almost complete.

Janine Altounian, in her exploration of the transgenerational trauma of the Armenian genocide, notes the unhappy coalition between hunger and silence in the minds of the survivors:

> There would be, then, a close connection between *dying of hunger* and *lacking the words* to speak about oneself, to think for oneself, to name who one is and to make the world meaningful in one's own language.
>
> *(Altounian, 2012: 149) (her own emphasis)*[1]

Famine, in a sense, is a mortal attack on two primary functions of orality: eating and speaking. When one function of orality—nourishment—is faced with a lethal threat to its viability, it is less than surprising that the other—communication—is irreparably damaged. Barry McCrea has described in his recent work *Languages of the Night* (2015) the linguistic collapse of part of post-famine Ireland—the county of Mayo—where parents refused to speak to their children in their own language, haunted by the spectre of mouths that could not be fed, and determined to translate the next generation into the idiom of plenty. In his clinical journal, Sandor Ferenczi noted how a part of a person may die, but that if another part survives the trauma, they emerge 'with a gap in their memory' or 'a gap in their personality' (cited in Altounian, 2012: 39). The language that is left unspoken is the untouchable zone of psychic hurt, and part of the filial piety in the generational transmission of trauma is to remain faithful to the mutism of dispossession.

Language change, the translation of a people from one tongue to another, is not always amenable to capture by a particular kind of commemorative logic, and the limits of this logic may remind us both of what we may need to remember and what we may need to forget. In other words, the dark legacies of language loss are not always susceptible to capture by forms of thinking that fail to understand the internal dynamic of translation.

Blaise Pascal in his *Pensées* (1670) was not particularly hopeful about the constancy of affection. One day you wake up and the other is no longer the beloved, but a complete stranger:

> He no longer loves the person he loved ten years ago. I believe: she's not the same nor is he. He was young and so was she; she is completely different. Perhaps, he would love her still as she was then.
>
> *(Pascal (2000), II, 123)*[2]

For the French philosopher, the fickleness of human affections demands the durability of divine love. Underlying Pascal's description of the hapless lovers is a particular way of viewing events which is central to Western ontology. One moment the couple are in love, the next they are not. I am sitting or I am standing, but I cannot be doing both at the same time. Otherwise, I am in the realm of the paradoxical. The work of *logos* is to determine. The more the object is determined, the greater the sensation of the object's existence. As Hegel notes, as long as pure Being is indeterminate, it is indistinguishable from pure nothingness. It is a pure void. There is nothing to see and still less to say (Hegel, 2010: 60). Hence, the great movement in Western art in the early and late Renaissance, as E. H. Gombrich has pointed out, to give weight, heft and substance to the world through the determinations of the artist's brush (Gombrich, 2000). The more vivid the sense of the world on canvas, the more it could be said to properly exist. The difficulty is what to do with or how to think about transitional states, that position between one state, one language, and another.

Aristotle, in his *Physics*, tries to offer a definition of the colour grey and claims that it is black with respect to white, and white with respect to black (Aristotle, 1934: 77). There is a distinct uneasiness here about what is neither black nor white but something in between. The ontological fixation makes thinking about certain phenomena difficult or problematic. Can we say there is an exact moment when people fall out of love? Is there a precise minute or hour or day when I begin to grow old? Am I young at 11.55 am and middle-aged at 12? Can we specify the hour, the day, the year, when the Soviet Union entered irreversible decline?

Answering any or all of these questions is not easy and suggests that our own specific conceptual traditions may not always be adequate to the experiences that are the lot of humans. The French sinologist François Jullien advocates the usefulness of looking at other traditions as a way of both revealing blind spots in how we interpret the world and locating repertoires of thinking that allow us to capture important dimensions to subjective and social experience. In his case, he draws on the Chinese term biàntōng, which can be variously translated as 'to accommodate to circumstances', 'flexible', 'to act differently in different situations' (Jullien, 2009: 26–27) as a way of thinking about transition in a way that is not beholden to Western ontological assumptions. The two characters that make up the word refer to 'modification' and 'continuation'. At one level these are opposites but, at another, each is the precondition of the other. It is thanks to 'modification' that a process engaged in does not exhaust itself, but is renewed and can 'continue', and it is thanks to 'continuation' that modification can communicate itself, can make sense in the context of the overall process. By way of illustrating what he means by 'silent transformations', Jullien selects one of the abiding themes of classical Chinese art, the passage of the seasons:

> The 'modification' comes in the passage from winter to spring, or from summer to autumn when the cold changes to warm or the warm changes to cold; the 'continuation' is apparent in the passage from spring to summer or from autumn to winter when the warm becomes warmer or the cold colder.

> Each moment of modification or communication alternates, but even modification, by repairing through the other the factor that is exhausting itself, operates to the benefit of the other and allows the whole process to continue.
>
> *(Jullien 2009: 27)*[3]

From this standpoint, it is not defining being or substance (offering precise definitions of what constitutes winter, spring, summer or autumn) that matters, but rather the actual process of change itself. What the binomial term with its polar opposites attempts to account for is the nature and coherence of the transition, just as each word I am writing is new (modification) but I am still (I hope) making sense (continuation). Thus, to return to Pascal's example, the focus is not on the subject, the lover who no longer loves or is loved, but on the process that leads to this state of affairs. The process itself becomes the true subject of enquiry. This enduring Western ontological prejudice is powerfully reinforced in the contemporary moment by the binary logic of the digital—one/zero, on/off. The focus on epochal moments of rupture—'Ten Days that Shook the World'—is inimical to the ontological status of translation, which is infinitely more akin to Jullien's paradigm of silent transformations—the gradual shift from one state to another through the cumulative effects of a multiplicity of minor changes. This makes the relationship between translation and social change often difficult to account for, as translation does not lend itself easily to the schismatic ontological drama of the Great Turning Point or the Revolutionary Event (see Meylaerts and Gonne, 2014: 133–151 for an example of the gradual nature of translation agency). On the other hand, in offering a more credible pointer as to how change actually occurs—whether this involves the dissemination of Buddhist teachings in China or the spread of Reformation thinking in Western Christendom—translation can help us to think through implications of changes in knowledge organisation as a result of complex causality of climate change. In order to do this, I want to sketch out a brief history of university development before asking what position translation might occupy in the knowledge scapes of the future. The aim here is to suggest that more relevant forms of knowledge organisation are necessary if translation studies, along with other branches of the human and social sciences, are not to find themselves lost in the perpetual darkness of species extinction and climate meltdown.

Changing the university

In his famous work on European literature and the Latin Middle Ages, Ernst Robert Curtius claimed that European universities were the 'original creations of the Middle Ages' (Curtius, 1948: 62). The distinctiveness of these institutions, for Curtius, lay both in their wetware and their hardware. Wetware, in that they were a community of teachers and scholars—an *universitias magistrorum et studentium*—and hardware in the form of lecterns, libraries and private mail systems. Though these emergent universities in Bologna, Paris, Oxford and Prague largely originated from pre-existing monasteries or cathedral schools, they represented the beginning of a sundering of education from the clerical hegemony that had been a hallmark of Western Christendom for centuries. Even if the clergy would continue to exercise considerable influence, the university became increasingly aligned with secular power, and sovereigns were soon to spot the political advantages in having an educated class that was prepared to support its economic, social and military interests against those of an often predatory papacy. Thus, we might label this first form of university organisation the monarchical university, to indicate the nature of ducal or regal patronage that allowed the universities to develop an autonomous identity outside the perimeter fences of ecclesiastical institutions. In terms of knowledge organisation, it is important to remember that a crucial element of continuity was the transmission of Latin manuscripts which permitted the *translatio studiorum*, the carrying of classical antiquity to the High Middle Ages (Kittler, 2004: 245). It was not enough to store this knowledge, of course; it had to be transmitted, processed and recorded. The data-processing lecture, the data-storing university library and the data-transmitting mail service were part of an overall media system that would allow for the cumulative and recursive production of knowledge over several centuries.

The changing nature of monarchy would ultimately usher in a form of knowledge organisation that would spell the end of monarchy itself as a dominant form of political expression. A characteristic of the British and French monarchies in the sixteenth and seventeenth centuries is the shift to a more strongly territorial notion of power consolidated around notions of cultural and linguistic specificity. Henry VIII with the Act for the English Order, Habit and Language in 1537, and François 1er with the *Ordonnance de Villers-Cottêrets* in 1539 that makes French the sole legislative language on French territory, signal the consolidation of royal power around emerging notions of national identity. When the French Revolution puts an end to royal power, the natural context for new institutionalised forms of knowledge is the nation-state. Thus, we get the foundation of the *École Polytechnique* in 1794, the clear intention being to produce an educated group of graduates who would minister to the technical needs of the emergent republic. The Prussian King gives university professors and high teachers the status of civil servants, and the conditions are right for the emergence of what Bill Readings calls the 'Humboldtian' university (Readings, 1996). The purpose of this university, what I am going to call the 'national university', is to prepare students to be future citizens of the state. The *Bildung* that is dispensed is not simply a matter of individual character formation, but it is designed to prepare the future graduate for public service, hence the increasing emphasis on the teaching of national language, history, geography and literature. Insurgent nationalism, the collapse of empire and the anti-imperial and anti-colonial struggles in different parts of the globe ensured the centrality of the paradigm of the national university to knowledge organisation in developed and developing nations until the closing decades of the last century.

From the 1980s onwards, a radical reorganisation of the world economic system, loosely referred to as globalisation, created pressures for new forms of knowledge organisation. Five main features of the globalisation era have been:

the growing frequency, volume and interrelatedness of cultures, commodities, information and peoples across time and space; the increasing capacity of information technologies to reduce and compress time and space; the diffusion of routine practices for processing global flows of information, money, commodities and people; the emergence of institutions and social movements to promote, regulate, oversee or reject globalisation, and the emergence of new types of global consciousness or ideologies of globalism which give expression to new forms of social connectedness described as cosmopolitanism (Beckford, 2003: 119; Turner and Holton, 2016: 10). Important geopolitical contexts for the emergence of globalisation have been the collapse of the Soviet Union in the early 1990s and the spectacular emergence of the Asian economies—Japan, China, South Korea and Singapore—which has led to a fundamental shift in the global basis of economic production. Not surprisingly, the relentless drive towards deregulation and the globalisation of production and consumption created unprecedented pressures for the traditional nation-state paradigm and its form of knowledge organisation.

As Thomas Docherty claims in *Universities at War* (2014), '[v]irtually every university institution nowadays presents itself as somehow shaped or determined in its fundamental values and activities by globalization' (Docherty, 2014: 75). The most public face of the university is ritually expressed in the 'mission statement', which mixes the evangelising zeal of monotheisms with the corporate outreach of the transnational business enterprise. The internationalisation of university rankings, the institutional implantation of campuses in different geographical territories, the active recruitment of foreign students (only, of course, if the students are prepared to pay dearly for this education) and the vertiginous rise in the control and surveillance logic of corporate managerialism all point to the estrangement of the university from the earlier nation-state paradigm. This is not to say that the national university has been totally usurped by the corporate university, any more than the national university in Europe in the nineteenth century signalled the immediate end of the monarchical university. Forms inevitably overlap, but the core argument here is that forms of knowledge organisation inevitably respond to broader societal changes.

The Australian theorist McKenzie Wark has argued that the 'production and reproduction of our species-being, whatever it may be, has to be a central concern of any critical knowledge' (McKenzie Wark, 2015: 134). The challenge of the Anthropocene—the era of human-induced climate change—is precisely the need to question deeply-held assumptions, to think the unthinkable and to develop new forms of knowledge, responsive not just to our current predicament, but to the planet which will be inherited by those who come after us. The need to orient knowledge to different ends by taking means seriously requires, among other things, that we reconsider the infrastructures of knowledge, in particular those whose avowed aim is the support and promotion of research: universities. It might be asked whether universities as they are currently constituted are capable of the development of a critical knowledge that meets the current and future needs of the 'production and reproduction of our species-being'? The difficulty is that the employment needs, the nutritional needs, the educational needs of the planet's inhabitants cannot be met by a growth model which is predicated on the unsustainable and destructive use of increasingly scarce resources, whether this be water, land, food or knowledge itself, corralled off in the auction rooms of the patents market.

This is where we might speculate on the emergence of the transitional university, a form of knowledge organisation that is directed to the creation of a carbon-neutral, sustainable and resilient economy and society. In what follows I will try to suggest why, at a conceptual level, the transitional university represents a radical departure from conventional ways of accommodating environmental issues. I will then argue that consideration of the notion of translation can potentially help us to engage with a number of core concerns in new critical forms of knowledge organisation.

Any organisation is at its most basic level a process that creates an environment. It allows you to draw general lines in the fabric of the whole (Holt and Mueller, 2011: 68). You make some kind of cut in the universe, to simultaneously create and order an inside from an outside. So what kind of cut do we make when dealing with climate change? Let us first consider this definition of climate change from the organisation theorist Norah Campbell:

> Climate change is the moment I turn on the engine of a car and ignite the 165 million-year-old microscopic fossil faunae, connecting me to the 35 billion ancient barrels that are drilled, fracked, refined, and transported every single year. Climate change is in the 100 trillion objects that are in, that are the Earth, traversing the stomach lining of the Burmese python and the Atlantic Meridional Overturning Circulation, which churns a quarter of the planet's heat flux. Climate change is the embodied and enacted operations of simplification, extraction, purification, replication, and acceleration—all of which are needed to create the philosophy of progress that is embodied by nearly every human in this world. Climate change is so unimaginably vast and complex that, to quote George Eliot, 'if we had a keen vision of all feeling and all ordinary human life, it would be like hearing the grass grow and the squirrel's heart beat and we should die at the roar which lies on the other side of silence'. In such a reckoning, climate change is the end of demarcation, the end of a background.
>
> *(Campbell, 2018: 1)*

Climate change as expressed here is one of Timothy Morton's 'hyperobjects' which enjoy vast extension in space and time. Three constitutive features of climate change pose particular problems for organisational response—unboundedness, incalculability and unthinkability. Unboundedness, because we can never be sure what can be included in climate and what cannot be. As Morton puts it in the heading to chapter two in *Being Ecological* (2018), 'And the Leg Bone's

Connected to the Toxic Waste Bone', and the list of connections goes on and on. Incalculability, because climate change involves complex, non-linear systems that generate untotalisable effects that defy known forms of planning and organising. Unthinkability, because we are continually frustrated in our desire to capture it empirically, organisationally or psychologically, as indeed I am trying to do now. What all of this implies is that climate change is not some 'thing' that can be recuperated into existing institutional and infrastructural frameworks. As Norah Campbell argues, the ontologisation of climate change means that it is not so much a problem within the world we live in but that it now constitutes that world. Climate change, in other words, is so unbounded that it is not something 'outside' that can be internalised by an organisation. Organisations can only exist within it, as nothing can exist outside of it. If, as the British sociologist John Urry has claimed, climate change entails the 'total reorganisation of social life, nothing more and nothing less' (2010: 8), then can we simply consider the matter of the environment as simply one other topic among others that can be safely accommodated in our existing institutional structures and research programmes?

To put this into context, I want to allude briefly to the notion of 'advents' that the French philosopher Quentin Meillassoux has developed in *L'Inexistence divine*. Meillassoux's argument is that there are three specific points in the history of the universe where there has been the emergence *ex nihilo* of distinct worlds—the World of the material, the World of life and the World of thought:

> So far there seem to have been three [Worlds] of irreducible facts: matter (reducible to what can be theorized in physico-mathematical terms), life (understood more specifically as a set of terms, that is, affections, sensations, qualitative perceptions, etc., which cannot be reduced to material processes), and finally thought (understood as a capacity to arrive at the 'intelligible contents' bearers of eternity, and which as such is not reducible to any other terms).
>
> *(Meillassoux 2011: 221)*

Advents, for Meillassoux, are forms of emergence without precedent. In the transition from non-life to life, the laws of biological life were not somehow contained in the pre-life world. Combinations that were inherent in the organisation of the living could be imagined as possible cases of the World of matter but not as latent in it, as if it were a ghostly potential force. In the transition from the Holocene to the Anthropocene, we are arguably living through one of these radical discontinuities in the fabric of what has come before, an Advent period that ushers in a new World. When we pause to think of what the Holocene brought in its wake—agriculture, advanced forms of technology, urbanisation, animal domestication, the births of languages and religions and translation —the entry into a new geological era characterised as we noted earlier by unboundedness, incalculability and unthinkability poses fundamental challenges to our habitual forms of knowledge organisation and institutional expression. So what future then for the university? How might we transition to the transitional university? And where does translation come into this picture of epochal shift?

Changing the subject

The ontologisation of climate change or the apprehension of it as hyperobject—where throwing away a styrofoam cup now can impact on life four hundred years into the future—means that treating our ecological condition as yet another research topic or disciplinary sub-interest is clearly not feasible. Climate change is the outside that cannot be internalised in this way. Similarly, Green Campus initiatives that encourage ecological good practice, while laudable and necessary, should not be confused with the more daunting task of finding a form of knowledge organisation that is adequate to our predicament. The biologist Edward O. Wilson, in *The Future of Life* (2003), sees specific, long-range historical thinking as crucial to curbing humanity as 'planetary killer, concerned only with its short-term survival' (Wilson, 2003: 202). Wilson argues it is only when humans begin to think of themselves as a species that they can begin to take the longer view, not only as an important exercise in critical self-understanding, but as a means of securing the future. For Rosi Braidotti, this move towards species awareness is a necessary step towards post-anthropocentric identity. Critical at the present moment is the de-centring of *anthropos*, 'the representative of a hierarchical, hegemonic and generally violent species whose centrality is now challenged by a combination of scientific advances and global economic concerns' (Braidotti, 2013: 65). Being 'matter-realist', to use her term, is to take seriously our multiple connections to natural and material worlds. If we conceive of the notion of subjectivity to include the non-human, then the task for critical thinking is, as Braidotti herself admits, 'momentous'. This would involve visualising the subject as 'a transversal entity encompassing the human, our genetic neighbours the animals and the earth as a whole, and to do so within an understandable language' (Braidotti, 2013: 82). If we bear in mind what Braidotti has to say about new, emergent forms of subjectivity, 'a transversal entity encompassing the human, our genetic neighbours the animals and the earth as a whole', the emphasis is clearly on extended forms of relatedness.

Though Braidotti does not state this anywhere, this transversal subjectivity obviously demands translation if the relatedness is to be anything other than simple contiguity. The transversal connections are only possible if there is communication across difference. Otherwise entities are condemned to monadic solitude. If translation has traditionally been regarded as one of the disciplines in the humanities, the challenge of climate change and transversal subjectivity is to stress the (in)humanity of translation, its capacity as a form of thought to engage with questions of meaning, representation and transformation across lines of radical difference between the human and the non-human. It is in this context that we might imagine for a moment a very different organisation of the current university that focuses on the Commons—those shared goods such as air or water which have often been regarded as mere externalities in market capitalism and which, because they were shared, were not valued and recklessly polluted. In this Elemental University we might have a Faculty of Air, a Faculty of Fire, a Faculty of Earth and a Faculty of Water. Recasting our institutional arrangements means, at one level, shifting the focus to the neglected externalities that make up life support systems on the planet. If we have the physicists, the biologists, the engineers, the medical faculty, the computer science specialists, the philosophers, the comparative literature scholars all working together, for example, in a Faculty of Water—one of the most vital and endangered resources on our planet at present—then we have the potential coming-together of anthropological and materialist approaches which are so necessary to holistic approaches to climate awareness. What this coming-together begs, however, is the question of translation, or communicability across difference.

This question is irredeemably complex, but one way into it is through Gilbert Simondon's conceptualisation of individuation. Simondon was resolutely opposed to 'the hierarchical subordination of matter to a transcendent form', where 'the constituted individual is considered to be explicable on the basis of a principle of individuation anterior to it' (Sauvagnargues, 2016: 57). From an Aristotelian perspective, in order to create anything you have to bring together form (*morphe*) and matter (*hyle*). In this hylomorphic model of creation, form was imposed by an agent with a particular design in mind, and matter itself was passive and inert, that which was imposed upon (Kirby, 2011). The extraordinary success of Albertian principles in architecture, the rise of the printing press, and the Faustian energies unleashed by mass production seemed to be incontrovertible proof of the validity of the hylomorphic model, where the architect's blueprint, the printer's hot plate and the manufacturer's cast were the tangible proof of the power of a preconceived design to be imprinted many times over on supine matter (Cronin, 2013: 67–69). In this transitive model of production, human activity is regarded primarily as the instrumental outcome of preconceived plans.

For Simondon, the difficulty with this approach is that it sees becoming as the becoming of individuated being rather than the becoming of the individuation of being. What constitutes individuation in his eyes is the 'solution of a conflict, the discovery of an incompatibility, the invention of a form' (Simondon, 1989: 77). He describes this process in terms of a problematic 'disparation', as an act of relation. Simondon takes the term from the psychophysiology of perception, where it designates the production of depth in binocular vision. Each retina is covered by a bi-dimensional image, but the two images do not coincide due to the difference in parallaxes (you can observe this by closing one eye and then the other). There is no optically available bi-dimensional image than can resolve the lack of coherence between the two images. The human brain deals with this bi-dimensional disparation by integrating it as the condition of coherence of a new axiom, tri-dimensionality. Volume or depth perception resolves the bi-dimensional conflict by actively creating a new dimension, tri-dimensionality, in the absence of the retinal image. The perceptual discovery is not a reductive abstraction but an integration, an amplifying operation. In-depth perception is achieved not through the elimination of disparity, the elimination of the difference of the parallaxes, 'but rather though an operation, an inventive construction that adds a new dimension that the isolated retinal image does not contain. It is the pair of disparate retinas that require this amplifying operation, which is what constitutes "disparation"' (Sauvagnargues, 2016: 63).

Disparation is thus simultaneously 'problematic' and creative. 'Problematic' refers to the disparity, the difference, between the retinal images in so far as this difference is not reduced, but, on the contrary, provides the opportunity for the constitution of a new dimension (Sauvagnargues, 2016: 63). Rather than seeing disparation as a specifically psychophysiological phenomenon, Simondon extends it to any production of existence on whatever scale one is situated (physical signal, living being, collective body, idea). Problematic disparation, which is remarkably analogous to translation—a new entity emerging in the problematic gap between different languages—produces singularity. Crucially, however—and this brings us back to transversal subjectivity—it suggests a way of dealing with relatedness across difference that does not lead to the extinction of difference. Other examples Simondon provides comes from the process of crystallisation and the operation of cell membranes. Crucial from the point of view of what might underpin the operations of translation and the transitional university is that we find a line of thought going from Spinoza to Bergson to Raymond Ruyer, Gilbert Simondon, Félix Guattari, Gilles Deleuze, Rosi Braidotti, Val Plumwood and Timothy Morton which professes a form of continuism. This places matter, organism, psychic and collective individuation on the same plane and in the words of Morton, 'the fact that interconnection is also a thing, not just an abstraction or convenient idea, has really surprising deep implications' (Morton, 2018: 78). It is precisely the collapse of continuism, the dualistic separation of subjects and objects, the instrumentalist, extractivist ideology of an inanimate universe that can be manipulated by a select animate species that has brought us to our sorry ecological pass. One of the roles of the transitional university would be look to ways of making that continuism a constituent part of intellectual enquiry and pedagogical practice. Translation as disparation is a way of aligning translation thinking with a form of thought that allows for emergence, creativity, singularity, but not at the cost of eliminating difference.

After mapping out, however allusively, the ontological and conceptual backdrop to the transitional university I would mention briefly three specific areas where translation and translation studies would have a role to play in development of this new organisational enterprise:

Translation and the indigenisation of knowledge

As Naomi Klein has pointed out in *This Changes Everything*, one of the most striking features about major sites of resource extraction around the world is that they are often inhabited by impoverished, marginalised peoples frequently speaking lesser-used languages (Klein, 2014). Their material dispossession and linguistic marginalisation makes the inhabitants of these 'sacrifice zones' particularly vulnerable to exploitation and acculturation. It is precisely these groups, however, that have an understanding of the relationship of the human to the non-human world which becomes especially valuable in an era of environmental degradation. Elizabeth Povinelli has coined the term 'geo-ontology' to speak about the worldview of many indigenous groups in Australia who do not establish rigid conceptual and hierarchical distinctions between the human and the non-human. Treating rock formations as inert, inanimate matter does not make sense from their geo-ontological perspective, where the world in all its variousness is an active part of an animate cosmos (Povinelli, 2016). The political theorist Jane Bennett, in *Vibrant Matter: A Political Ecology of Things*, argues for a 'vital materiality' that runs through and across bodies, both human and non-human. She claims that the 'quarantines of matter and life encourage us to ignore the vitality *of* matter and the lively powers of material formation' (Bennett, 2010: vii). The implications for translation studies in the age of the Anthropocene are twofold. Firstly, while efforts have been made in recent decades to try and remedy the North American and Eurocentric bias of translation studies, it is remarkable how rarely indigenous peoples or endangered languages have been centre-stage in TS debates. It is time that this balance was redressed so that crucial parts of the planet's knowledge infrastructure are appropriately recognised and valued. Secondly, such an engagement implies rethinking the conventional understandings about what it is that translation is supposed to do, namely that translation is exclusively an activity that takes place between, and comprises, animate human subjects. In pushing the boundaries of how we might think about translation (while drawing on its immeasurably rich tradition of thinking about and engaging with difference), the subject of translation and indigenous peoples should not be seen as an exercise in salvage archaeology. The point is not a kind of appropriative exoticism which sees endangered languages as the receptacles of past greatness or vanished worlds, but an approach that construes the languages and cultures as part of future-oriented cosmologies (Danowski and Viveiros de Castro, 2014: 221–339; Latour, 2017). Thus, it is not simply a question of revealing through translation the depth and complexity of different indigenous epistemes or mobilising translation to make language use a viable proposition for indigenous peoples across different domains, but making manifest a way of engaging with the planet that alters translation studies modes of conceptualisation and operation.

Translation and projective citizenship

A common economic and political assumption in market economies and societies is that individuals are isolated entities who seek to maximise their personal gain. In so doing—making profits from producing as much bread as possible, for example—the pursuit of individual self-interest contributes to the collective good: more bread is produced, which increases the supply for everyone (Brown, 2015). In this view, the function of the university is to treat the student as a paying customer whose primary aim is to use the university as a means of maximising individual economic self-interest. The payoff is clearing the student loan and a lifetime of added value. As Thomas Docherty argues, the university becomes a simple forum where unrelated individuals 'come, engage as if in a market or commercial enterprise in the seeking of personal gain and then leave again, returning once more to their prior identity' (Docherty, 2014: 100). In this respect, the university is akin to a shopping mall or a gambling den, where the focus is exclusively on material self-enrichment. In a sense, this is a clearly extractivist logic where the focus is on individual gain, not on the public good, and there is a consequent disregard for the commons: those goods that because they are collectively shared are deemed to be privately worthless. This guiding fiction of the corporate university, of course, ignores the real conditions of people where they are already a constituent part of society. 'That public thing, that *res publica* is there entirely because of our previously existing social relations, our being-together. Instead of arithmetic, think geometry—literally the measuring of the earth and its constructed shape as an intrinsic and integrated whole' (Docherty, 2014: 100). Docherty draws on the thinking of the American poet Charles Olson, who saw in projective geometry a way of thinking about literature and the world. In projective geometry, objects are understood to make space for themselves in the world but in relation to others. Translation, as a praxis that makes connections, explores the manifold forms of relatedness, contests an additive, arithmetical notion of human or cultural contiguity and shows how translations make projective spaces for themselves in other cultures, but always in relation to these cultures. As Milan Kundera noted, 'it was to Rabelais that Laurence Sterne was reacting, it was Sterne who set off Diderot, it was from Cervantes that Fielding drew constant inspiration, it was against Fielding that Stendhal measured himself' (cited in Wynne, 2018: n.p.), and the list goes on. In the context of the shift to the transitional university, where the emphasis is no longer on the virtual profiteering of the *hors-sol* but on the real-life predicaments of the *terrestres* (Latour, 2018), the study and practice of translation can help to underpin a notion of 'projective citizenship' that has global consequence.

Translation kinetics

The German sociologist Hartmut Rosa, in his most recent work *Resonanz: Eine Soziologie der Weltbeziehung* (2016), speaks of the fundamental social formation of modernity which is oriented towards an ever-accelerating culture of infinite growth. The increasingly rapid accumulation of resources is based on a basic reorientation in modernity away from a society where there were fixed or preordained positions or ranks in life towards a society where there is basically a privatisation of what constitutes the good life. What Rosa means by this is that each individual must determine what the good life is and organise access to the resources—health, wealth, human connections—that will ensure that this life becomes a possibility. The difficulty for the modern self, however, is twofold.

Firstly, getting access to resources is more and more fraught as the basic principle of competition in contemporary societies means that the individuals are constantly asked to reinvent themselves—to become smarter, fitter, healthier, more performative—in an increasingly accelerated cycle of entrepreneurial self-invention. Secondly, the fixation on resources becomes an end in itself so that what these resources might be for is lost sight of, and the increasingly desperate effort to procure the resources means that the ends they serve—physical, mental and social wellbeing—are increasingly remote. The faster you go, in effect, the more instrumental your relationship to self and your environment. You have less time to attend to your inner self and to your external world. The social consequences are a triple form of dissonance: ecological, social and psychological. Ecological, because the kinetic inferno of material growth ignores the limits to the natural sustainability of the planet. Social, because the dehumanisation of technological and market instrumentalism mean that more and more citizens feel left behind in the backwaters of political exclusion. Psychological, because the explosion of mental health issues in contemporary societies and the anti-depressants epidemic in the developed world detailed by Mark Fisher in *Capitalist Realism: Is There No Alternative?* (2009) point to the heavy toll on individual wellbeing of the pumping iron productivism of the modern corporatised workplace. Maggie Berg and Barbara Seeber in the *The Slow Professor* (2016) have detailed the consequences of cultures of accelerated productivity for universities and the continual erosion of the spaces and possibilities of deep thought. As the transitional university demands decelerationist, long-term, non-extractivist thinking and practice, it suggests that we look to translation as an activity which potentially offers careful, attentive, time-rich attention to language and text. The French translator Mireille Gansel describes how she initially retranslated *Sensible Wege*, the title of a poem by Reiner Kunze, as 'Fragile Paths' and then thirty years later retranslated it as 'Sensitive Paths'. A change in one word reflected three decades of reading and experience, and she notes that, at the moment of making the change, 'I understood translation both as risk taking and continual re-examination, of even a single word—a delicate seismograph at the heart of time' (Gansel, 2018: 36). This concern for time and the requirement to respect the time necessary for translation expressed by certain translators (Schwartz, 2017) is easily mocked by the pragmatico-realists of the translation industry, but it is the intrinsic temporal logic of the latter that will precipitate ecological mayhem not the thoughtful deliberateness of the former. The championing of a different kind of translation kinetics—one that values an investment in the long now—should no longer be seen as a quaint throwback to a world of unearned privilege, but as the only feasible way of creating a world based on long-term sustainability. For translation to have a future, it must reflect on how it might contribute to that future. Challenging fundamental ontological prejudices, helping to elaborate new forms of knowledge organisation and focusing on the development of a terracentric as opposed to a geocentric or ethnocentric translation studies are all within the remit of translation. If Frank Wynne has argued that 'translators are the beating heart that make it possible for stories to flow beyond borders and across oceans' (Wynne, 2018: n.p.), the time is upon us to take notice of what is happening to those oceans and to the planet more generally if those hearts are going to continue to beat. The true dark side of translation studies must be ignorance. If we fail to acknowledge changed contetxs, then we will indeed 'degenerate and decay' and there will be nobody left to wait for us on the other side of our dead rivers.

Notes

1 Il y aurait ainsi un lien étroit entre *mourir de faim* et *manquer de mots* pour se dire, pour se penser, pour nommer qui on est et signifier le monde dans sa propre langue.
2 Il n'aime plus cette personne qu'il aimait il y a dix ans. Je crois bien: elle n'est plus la même, ni lui non plus. Il était jeune et elle aussi; elle est tout autre. Il l'aimerait peut-être encore, telle qu'elle était alors.
3 La 'modification' intervient de l'hiver au printemps, ou de l'été à l'automne, quand le froid s'inverse et tend vers le chaud, ou le chaud vers le froid; la 'continuation', quant à elle, se manifeste du printemps à l'été, ou de l'automne à l'hiver, quand le chaud devient plus chaud ou le froid plus froid. L'un et l'autre moment alternent, de modification ou de continuation, mais même celui de la modification, en réparant par l'autre le facteur qui s'épuise, opère au profit de son autre et sert à la continuation d'ensemble du procès.

References

Altounian, J. (2012) *De La Cure À L'écriture: L'élaboration D'un Héritage Traumatique*, Paris: PUF.
Aristotle (1934) *Physics Books 5–8*, trans. P. H. Wicksteed and F. M. Cornford, Cambridge MA: Harvard University Press.
Beckford, J. (2003) *Social Theory and Religion*, Cambridge: Cambridge University Press.
Bennett, J. (2010) *Vibrant Matter: A Political Ecology of Things*, Durham and London: Duke University Press.
Berg, M. & B. Seeber (2016) *The Slow Professor: Challenging the Culture of Speed in the Academy*, Toronto: University of Toronto Press.
Braidotti, R. (2013) *The Posthuman*, Cambridge: Polity.
Brown, W. (2015) *Undoing the Demos: Neoliberalism's Stealth Revolution*, London: Zone Books.
Campbell, N. (2018) *Climate Change is Not A Problem: Speculative Realism at the End of Organization*, unpublished MS: cited with author's permission.
Cronin, M. (2013) *Translation in the Digital Age*, London: Routledge.
Curtius, E. R. (1948) *Europäische Literatur und Lateinisches Mittelalter*, Bern: Francke Verlag.
Danowski, D. & E. Viveiros de Castro (2014) 'L'Arrêt de monde', In (É. Hache.), *De l'univers Clos au Monde Infini*, Bellevaux: Éditions Dehors, 221–339.
Docherty, T. (2014) *Universities at War*, London: Sage.
Fisher, M. (2009) *Capitalist Realism: Is There No Alternative?*, Washington: Zero Books.
Gansel, M. (2018) *Translation as Transhumance*, trans. R. Schwartz., London: Les Fugitives.
Gombrich, E. H. (2000) *Art and Illusion: A Study in the Psychology of Pictorial Presentation*, Princeton: Princeton University Press.
Hegel, G. W. F. (2010) *The Science of Logic*, trans. G. Di Giovanni., Cambridge: Cambridge University Press.

Holt, R. & F. Mueller (2011) 'Wittgenstein, Heidegger and Drawing Line in Organization Studies', *Organization Studies* 32: 67–84.
Jullien, F. (2009) *Les Transformations Silencieuses: Chantiers, I*, Paris: Livre de Poche.
Kirby, J. (2011) *Aristotle's Metaphysics: Form, Matter and Identity*, London: Continuum.
Kittler, F. (2004) 'Universities: Wet, Hard, Soft, and Harder', *Critical Inquiry* 31(1): 244–245.
Klein, N. (2014) *This Changes Everything: Capitalism vs. the Climate*, London: Allen Lane.
Latour, B. (2017) *Facing Gaïa: Eight Lectures on Climate Change*, Oxford: Polity.
Latour, B. (2018) *Down to Earth: Politics in the New Climactic Regime*, Oxford: Polity.
McCrea, B. (2015) *Languages of the Night: Minor Languages and the Literary Imagination in Twentieth-Century Ireland and Europe*, New Haven: Yale University Press.
McKenzie Wark, K. (2015) *Molecular Red: Theory for the Anthropocene*, London: Verso.
Meillassoux, Q. (2011[1997]) 'Appendix: Excerpts from L'Inexistence divine', In (G. Harman.), *Quentin Meillassoux: Philosophy in the Making*, Edinburgh: Edinburgh University Press, 177–238.
Meylaerts, R. & M. Gonne (2014) 'Transferring the City—Transgressing Borders: Cultural Mediators in Antwerp (1850–1930)', *Translation Studies* 7(2): 133–151.
Morton, T. (2018) *Being Ecological*, London: Penguin.
Ó Tuathaigh, G. (2015) *I mBéal an Bháis: The Great Famine and the Language Shift in Nineteenth-Century Ireland*, Hamden (CT): Quinnipiac University Press.
Palmer, P. (2001) *Language and Conquest in Early Modern Ireland*, Cambridge: Cambridge University Press.
Palmer, P. (2011) *The Severed Head and the Grafted Tongue: Literature, Translation and Violence in Early Modern Ireland*, Cambridge: Cambridge University Press.
Pascal, B. (2000) *Pensées* [1670], Paris: Livre de Poche.
Povinelli, E. (2016) *Geontologies*, Durham NC: Duke University Press.
Readings, B. (1996) *The University in Ruins*, Cambridge MA: Harvard University Press.
Rosa, H. (2016) *Resonanz: Eine Soziologie der Weltbeziehung*, Berlin: Suhrkamp Verlag.
Simondon, G. (1989) *L'individuation psychique et collective : à la lumière des notions de forme, information, potentiel et métastabilité*. Aubier, Paris.
Sauvagnargues, A. (2016) *Artmachines: Deleuze, Guattari, Simondon*, S. Verderber & E. W. Holland., Edinburgh: Edinburgh University Press.
Schwartz, R. (2017) 'How Long Will It Take You to Type This in English?', in *ATA Chronicle*: www.atanet.org/chronicle-online/featured/how-long-will-it-take-you-to-type-this-in-english (viewed 15/11/2018).
Tokarczuk, O. (2018) *Flights*, trans J. Croft., London: Fitzcarraldo.
Turner, B. S. & R. J. Holton (2016) 'Theories of Globalisation: Issues and Origins', In B. S. Turner & R. J. Holton (eds.), *The Routledge International Handbook of Globalization Studies*, 2nd edition London and New York: Routledge, 3–23.
Urry, J. (2010) 'Consuming the planet to excess', *Theory, Culture and Society*, 27(2–3): 191–212.
Wilson, E. O. (2003) *The Future of Life*, London: Abacus.
Wynne, F. (ed) (2018) *Found in Translation*, London: Head of Zeus.

6
CLIMATE CHANGE AND THE DARK SIDE OF TRANSLATING SCIENCE INTO POPULAR CULTURE

Alexa Weik von Mossner

A cartoon by Tom Dunne shown on the website of the *American Scientist* is neatly divided down the middle, showing four figures labelled as 'scientists' on the left side of the image and a dense mass called 'the public' on the right. The speech balloon above the scientists contains no words, but a few apples instead (Dunne, 2015). The speech balloon above the public is filled with a great many oranges. This, Dunne suggests, is science communication. His cartoon illustrates a blog by Katie L. Burke that seeks to clarify '8 Myths About Public Understanding of Science' (Burke, 2015). The myths themselves include the (false) beliefs that '[p]eople need more information to understand science of concern to the public' and that '[a]rguments supported by facts and evidence will change people's beliefs'. Dunne's interpretation of the situation, however, seems much more radical: in his cartoon, scientists and the public speak apples and oranges, and so what is needed is some major acts of *translation* from one fruit into the other, so to speak, by someone who understands and speaks both apples and oranges.

Dunne's point is exaggerated but well-taken: scientists often express their findings in a language that is not easily accessible to the general public. This is a problem because many of these findings have far-reaching implications for individuals, groups or whole societies, which is why institutions and journalists have tried to translate scientific findings into a language that can be more widely understood, appreciated and applied. As communication scholars Sarah Davies and Maja Horst have observed, '[s]cience communication is not simply about making difficult things more simple, and it is something more than the exchange of scientific knowledge from those who know to those who know not' (Davies and Horst, 2016: 2). The acts of translation involved have, in fact, important implications for 'the welfare of individuals, organizations, and nations' (ibid.: 1) and, in some cases, they even have consequences for the survival of a species, an ecosystem, or the planet as a whole. The latter argument has been frequently made in relation to climate change communication, where there is an urgent sense that scientific insights must be communicated to lawmakers, industry leaders, and the general public before it is too late to avoid planetary disaster. As Burke notes, 'facts and evidence' are not enough to 'change people's beliefs' (Burke, 2015) and so, in recent years, there have been increased efforts by scientists, journalists, novelists, and filmmakers alike to translate dry science into emotionally moving stories that engage people on a different level. However, a frequent complaint against this endeavour has been that such translations display a problematic proclivity towards dark, even apocalyptic storytelling that cues negative emotions such as anger, sadness, fear, guilt, and shame, rather than hope or desire for a better way of being. Such negative feelings, it is feared, will push people into apathy, depression, and desperation, leaving them unable to *do* anything about the situation.

In this essay, I want to pick up some of these complaints and discuss their validity, and I want to do so with reference to two of the meanings of 'dark translation' that Federico Italiano discusses so eloquently in his introduction to this book. Firstly, the notion of *opacity* as that which is invisible, hidden from view, that which gets lost in translation—for example, the complexities and uncertainties of a given scientific model. And, secondly, the notion of *emotional darkness* that may be evoked by populist acts of science translation that emphasise the dangerous and catastrophic over the moderate and optimistic. As we will see, the feelings evoked by such translations must not necessarily be bad or painful, nor must they lead to apathy or despair. And yet, journalists and scholars alike tend to conceptualise the dark side of climate change communication as deeply problematic, if not debilitating. In what follows, I will take a look at some of the ecocritical and psychological research on the matter and relate it to a number of cultural texts that deliberately employ emotional darkness in their popular translations of climate science.

The dark side of climate change communication: attempts at eco-translation

Translations of scientific findings about the changing climate of planet Earth into a language that can be understood by the general public arguably belong into the larger field of what translation scholar Michael Cronin has called *eco-translation* (Cronin, 2017: pos. 2). In Cronin's deliberately broad definition, eco-translation is 'a body of ideas and a set of practices [that] is central to any serious or sustained attempt to think about [our] interconnectedness and vulnerability in the age of human-induced climate change' (ibid.: pos. 137). As such, it 'covers all forms of translation thinking and practice that knowingly engage with the challenge of human-induced environmental change' (ibid.: pos. 148). In his book, Cronin explores eco-translation in relation to specific ecological issues such as our relationship to food and to non-human animals, while anthropogenic climate change emerges as the vast backdrop for all acts of translation. 'When we think about the future of translation,' he writes, 'it involves inescapably the question of climate change which will leave no area of human and non-human being untouched' (ibid.: pos. 164). Following the environmental philosopher Timothy Morton, Cronin understands climate change as a 'hyperobject' (ibid.: pos. 150) that is simply too vast and too complex to be grasped in its totality by the human mind.[1]

Indeed, we could argue that translating climate change into a language that can be understood by the general public involves at least two important steps of translation. In the first step, scientists translate physical phenomena that are either observed, reconstructed or expected into the language of science. In the second step, that scientific language then gets translated into a range of texts and images that are accessible to lay people. Both steps inevitably involve a loss of data, leading to the kind of *opacity* that Italiano considers typical for many acts of translation: for the sake of clarity and relevance, parts of the information are simplified or completely left out. This simplification may be a deliberate decision, or it may be the result of the translator's limited understanding of the original data. In addition, the translated data will be *framed* in certain ways in order to give it meaning within a specific context. If we look at actual climate change communication, we can't help but notice that much of it is framed in a way that is likely to cue a range of *dark emotions* in recipients. At the same time, there is an ongoing debate around the potential problems involved in dark translations of this kind.

A typical example is the controversy around a long-form article published by David Wallace-Wells in the *New York Magazine* on July 9, 2017 (Wallace-Wells, 2017a).[2] Entitled 'The Uninhabitable Earth', the article made what some readers considered an alarmist argument about the need to face the threat posed by climate change rather than clinging to the idea that humanity will find some kind of technological fix before things gets really bad. 'It is, I promise, worse than you think', writes Wallace-Wells at the beginning of his deliberately provocative piece:

> If your anxiety about global warming is dominated by fears of sea-level rise, you are barely scratching the surface of what terrors are possible, even within the lifetime of a teenager today. And yet the swelling seas—and the cities they will drown—have so dominated the picture of global warming, and so overwhelmed our capacity for climate panic, that they have occluded our perception of other threats, many much closer at hand. [...] Indeed, absent a significant adjustment to how billions of humans conduct their lives, parts of the Earth will likely become close to uninhabitable, and other parts horrifically inhospitable, as soon as the end of this century.
>
> *(Wallace-Wells, 2017a)*

This apocalyptic scenario of a 'horrifically inhospitable' Earth by the end of this century is not dystopian fiction, argues Wallace-Wells, but rather based on the worst-case scenarios of published scientific research on climate change. It is this combination of emotionally dark storytelling and a claim to scientific accuracy that hit a nerve with readers.

Within hours of its publication, 'The Uninhabitable Earth' caused a storm of indignation not only in the comments section of the article's online version, but also in a range of social media and major publication outlets (the *New York Magazine* later published an annotated version of the article), the main criticism being that Wallace-Wells was trying to scare people and could well succeed. Some of the most damning and remarkable responses came from the climate science community. The American climatologist Michael Mann called the tone of the article 'counterproductively doomist', adding that while

> [i]t is important to be up front about the risks of unmitigated climate change [...] there is also a danger in overstating the science in a way that presents the problem as unsolvable, and feeds a sense of doom, inevitability and hopelessness.
>
> *(Mann, 2017)*

Mann proceeded to assert that '[t]he article paints an overly bleak picture by overstating some of the science', suggesting that the problem was a mistranslation, in this case an overstatement, of scientific language ('apples' in the terminology suggested by Tom Dunne's cartoon) into the language a journalist uses to engage a mass readership of lay people (who, in Dunne's terminology, speak oranges). He supported his criticism with a number of corrections of 'translation errors' he noticed in Wallace-Wells's article, complete with links to the science blog *Real Climate* and a peer-reviewed article in the scientific journal *Nature Geoscience* that are supposed to provide readers with more accurate scientific knowledge in the words of scientists, rather than those of a journalist. Such words, he implied, are considerably less alarmist than Wallace-Wells' dark translation of them.

Wallace-Wells responded to Mann's criticism by acknowledging that his article was deliberately alarmist because it is high time for alarm. Stressing the importance of storytelling in human processes of comprehension, he insists that

> we have suffered from a terrible failure of imagination when it comes to climate change [...] and that is in part because most of us do not understand the real risks and horrors that warming can bring, especially with unabated carbon emissions.
>
> *(Wallace-Wells, 2017b)*

To corroborate his point, Wallace-Wells also included the unedited transcript of his own interview with Mann, in which Mann talks freely about the tendency among climatologists to 'understate [...] the potential risks [of climate change] and the timeframe on which they may unfold because of [a] combination of innate conservatism among scientists and [the] assault on science by climate-change deniers' (Mann, quoted in Wallace-Wells, 2017b). So there are things, then, that climatologists deliberately downplay or omit when translating their findings for the general public, things that get lost in translation not only because the public cannot grasp scientific jargon, but also because scientists are careful, conservative, or cautious. In this context, it is revealing that Mann also says in the same interview that 'it's critical to not just consider the most likely impacts, but those sort of low-probability but catastrophic sort of cost scenarios. What we call the so-called tails of the probability distribution' (Mann, quoted in Wallace-Wells, 2017b). These are precisely the kind of worst-case scenarios that Wells describes in 'The Uninhabitable Earth', and yet as soon as it is out in published form, Mann himself attacks that translation of science for being 'doomist' and 'counterproductive'. Whether he does so because he fears it will scare lay readers into apathy, or whether he himself is afraid of a potential backlash against climatologists, we cannot know.

Mann's weariness with the potential effects of the dark side of eco-translations echoes some concerns voiced by Timothy Morton in his 2016 *Dark Ecology*. In the first pages of the book, Morton explains that, in his definition, 'dark ecology' is synonymous with 'ecological awareness', which is 'dark-depressing' but also 'dark-uncanny' and even 'dark-sweet' (Morton, 2016: 5). As an eco-critically inclined philosopher, Morton is interested in all three of those dimensions of meaning, but he most fervently embraces the third one, with its somewhat positive connotation, over the more negative ones. 'Nihilism', writes Morton, 'is always number one on the charts these days. We usually don't get beyond the first [depressing] darkness, and that is if we even care' (ibid.: 5). Morton, however, does not stop at just criticising forms of ecological awareness that are nihilistic or depressing. Instead, he suggests that we should try 'to get to the third darkness, the sweet one, through the second darkness, the uncanny one' and adds: 'Don't be afraid' (ibid.: 5). The implied suggestion is that, instead of remaining at the level of nihilism, we should walk through the uncanny—which, in his understanding, involves recognising that as a collective, humanity is a 'zombie' and that as an individual one is inevitably part of it—to eventually 'find the sweetness in the depression' of ecological awareness. 'Find the joy', Morton writes, 'without pushing away the depression, for depression is accurate' (ibid.: 117). Even for Morton, then, the dark-depressive response is *appropriate* in the face of our current ecological situation; but it is unhelpful, which is why he hopes to train his readers in the art of finding and developing positive emotions such as joy within the darkness. Whether that is truly possible without falling back to the stance that he criticises at the very beginning—the lack of care most researchers describe as a state of apathy—remains an open question.

In the world of climate science, one is hard-pressed to find any expressions of the 'dark sweetness' in the midst of environmental decline and disaster that Morton wants us to find. And yet, searching for the emotionally pleasant in the midst of disaster is nothing strange or uncommon for those who produce popular culture narratives, regardless of whether we look at literature, film, or other media. Authors, filmmakers and producers are inevitably confronted with the need to make their stories *attractive* to audiences, since only very few people are willing to subject themselves voluntary to stories that cue exclusively negative and painful emotions. Most of us look for some kind of pleasurable experience when we go to the movies, pick up a book, play a video game, or engage in some other form of storytelling, even if—or, in some cases, precisely because—the story we are engaging with is dark, depressing, or even horrifying. This phenomenon, labelled by David Hume as 'the paradox of tragedy' (Hume, 1965 [1793]), also holds true for dark popular culture translations of climate science. A quick look at the emerging genre of popular climate change narratives reveals that even the most doomist and dystopian of them cue a range of pleasurable emotions in audiences. Moreover, it opens up an important question: is it really true that dark translations of climate science are inherently problematic?

Dark-sweet climate fiction and the paradox of emotional darkness

Perhaps the most appropriate starting point for an exploration of the emotional value of dark climate change fiction is Roland Emmerich's 2004 *The Day After Tomorrow*, a film that translates a scientific scenario into a popular film by greatly exaggerating the expected effects and adding features of melodrama and disaster narrative to engage viewers in an apocalyptic story about abrupt climate change. Despite its many scientific inaccuracies, Emmerich's movie stands out as the first Hollywood mega-blockbuster that was self-consciously about climate change, rather than just using a climatically changed environment as narrative setting and background. More recent climate-themed films such as Bong Joon-ho's *Snowpiercer* (2012) and George Miller's *Mad Max: Fury Road* (2015) feature spectacular environments that severely limit what their protagonists can and cannot do, but these protagonists are not scientists, nor do those films aim to translate, as *The Day After Tomorrow* does, an actual scientific scenario such as the shutdown of the Atlantic Meridional Overturning Circulation into an economically successful piece of popular culture.[3]

Countless commentators, scientists and otherwise, have stressed that the spectacular disasters on show in *The Day After Tomorrow* are not actually part of this or any other serious scientific scenario. Just as in the case of David Wallace-Wells's 'The Uninhabitable Earth', which was published thirteen years later, climatologists were highly concerned about the possible effects of Emmerich's dark translation of climate science into a spectacular disaster narrative, although their concerns were somewhat different. Upon the film's release on Memorial Day weekend in 2004, research centres around the world put up information sheets on their websites that commented on the film's scientific inaccuracies and sought to assure readers that such drastic climatic changes could never happen that fast in reality. As the psychologist Anthony Leiserowitz puts it in his survey of the impact of Emmerich's film in the United States, '[s]ome commentators feared that the catastrophic plotline of *The Day After Tomorrow* would be so extreme that the public would subsequently dismiss the entire issue of global warming as fantasy' (Leiserowitz, 2004: 23). Just as in the case of Wallace-Wells's article, the underlying assumption was that an overly dark translation of science would negatively affect the public's understanding of climate change, but here the assumption was not that a 'counterproductively doomist' narrative would feed 'a sense of doom, inevitability and hopelessness' in the general public (Mann, 2017). Rather, scientists feared that *The Day After Tomorrow* might lead people to dismiss climate change entirely.

This fear, however, turned out to be mostly unfounded. The results of Leiserowitz's survey showed that Emmerich's film 'had a considerable impact on the global-warming risk perceptions of those who saw the movie' (Leiserowitz, 2004: 28). It 'did not lead moviegoers to suddenly adopt an extreme model of climate sensitivity' (ibid.: 29), nor did it lead them to dismiss the idea of anthropogenic climate change entirely. Four other studies, conducted in Japan, the UK and Germany, came to somewhat different but similar conclusions (Reusswig, 2004a: 42; 2004b).[4] Even more interesting is the fact that many scientists used the hype around the film to educate the public. In a 2004 blog post, the renowned climatologist Stefan Rahmstorf writes that *The Day After Tomorrow* 'presents an opportunity to explain that some of the basic [scientific] background is right: humans are indeed increasingly changing the climate and this is quite a dangerous experiment, including some risk of abrupt and unforeseen changes' (Rahmstorf, 2004). And, as Michael Svoboda has attested in a contribution to *Yale Climate Connections* (2014), this still holds true more than ten years after the film's release. Several people involved in climate change communication whom Svoboda interviewed confirmed that the film continues to facilitate their translation work, suggesting that—rather than being counterproductive because of its cueing of dark emotions—Emmerich's apocalyptic narrative continues to be an effective tool in climate change communication.[5]

What are the crucial differences, then, between Wallace-Wells's article and Emmerich's film, given that both paint a lively picture of a more or less 'uninhabitable Earth' based on equally dark eco-translations of climate science? Why is it that one of them—the improbable disaster science fiction—is used in science communication to this day, while the other one is labelled as 'counterproductively doomist'? Issues of genre, mode, and medium are an important part of the answer to this question but, before we get to that, I first want to briefly address the more immediate question of why it is that a film that centres on abrupt and catastrophic climate change can become a box-office hit at all. Common sense would tell us that showcasing the utter destruction of the Northern Hemisphere and implying the death of millions, if not billions of people cannot be particularly entertaining, and yet it is not only the disaster film genre that excels in doing just that. There are also many other genres, among them the thriller, the horror film, and the melodrama, that succeed in making emotional darkness *enjoyable* for their audiences. In his seminal essay 'Of Tragedy' (1965 [1793]), David Hume writes that

> [i]t seems an unaccountable pleasure, which the spectators of a well written tragedy receive from sorrow, terror [...] and other passions, which are in themselves disagreeable and uneasy. The more they are touched and affected, the more are they delighted with the spectacle.
>
> (Hume, 1965 [1793]: 216)

Aristotle explained what has become known as the 'paradox of tragedy' with the idea of *catharsis*, but some of the more recent explanations aim to reveal the source of what Morton calls the 'sweetness' in the dark and depressing, in the very nature of our emotional engagement with fiction.[6]

Building his argument on Hume's deliberations, the cognitive film scholar Carl Plantinga has argued that filmmakers use various techniques to make the eliciting of negative emotions enjoyable. In his astute analysis of these techniques in James Cameron's *Titanic* (1997), Plantinga demonstrates that, in Hollywood film, negative emotions such as sadness and empathetic pain tend to be balanced and attenuated with a range of *positive* emotions (Plantinga, 2009: 187). And indeed, even the most cursory look at the storyline of *The Day After Tomorrow* makes clear that Emmerich's film stays true to this tradition, mixing the negative emotions that may be cued by the depicted disaster and loss of life with positive emotions, such a sympathy and admiration for the two main protagonists (played by Dennis Quaid and Jake Gyllenhaal, two major stars at the time), curiosity and excitement about the spectacular visualisation of climate disaster, and happiness about the reunion of father and son at the end of the film's family reunification plot. As several scholars have shown (Ingram, 2005; Murray and Heumann, 2009; Weik von Mossner, 2017), it is this family-oriented plot that is foregrounded in the film, not the terrible deaths of millions of people; and yet, the dark background of climate catastrophe is needed in order to raise the stakes for the family that's about to be reunited.

It is, in fact, no coincidence that many of the commercially most successful films revel in emotional darkness in order to make things more difficult for their protagonists and thus more exciting for their audiences. In a 2017 study introducing the 'Distancing-Embracing Model of the Enjoyment of Negative Emotions in Art Reception', Winfried Menninghaus et al. explain that 'negative emotions have been shown to be particularly powerful in securing attention, intense emotional involvement, and high memorability, and hence is [sic] precisely what artworks strive for' (Menninghaus et al., 2017: 1). And while the comments the authors received in response to their proposed model from researchers in a range of fields from psychology to literary studies impressively demonstrates that there is no universally agreed-upon explanation for the paradox of tragedy, they emphatically confirm the central importance of emotional darkness in fictional storytelling for audience enjoyment.[7] With this in mind, let's return to the question why climatologists have responded more harshly to Wallace-Wells's *New York Magazine* article than to Emmerich's blockbuster film, regardless of the fact that, if anything, the film depicts the darker scenario.

Fiction, nonfiction and the dark side of climate science translation

The complaints levelled against the 'doom and gloom messaging' of Wallace-Wells's 'The Uninhabitable Earth' seem to tacitly assume that nonfiction accounts, such as a magazine article, will be understood in way that is categorically different from fiction, presumably because the audience believes them to be accounts of the actual world rather than free inventions. However, in the age of alternative facts, even the most cursory glance at news reporting will promptly remind us that the general public is quite aware that not everything they see and read in the news is factual. This is particularly true for reports about climate change, which, as Naomi Oreskes and Erik Conway (2010) have demonstrated, are notoriously plagued by politically motivated mistranslations of scientific findings.[8] If anything, the cueing of negative emotions such as anger and fear is even more common in news reporting, and thus in *non*fiction, than it is in popular fiction.

It should thus not surprise us that, in their response to Menninghaus et al., psychologists Deena Skolnick Weisberg and Stacie Friend argue that there is no reason to exclude nonfiction from any consideration of the enjoyment of negative emotions, since 'consumers can have similar responses to nonfictional representations' (Skolnick Weisberg and Friend, 2017: 43). And once we look at the long list of nonfiction treatments of climate change in both literature and film, it becomes obvious that most of them, too, provide readers and viewers with emotionally dark and doomist translations of climate science. That is true for many of the popular science books that cater to a lay readership, from Elizabeth Kolbert's *Fieldnotes from a Catastrophe* (2006) and Peter Ward's *The Flooded Earth* (2010) to Jeff Goodell's *The Water Will Come* (2017). Even more remarkable, perhaps, is James Hansen's *Storms of My Grandchildren* (2009), in which the acclaimed climatologist and former head of NASA pauses his detailed scientific argument about the coming climate disaster to include a post-apocalyptic science fiction story, to allow readers to experience on the imaginary level what it would be like to push our planet all the way into Condition Venus. The inclusion of emotionally dark elements in popular science books about climate change has been a growing trend in recent years.

The same is true for documentary film. From Davis Guggenheim's *An Inconvenient Truth* (2006) and Leila Conners Petersen and Nadia Conners's *The 11th Hour* (2007) to Fisher Stevens' *Before the Flood* (2016), climate change documentaries make use of a broad spectrum of dark affective appeals, translating scientific findings in ways that cue anxiety, fear, or anger. The most notable of them, in this regard, is Franny Armstrong's crowd-funded documentary-fiction-hybrid *The Age of Stupid* (2009). Armstrong initially conceptualised her film as a straightforward documentary. It was only after test screenings showed that it was not engaging enough for viewers that she decided to add a fictional dystopian frame narrative set in a devastated 2055, in which an old archivist, played by Pete Postlethwaite, looks back to our time—to the age of stupid—when people could have saved themselves but didn't. The rhetoric employed in the frame narrative is downright apocalyptic, whereas the six documentary strands of the film are suffused with bitter irony and brief moments of comic relief. Unlike many of the other climate change documentaries shown earlier, Armstrong even resists the final turn to the hopeful in the last few minutes of the film. Instead, it ends on a dark and depressing note.

The British researcher Rachel Howell conducted research on the film's reception during 21 screenings at the Edinburgh Filmhouse, and concluded that the often-suspected depoliticising effect of dark storytelling

> largely does not appear to have happened in this case. Respondents emerged from the film with an increased motivation to take action, and an increased belief that they could do something to prevent climate change getting worse, along with the sense that they are not already doing everything they can.
>
> *(Howell, 2011: 184)*

Only a very small percentage of respondents (about ten percent) 'expressed a sense of depression' (ibid.: 181). It seems then, that dark eco-translations of climate science in *nonfiction* narratives are also not necessarily as problematic as is often claimed, and that filmmakers and writers have good reason to rely on the dark emotions if they want to reach a large audience. As it turns out, 'The Uninhabitable Earth' became the most-read story in the history of *New York Magazine* (Roberts, 2017), and it was its sheer popularity that led some scientists to reconsider their stance on dark storytelling. Andrew Dessler, a climate scientist at Texas A&M whose first reaction to the article was very critical, later wrote:

> My initial impression of the article was negative—I thought it presented a worst, worst, worst case scenario as being far more likely than the science indicates. As time went on, however, I was amazed to see the strong reaction to the article and the amount of discussion it fostered. I think it engaged people and made them think about the well-established risks that climate change poses to humanity. I do hope, however, that no one comes away from the article despairing that all hope is lost.
>
> *(quoted in Comments, 2017)*

Emotional darkness seems to hold a deep fascination for us that cannot be easily resisted, and as long as dark translations of scientific facts are at least somewhat faithful, there may be no reason to be too concerned about them. As Michael Cronin points out, 'gaining people's attention' (Cronin, 2017: pos. 599) is one of the most crucial and most difficult tasks for any communicator in our day and age, and if dark storytelling gets people to pay attention to climate change, it may be of greater value than is often acknowledged.

Conclusion

In the attempt to translate scientific apples into popular oranges, then, emotional darkness is not only common but also potentially useful when it comes to drawing people's attention to the subject of climate change. However, it is nevertheless worth adding a word of caution by way of conclusion. As psychologists Chapman et al. maintain in their commentary on the controversy around Wallace-Wells's article, '[d]ebate over effective climate change communication must be grounded in rigorous affective science' (Chapman et al., 2017: 850). And affective science suggests that, rather than treating emotions 'as simple levers to be pulled to promote desired outcomes', they 'should be viewed as one integral component of a cognitive feedback system guiding responses to challenging decision-making problems' (ibid.: 850). Furthermore, Chapman et al. reiterate a point that has also been made by Leiserowitz and Howell: namely, we know only very little 'about how emotional responses to climate change evolve over time or how those changes prospectively predict shifts in beliefs, attitudes, and behaviour' (ibid.: 851). The journalist David Roberts has made the same observation, concluding that '[w]hat matters in an overall assessment of someone's disposition toward climate change is not their raw feelings in the immediate aftermath of an emotionally significant experience (living through a hurricane, say, or reading a scary magazine story), but how those responses are reinforced and strengthened (or not) over the course of the following days and years' (Roberts, 2017). Roberts concludes that there is room for as many stories about climate change 'as there are people, room for fear and hope and wonder and suspense and sadness and curiosity and all the rest of human experience' (ibid.). Some people might respond well to pleasant fear cued by dystopian or apocalyptic storytelling, and others might be inspired by more positive emotions such as wonder and hope.

This raises a question that might seem like heresy in a book about the dark side of translation: what about the bright side? Aren't there any popular culture texts that aim to translate climate science into positive, hopeful stories? There are such translations, in fact, but not very many. In popular film, practically none, although recent years have seen a few attempts in the realm of nonfiction: among them Josh Fox's *How to Let Go of the World* (2016) and Bonni Cohen and Jon Shenk's *An Inconvenient Sequel* (2017).[9] In popular literature, the trend is also towards dystopian translations of climate science, but there are some storytellers that seek to capture a form of the 'sweetness' within the dark-depressing that Timothy Morton has ask us to search for and unveil. The most notable example is Kim Stanley Robinson, whose science fiction novel *New York 2140* paints a sweeping panorama of a Venice-like New York City more than a hundred years from now, portraying the lives of a group of people who simply live out their existences in this climate-changed world. Perhaps we will see more of these somewhat brighter translations of climate science in the future, storytelling that also seems to speak to the call, voiced recently by the environmental psychologist Renee Lertzman, that 'a more nuanced—that is to say, a more authentic and more human—mode of communication can actually enhance people's capacities for response' (Lertzman, 2017). In Lertzman's view, changing people's minds about climate change is 'not about hope or despair or solutions versus warnings. It's about openly acknowledging that climate change is a classic both-and situation' (ibid.). Translating the science of climate change for a lay audience may mean helping people acknowledge the dark side of its insights without extinguishing the light.

Notes

1 Morton names climate change as a typical example of a hyperobject in his book *Hyperobjects: Philosophy and Ecology after the End of the World* (2013). In Morton's definition, 'the term hyperobjects refers to things massively distributed in time and space relative to humans' (Morton, 2013: 1).
2 For a good overview of the controversy, see Kevin Drum's 'Our Approach to Climate Change Isn't Working. Let's Try Something Else' (2017).
3 The Atlantic Meridional Overturning Circulation (AMOC) is a system of currents in the Atlantic Ocean that is an important component of the Earth's climate system. In recent years, researchers have expressed concerned over what is often called a 'cold blob' in the North Atlantic, which may signal a potentially catastrophic weakening of the AMOC (Hansen et al., 2016: 3761), though a complete shutdown in the twenty-first century—as depicted (in an exaggerated and highly accelerated fashion) in *The Day After Tomorrow*—is considered highly unlikely by most researchers. At this point, the stability of the AMOC remains an open question. For more information, see Robinson Meyer (2017) 'The Atlantic Ocean and an Actual Debate in Climate Science', in *The Atlantic*, 7 January: www.theatlantic.com/science/archive/2017/01/what-a-real-debate-looks-like-in-climate-science/512444 (viewed 26/09/2019).
4 For an evaluation of the impact of *The Day After Tomorrow* on the American public's understanding of climate science, see also Matthew Nisbet (2004).
5 However, this does not have to mean that the impact of dystopian films must always be constructive. Matthew Schneider-Mayerson (2013) has shown that, historically, disaster movies have also encouraged eco-apocalyptic beliefs in the United States.
6 Aristotle used the metaphor of a cathartic process in the *Poetics* to describe the effects of true tragedy on the spectator. In his definition, catharsis is defined as a process in which we inflict upon ourselves some form of punishment so that we find relief from negative emotions we have experienced in real life.
7 The comments are all included in the cited 2017 edition of Menninghaus et al.'s study.
8 In *Merchants of Doubt* (2010), Oreskes and Conway demonstrate how, over four decades, a group of high-level scientists with extensive political connections ran effective campaigns to mislead the public and deny well-established scientific knowledge. See also Robert Kenner's 2014 documentary film of the same title, which is based on the Oreskes and Conway's research.
9 Josh Fox's *How to Let Go of the World* begins with a familiar narrative of climate gloom and doom and then travels around the world to visit communities that have become climate activists on the local, national or global level. Bonni Cohen and Jon Shenk's *An Inconvenient Sequel*, featuring Al Gore, focuses on the progress made to tackle global climate change since the release of *An Inconvenient Truth* and Gore's global efforts to persuade governmental leaders to invest in renewable energy. The film's narrative arc culminates in the landmark signing of 2016's Paris Agreement, though it had to be re-edited (leading to a somewhat darker overall message) after Donald Trump's announcement that the United States would leave the Paris Agreement.

References

The 11th Hour (US 2007/D: Leila Conners Petersen and Nadia Conners).
The Age of Stupid (UK 2009/D: Franny Armstrong).
Before the Flood (US 2016/D: Fisher Stevens).
Burke, K. L. (2015) '8 Myths About Public Understanding of Science', in *American Scientist*, 9 February: www.americanscientist.org/blog/from-the-staff/8-myths-about-public-understanding-of-science (viewed 14/ 08/2019).
Chapman, D. A., B. Lickel & E. M. Markowitz (2017).'Reassessing Emotion in Climate Change Communication', in *Nature Climate Change* 7: 848–852.
'Comments' (2017) *New York Magazine* (July 24): http://nymag.com/nymag/letters/comments-2017-07-24/(viewed 14/08/2019).
Cronin, M. (2017) *Eco-Translation: Translation and Ecology in the Age of the Anthropocene*, New York and London: Routledge.
Davies, S. R. & M. Horst (2016) *Science Communication: Culture, Identity and Citizenship*, Basingstoke: Palgrave Macmillan.
The Day After Tomorrow (U.S. 2004/D: Roland Emmerich).
Drum, K. (2017) 'Our Approach to Climate Change Isn't Working. Let's Try Something Else', in *Mother Jones*: www.motherjones.com/kevin-drum/2017/07/our-approach-to-climate-change-isnt-working-lets-try-something-else/(viewed 14/08/2019).
Dunne, T. (2015) 'Science Communication', cartoon on the *American Scientist* website: www.americanscientist.org/blog/from-the-staff/8-myths-about-public-understanding-of-science (viewed 14/ 08/2019).
Goodell, J. (2017) *The Water Will Come: Rising Seas, Sinking Cities, and the Remaking of the Civilized World*, New York: Little Brown and Company.
Hansen, J. (2009) *Storms of my Grandchildren: The Truth about the Climate Catastrophe and Our Last Chance to Save Humanity*, New York: Bloomsbury.
Hansen, J., M. Sato, P. Hearty, R. Ruedy, M. Kelley, V. Masson-Delmotte, G. Russell, G. Tselioudis, J. Cao, E. Rignot, I. Velicogna, B. Tormey, B. Donovan, E. Kandiano, K. von Schuckmann, P. Kharecha, A. N. LeGrande, M. Bauer & K.-W. Lo (2016) 'Ice Melt, Sea Level Rise and Superstorms: Evidence from Paleoclimate Data, Climate Modeling, and Modern Observations that 2°C Global Warming Could be Dangerous', *Atmospheric Chemistry and Physics* 16: 3761–3812.
How to Let Go of the World and Love all the Things that Climate Can't Change (US 2016/D: Josh Fox).
Howell, R. A. (2011) 'Lights, Camera … Action? Altered Attitudes and Behaviour in Response to the Climate Change Film' *The Age of Stupid*, *Global Environmental Change* 21 (1): 177–187.
Hume, D. (1965 [1793]) 'Of Tragedy', in J. V. Lenz (ed), *Of the Standard of Taste and Other Essays*, Indianapolis: Bobbs-Merrill, 29–37.
An Inconvenient Sequel: Truth to Power (US 2017: D: Robert Kenner).
An Inconvenient Truth (U.S. 2006/D: Davis Guggenheim).
Ingram, D. (2005) 'Hollywood Cinema and Climate Change: *The Day After Tomorrow*', in M. Devine & C. Grewe-Volpp (eds), *Words on Water: Literary and Cultural Representations*, Trier: Wissenschaftlicher Verlag Trier, 53–63.
Kolbert, E. (2006) *Fieldnotes from a Catastrophe: Man, Nature, and Climate Change*, London: Bloomsbury.
Leiserowitz, A. A. (2004) 'Before and after *The Day After Tomorrow*: a U.S. Study of Climate Risk Perception', *Environment* 46(9): 23–37.

Lertzman, R. (2017) 'Can We Talk About Global Warming?', in *Sierra: The National Magazine of the Sierra Club*, 19 July: www.sierraclub.org/sierra/how-can-we-talk-about-global-warming (viewed 14/ 08/2019).

Mad Max: Fury Road (Australia 2015/D: George Miller).

Mann, M. (2017) Post 7 July, Facebook: www.facebook.com/MichaelMannScientist/posts/1470539096335621 (viewed 26/ 09/2019).

Menninghaus, W., V. Wagner, J. Hanich, E. Wassiliwizky, T. Jacobsen & Stefan Koelsch (2017) 'The Distancing-Embracing Model of the Enjoyment of Negative Emotions in Art Reception', *Behavioral and Brain Sciences* 40: 1–15.

Merchants of Doubt (US 2014/D: Robert Kenner).

Meyer, R. (2017) 'The Atlantic Ocean and an Actual Debate in Climate Science', in *The Atlantic* (January 7): www.theatlantic.com/science/archive/2017/01/what-a-real-debate-looks-like-in-climate-science/512444/(viewed 14/08/2019).

Morton, T. (2013) *Hyperobjects: Philosophy and Ecology after the End of the World*, Minneapolis: University of Minnesota Press.

Morton, T. (2016) *Dark Ecology: For a Logic of Future Coexistence*, New York: Columbia University Press.

Murray, R. L. & J. K. Heumann (2009) *Ecology and Popular Film: Cinema on the Edge*, Albany: State University of New York State University of New York Press.

Nisbet, M. (2004) 'Evaluating the Impact of *The Day After Tomorrow*: Can a Blockbuster Film Shape the Public's Understanding of a Science Controversy?', in *CSICOP On-Line: Science and the Media*: www.csicop.org/specialarticles/show/evaluating_the_impact_of_the_day_after_tomorrow/(viewed 14/ 08/2019).

Oreskes, N. & E. M. Conway (2010) *Merchants of Doubt: How a Handful of Scientists Obscured the Truth on Issues from Tobacco Smoke to Global Warming*, London: Bloomsbury Press.

Plantinga, C. (2009) *Moving Viewers: American Film and the Spectator Experience*, Berkeley: University of California Press.

Rahmstorf, S. (2004) '*The Day After Tomorrow*—Some Comments on the Movie': www.pik-potsdam.de/~stefan/tdat_review.html (viewed 14/ 08/2019).

Reusswig, F. (2004a) 'The International Impact of *The Day After Tomorrow*', *Environment* 46 (9): 41–43.

Reusswig, F. (2004b) 'Climate Change Goes Public: Five Studies Assess the Impact of 'The Day After Tomorrow in Four Countries', Potsdam Institute for Climate Research: www.upf.edu/pcstacademy/_docs/200410_climatechange.pdf (viewed 14/ 08/2019).

Roberts, D. (2017) 'Does Hope Inspire More Action on Climate Change than Fear? We Don't Know', in *Vox*, 5 December: www.vox.com/energy-and-environment/2017/12/5/16732772/emotion-climate-change-communication (viewed 14/ 08/2019).

Robinson, K. S. (2017) *New York 2140*, New York: Orbit Books.

Schneider-Mayerson, M. (2013) 'Disaster Movies and the "Peak Oil" Movement: Does Popular Culture Encourage Eco-Apocalyptic Beliefs in the United States', *Journal for the Study of Religion, Nature, and Culture* 7(3): 289–314.

Skolnick Weisberg, D. & S. Friend (2017) 'Embracing Nonfiction: How to Extend the Distancing-Embracing Model', *Behavioral and Brain Sciences* 40: 43–44.

Snowpiercer (KR/CZ 2013/D: Bong Joon-ho).

Svoboda, M. (2014) 'The long melt: The lingering influence of *The Day After Tomorrow*', in *Yale Climate Connections*: https://www.yaleclimateconnections.org/2014/11/the-long-melt-the-lingering-influence-of-the-day-after-tomorrow/(Wednesday, November 5, 2014).

Titanic (US 1997/D: James Cameron).

Wallace-Wells, D. (2017a) 'The Uninhabitable Earth' in *New York Magazine*: http://nymag.com/daily/intelligencer/2017/07/climate-change-earth-too-hot-for-humans.html (viewed 14/ 08/2019).

Wallace-Wells, D. (2017b) 'Scientist Michael Mann on "Low-Probability But Catastrophic" Climate Scenarios', in *New York Magazine*, 11 July: http://nymag.com/daily/intelligencer/2017/07/scientist-michael-mann-on-climate-scenarios.html (viewed 14/ 08/2019).

Ward, P. D. (2010) *The Flooded Earth: Our Future in a World Without Ice Caps*, New York: Basic Books.

Weik von Mossner, A. (2017) *Affective Ecologies: Empathy, Emotion, and Environmental Narrative*, Columbus: Ohio State University Press.

7

DARKNESS, OBSCURITY, OPACITY

Ecology in translation

Daniel Graziadei

You may be reading this in daylight, or with the help of artificial light. Whatever the case, I would like to invite you to follow me into the dark side. Or, rather, into an observation of the absence of light and the hidden qualities suggested by this volume's title, *The Dark Side of Translation*. I will begin this trajectory through darkness with some observations concerning this title, the general scope of the multiple meanings of darkness, and particularly 'the dark side'. My first tentative answer to the question of what are we actually translating when we translate darkness into metaphors, cultural concepts, etc., understands darkness as an embodied experience. After paying particular attention to the fear and insights this embodiment can trigger, I discuss physical as well as cultural aspects concerned with 'the dialectic of light and darkness' and its inherently positive evaluation of darkness' contrasting and dimming quality. In the following, I move from darkness in the sense of an absence of light to darkness in the sense of concealment, and from there to a discussion of the challenges *opacity* poses to (translation as perfect) understanding, but also to 'geopoetics' that unknowingly translate already 'translated natures' and the ecocide that follows these translations. The ecocritical practice of 'slow translation' proposed in order to generate 'eco-translation' (see Cronin, 2017) is then discussed as a way to re-evaluate complexity, opacity, obscurity, and darkness in a sustainable way.

The dark side of …

The title of this volume, *The Dark Side of Translation*, is an invitation to focus on the darkening and obscuring powers and qualities of translation. If we understand translation as a process or, as Michael Rössner and Federico Italiano propose, 'translatio/n' as 'a conflictual process of negotiation between elements of the old and the new contexts' (Rössner and Italiano, 2012: 12), which changes the target *and* the source context, then it is not easy to discern the different sides of such a process of translation, and even more difficult to assess their illuminations or densities. So where, and what, could the dark side possibly be? It appears that, in describing a process, 'side' and 'darkness' are used metaphorically and topologically.

In this vein, this volume's pop-culture-inspired differentiation between the 'Star Wars paradigm'—the centralising, concentrating, excluding energy' of the dark side of the Force (see Introduction, page 2)—and the 'Pink Floyd paradigm'—pointing to the invisible, latent, hidden, concealed (ibid.: 7) and the 'invisible, or covert or opaque or [...] unfathomable' (ibid.)—distinguishes cosmic infinitudes from psychic depths, total overview and insight from perspectivism and relationality, and the violent grasp for total control from the exploration of human psychopathology. Indeed, just as 'the Force' in the fictional world of *Star Wars* is an energy field that has a will of its own, 'the dark side of the Force doesn't refer to any part or aspect of the Force [...] but instead to its wilful misuse' (Eberl, 2015: 100; 110). This darkness is therefore based in the ethical dimensions of individual actions within a moral framework of binary conflict that has a long intertextual history. Contrary to this clear and bellicose moral framework, Pink Floyd's concept album *The Dark Side of the Moon* treats 'a variety of socially conscious themes, including escalating corporate greed, fears of ecological devastation, and pervasive insanity affecting both the power elite and popular opposition' (Demastes, 2015: 147). The connection the album creates between these instances of human lunacy[1] on earth and the dark side of the moon indicates an aspect of darkness that is not antagonistic to light, but hidden out of sight: the far side of the earth's satellite—that part of the moon that always faces away from Earth—is not always dark, but *is* always hidden. Only in 1959 did the Soviet Union's 'Luna 3 spacecraft [return] the first views ever of the far side of the Moon', and the very first image was taken at 03:30 UT on 7 October at a distance of 63,500 km, 'after Luna 3 had passed the Moon and looked back at the sunlit far side' (NASA, 2016). The impossibility of seeing the part of the satellite that is always turned away from Earth is evidently a different thing to the impossibility of perceiving the so-called 'new moon' without auxiliary optical means due to lunar night. Nonetheless, according to William Demastes, '[f]ar side and dark side were interchangeable terms during the lunar mania that captured our imaginations' (2015: 148). This interchangeability of '[t]he quality or state of being dark' is recorded among the nine different meanings of darkness the *OED* lists as the '[a]bsence or want of light' and the 'condition or environment which conceals from sight, observation, or knowledge'.[2] The conflation of the dark with the hidden begs questions about the relation between the sensory reception of physical phenomena and their translation into human language and thought: what are we actually translating? Are we translating day and night as well as matter and light, or are we translating the way we experience them? Are we even translating anything anew, or are we simply continuing the endless reproduction of texts, intertexts, cultural concepts, and discourses?

Embodied darkness—between fear and insight

According to Sky Marsen, the concepts human beings establish are based on bodily experiences and their translation into language, rather than being purely linguistic signifiers or mental categories with meanings ascribed to them freely and arbitrarily:

> Embodiment, that is, existence in a physical form, is vital in the meaning-making process. In fact, there seems to be general theoretical consensus on this: cognitive linguists [...], computer game theorists [...], and phenomenologists [...] agree that human conceptual forms are determined by embodied consciousness and a sensory experience of things. Although the language function provides important structures for conceptualizing and thinking, it is not necessary for our perceptions to be meaningful. [...] The verbal aspect would be an ulterior rationalization of the immediate sensation. The verbal component, however, does have a normative effect in that it will create a mental category (a set of expectations) that will activate when we experience the sensation another time or when we attempt to describe it to someone else.
>
> *(Marsen, 2008: 5)*

This process of making meaning through embodiment seems to be based on a negotiation between multisensory impressions, memory of experience and intertextuality, which also generates anticipations as well as imaginings. In the case of darkness, the multisensory impressions are based on the circling of planet Earth within the solar system, which creates a cyclical repetition of *gradual changes* in lighting due to its rotation and axial tilt (cf. Jóhannesson and Lund, 2017: 184). Arguably, the human body interacts with this continuum between darkness and (sun)light on the vegetative, corporeal, tactile levels of cognition long before its cultural valuation becomes verbally and conceptually accessible: 'the circuitry in our brains which imposes felt experience, and thereby creates much of what it is like to be ourselves, is truly ancient, a paleo-mammalian feature, shared with all our warm-blooded, mostly four-legged, mostly furry ancestors', while the 'cortex is a neo-mammalian add-on, which makes its judgements of the environment in entirely different terms' (Beecher, 2016: 33). Thus, the embodiment of darkness does not start with the ocular sense; from visual perception in a state of awakeness. However, among the senses that allow for an experience of darkness, the ocular sense is arguably most affected by the change of light, as its range is limited: 'Only electromagnectic radiation with a wavelength between 380 and 700 nm is visible to the human eye [...]. The width of the spectrum is determined primarily by the spectral absorbance of the photopigments in the eye' (Tovée, 1996: 11). Furthermore, within the human eye, 'the light-sensitive receptors on the retina are of two kinds, cones and rods, which respond to different wavelengths of light and consequently produce two different forms of vision' (Edensor, 2013: 452). We use our cones in the presence of daylight and develop a visual practice that scans 'a multitude of competing potential sights [that] deter orientation'. Contrarily, in darkness, we use night time rods and focus our vision more acutely on any available light, while losing the ability to discern colours (ibid.).

Nonetheless, towards the dark end of the spectrum of human sight, one extremely negative reaction recurs: nyctophobia, the fear of the dark, 'a fairly common fear experienced by nearly everyone at some point in his or her life' (Johnson, 1988: 179). Eric Johnson's 'phenomenological investigation' of nyctophobia via thirteen qualitative interviews finds that emotional corporeal reactions to darkness are connected to the limitations of the ocular sense it imposes on humans. Sight 'was a very important part of [the subjects'] feeling of maintained well-being', and without sight 'they felt they had lost a significant amount of control and inner comfort' (ibid.: 182).

> A constantly emphasized quality of darkness was its mystery. Being robbed of the sense of sight, nearly everyone stated that the dark frightened them simply because they did not know what was out there.
>
> (Johnson, 1988: 181)

This fear of the unknown, Johnson argues, is further increased by the heightened focus on less clearly intelligible and distinguishable sensations: 'one's hearing becomes the focus of attention' (ibid.: 183) and 'our proprioceptive sense gives more input' (ibid.: 184). While familiar sounds ease tension, every unfamiliar sound fuels both fear and our imagination of the feared object. Even the momentary absence of sounds—silence—remains ambiguous, as 'sound is time-bound and therefore fleeting' (ibid.: 183). Human reliance on sight, its diminished range in darkness, and the subsequent disadvantage and negative interpretation of other sensory input all seem to associate darkness with fear even before the imagination creates dangers and attackers out of unfamiliar noises, shadows and air. By impeding any rapid satisfaction of the urge to oversee, recognise and illustrate, the unknown darkness amounts to a physical and cognitive provocation. It creates the doubt that there may in fact be something to see and tell, which we are simply not able to perceive clearly due to our sensory and cognitive limitations.

Sensory limitations are, however, not necessarily and uniquely negative for cognition. Tim Edensor notes that the prayers of early Christian saints in their caves, and mystical devotions in later medieval and early modern times, are built upon darkness as a focus-enhancing quality (2013: 449–450). In *Walden*, the naturalist Henry David Thoreau uses the homophony of 'morning' and 'mourning' to connect 'dawning and grieving', while creating a 'specific linking of awakening with sleeping and with questioning' (Cavell, 2002: 112). Indeed, sleep is of 'unrivalled importance to the health of body, mind, and soul' (Handley, 2016: 3) and the circadian process that 'drives sleeping and waking activity within the body [is] sensitive to light and darkness' (Handley, 2016: 4–5). Furthermore, early modern sleeping habits show the prevalence of biphasic sleeping patterns, which is to say that many early modern people appear to have slept in two separate phases during the night, rather than in one single consolidated phase of sleep, which they termed their 'first' and 'second' sleeps.

(Handley, 2016: 5)

The time in between the first and the second sleep was apparently used for kindling the fire, but also for leisure (cf. Edensor, 2013: 450): a time for transgression without social control, a time to think without the noises of daytime ... And indeed, most of what you are reading right now has been thought of and written in the quiet of night.

The dialectic of light and darkness

Jóhannesson and Lund argue that the interactions between light and darkness 'are constantly changing due to more or less rhythmic variations in daylight during the course of the day, related to the rotation of the earth, weather and clouds as well as [...] man-made illuminations' and that they create 'lightscapes of affect' that 'human and more-than-human bodies utilise [...] to improvise both their regular and irregular rhythmic performances and choreographies'; that is to say, their relational ways to affect and be affected as well as their abilities to do so—on a bodily as well as on a socio-cultural level (2017: 184). In the same sense, Anna-Teresa Tymieniecka argues that the 'dialectic of light and darkness [...] as the essential element in the poiesis of life at large [...] unifies vital stirrings and moves with the specifically human experience' (Tymieniecka, 1992: viii). Päivi Mehtonen builds on her argument in pointing out that:

> clarity and obscurity are not merely *metaphors for* linguistic presentation, knowledge or ideology [...] they also constitute in *concrete fashion* modes and foundations for the analysis of language. The alternation of day and night, or the physical conditions associated with seeing and non-seeing, generate or conceal meaning.
>
> *(Mehtonen, 2003: 11, italics in the original)*

Similarly, Timothy Morton, while drawing a parallel between the codes of life forms and the code of human languages for operating via difference (Morton, 2014: 295), argues that darkness structures our experience in general: 'our experience of the environment contains difference—hidden dark sides that structure our experience of the side exposed to view' (ibid.: 291). Therefore, night time, the lunar night and the far side of the moon—impossible to perceive from Earth—become equally important parts of our human experience, and the interplay between darkness and light allows us to see and differentiate objects.

However, although plant and animal behaviour—*homo sapiens sapiens* and their cultures included—have evolved with the change of day and night, John

Jakle notes that 'landscape has been conceptualised primarily in terms of daytime use' and theories mostly imply daylight perception (Jakle, 2001: vii). Indeed, Western discourse shares a univocal preference for clarity and light, particularly since the seventeenth and eighteenth centuries, when rationalists and empiricists declared 'war on obscurity', as Mehtonen puts it (2003: 166).[3] According to Edensor, 'it is evident that in the West, the broadly negative conceptualisation of dark persists' (Edensor, 2013: 451), as the connotations of darkness with evil and devilish qualities that precede the godly light have been translated from Mosaic religion into scientific discourse and continue to shape our assessments of darkness in general. The preference for clarity and visibility within scientific discourse would thus be a bias that goes back to 'common biblical themes that often carry the assumptions that light is good and darkness is bad' (Stone, 2017: 102).[4] This clear-cut antagonism between different ranges of vision and different qualities of light—particularly perspicuous in the symbolic beacon of Enlightenment, penetrating every obscurity and opacity on the planet—is, however, not the full story of cultural attributions to darkness. Mehtonen traces a canon of obscurity from Longinus, who 'insists that greatness of style rests on the ability of the writer to conceal his techniques and devices beneath their very brilliance' (2003: 13), to Quintilian, who in book eight of his *Institutio* construes '*perspicuitas* (or *claritas*) and *obscuritas* [...] as mutually dependent linguistic and epistemological phenomena' (ibid.: 14). Mehtonen then focuses on the medieval cultures' *diglossia*, which gives new significance to obscurity and creates 'neologisms like *obscuratio, obscurificatio, obscuriloquium*' (ibid.: 15), before arriving at Edmund Burke, George Campbell and their German contemporary Alexander Gottlieb Baumgarten with his *Skiagraphia* as proponents of obscurity in the eighteenth century (ibid.: 17–20). What becomes apparent from this concise history of obscurity in rhetoric, poetics, philosophy and theology from antiquity to modernity is a constant negotiation between the contrasts and gradients. Western thought-systems seem to be built upon negotiations between clarity and obscurity, or light and darkness, rather than any absolute preference for only one aspect of the continuum. Along these lines, Mehtonen proposes that

> it is impossible to fully understand the enlightenments of Western culture, the predilection for the metaphysic and the metaphor of light or the centuries of post-mortems of Cartesian clarity if one does not raise alongside them the tradition of linguistic theories of obscurity. Nor do *claritas* and *obscuritas* come into their own in the history of concepts and doctrines except in conjunction.
>
> *(Mehtonen, 2003: 21)*

The obscure is thus impossible to conceive without its bright side and, more importantly, requires a negotiation of all the gradients in between the extremes. The constantly changing 'lightscapes of affect' and its inherent 'dialectic of light and darkness' can thus be said to generate or conceal meaning in a 'concrete fashion' along the spectrum between blinding brightness and blinding darkness.

A right to opacity

One strategy that goes a step further than reappraising the role and value of the dark side in its relation to the bright side might consist of focusing on opacity, which, in the sense of this volume's metaphor, would not relate to the lunar night but to the invisible far side of the moon. A plea for opacity can be found in the central part of Adorno's critique of positivism, through the refusal to accord primacy to clarity in philosophical discourse: opacity as a positive value arises from Adorno's suspicions regarding 'the drive for clarity and distinctness in philosophy' as well as a repudiation of 'the formal aim of consistency' (Finlayson, 2012: 6). Similarly, in his last philosophical oeuvre *La philosophie de la relation,* Martinican poet, philosopher, novelist and intellectual Édouard Glissant argues that the inextricable ways of the world allow for the inextricable quality of those contemporary literatures that are able to escape what he calls the consumed and obsolete yet still dominant transparencies of nationalism and generalising universality (cf. Glissant, 2009: 41). In other words, material and intellectual realities are highly complex and non-transparent, a fact that some literary oeuvres try to reflect; thereby becoming unavailable for narratives that try to encompass everything within an easy and transparent narrative. Glissant's examples of such narratives are the myth of the nation and that of universal truth. In thinking the thought of the opacity of the world—'La pensée de l'opacité du monde' (Glissant, 2009: 69)—Glissant denies author, narrator and reader the right to impose one singular transparency. Consequently, he advocates the right to a non-understandable opacity that neither defines itself nor comments on itself.[5] Gerard Aching argues that 'Glissant's defense of the right to opacity ultimately seeks to protect the subject against epistemologies that threaten to reduce him or her to an externally generated and imposed "truth"' (Aching quoted in Singh, 2014: 93). In this line of thought, Glissant does not just project the right to opacity onto interhuman or inter-species communication; rather, he directly addresses his readers, reminding them that 'you have a right to be obscure, firstly to yourself': 'Car tu as droit d'être obscur, d'abord à toi-même' (2009: 70).[6] Chapter eleven of *Philosophie de la Relation* (Glissant, 2009) insists that opacity receives and reflects the mystery and evidence of all poetics, of all the details of this earth and world, while claiming that opacity has its own forms of clarity and transparency, which are not imposed forms. The inextricable, while rooted in obscurity, directs non-imperative clarities (cf. ibid.: 69). In consequence, thinking the thought of the opacity of the world means to consider opacity as an attribute of being and existing while desisting from the urge to illuminate it: 'L'opacité est un attribut de l'être-comme-étant, dont la philosophie tient compte, sans l'éclairer' (ibid.: 70).[7] To take something into account without clarifying it, recognition without insight, appears to counter the demands of cognition and communication in general.

Thus, opacity poses a problem for translation, especially if one were to follow George Steiner into the dictum 'translating is understanding', or Marie-Claire Pasquier's 'reverse proposition [...]: understanding is translating. It is *already* translating. It is *already* telling stories, about the text or in relation to it, stories in your own language; it is telling yourself the text' (Pasquier, 2015: 194; italics in the original).[8] These two, apparently inextricable, cognitive actions—'translation is understanding' and 'understanding is translating'—are challenged by Glissant's notion of opacity. Indeed, Celia Britton stresses that Glissant proposes that opacity is a defence *against* understanding:

> Accepting the other's opacity means also accepting that there are no truths that apply universally or permanently. Relation and opacity work together to resist the reductiveness of humanism [...]. In this sense, opacity becomes a militant position [...] a defense against understanding [...]. The right to opacity, which Glissant claims is more fundamental than the right to difference [...] is a right not to be understood. [U]nderstanding appears as an act of aggression because it constructs the Other as an object of knowledge.
> *(Britton, 1999: 19)*

This militant position is quite problematic, because it goes against one of the subliminal assumptions about translation that has been expressed by Steiner and Pasquier (as cited above): namely, its fundamental relation to the cognitive process of understanding. Thus, Glissant disputes some of the basic presumptions about successful and peaceful communication and intercultural communication in particular. This alternative perspective is based on a more general deconstruction of the concept of truth or, rather, its temporal stability and spatial universality as well as its translatability. As a defence against the only superficially possible understanding, and as a way of accepting the incommensurability of the Earth and the human being in our multilingual world, this positive stance towards opacity opposes the simplicity as well as the clarity and fluidity celebrated in many reviews of literary translations. In this line of thought, Kavita Ashana Singh proposes 'key concepts of the heterolingual address and opacity' as well as 'the term translative' in order 'to theoretically frame [...] multilingual writing' (Singh, 2014: 92). She chooses

> translative to signify (1) a continuous and active demand that the reader engage not only as a receiver of but also as a participant in the experience of meaning creation, a doubled experience proper to translation, and (2) a continuous and active interaction between languages that is rarely peaceful, harmonious dialogue but instead marks again and again the confrontation with a historically entrenched hierarchy.
> *(Singh, 2014: 92)*

In her understanding, '[c]reolizing literature poses a challenge to the global tyranny of the transparent and recognizable' (Singh, 2014: 93) and '[t]he monolingualism of the colonial project, all the more sinister for its persistence in a time and space of undeniable linguistic diversity [...], imposed not only the colonizer's language but also the myth that a singular, unified epistemology would by definition be superior' (ibid.: 92–93). Thus, opacity is not only a right, but also a strategy against the extermination of difference and the celebration of uniformity. If it is true that '[t]he fate of language, as of perception and [...] of all relation, is forever to translate the dark and inward into the tangible and outward, a task at which it always comes up short given the infinite depth of things' (Harman, 2005: 105), then the acknowledgement of opacity without clarification offers more accurate a translation of the complexity of a world that can and will not be understood in every detail.

Geopoetics and natures in translation

Austrian author Valerie Fritsch proposes that we perceive her writing as an interface allowing her readers to access her individual translation of the Earth and the world.[9] The metaphor of the interface stresses something that is usually either taken for granted, or discarded for the sake of authorial superiority: that the communicative function of any literary text does include its implicit reader as well as its actual readers, merging them and the text 'into a single situation [where] meaning is no longer an object to be defined, but is an effect to be experienced' (Iser, 1980 [1978/1976]: 10). The ecologies translated into text are thus prepared for future interaction with cognitions that draw upon individual recollections, collective memories as well as their own mental categories, while mirror-neurons allow for a re-embodiment of these experiences. In this line of reasoning, one might discard the traditional metaphor of the reflecting mirror—and even that of the distorted mirror—that abounds in literary theory, and instead explain the relation between world and text as ongoing processes of de- and recontextualisation: as translations. The relation between human beings and the Earth, between cultures and natures, human expressions and human sensory impressions, could therefore be conceived as a continuous translation with impacts on both sides. In this respect, I have tried to show elsewhere that the different approaches to *geopoetics* by Kenneth White (1989), Stefan Günzel (2001), Federico Italiano (2009) and Daniel Maximin (2006) focus not only on how human conceptions and artistic productions construct and inform the perception of ecologies, but also how ecologies and natural disasters inspire human languages and arts (cf. Graziadei, 2011). Thus, both *mimesis*, the imitation or representation of aspects of Earth and world, and *poiesis*, the creative production of fictional worlds, are arguably intertwined and can be understood as acts of translation that allow us to grasp a 'world that is continually coming into being' and that has 'entangled the perceiving subject, entwining sensory data, memory and embodied imagination in an ongoing making sense of the world. Darkness is part of this flux' (Edensor, 2013: 462).

Clearly, this is not only true for darkness in the sense of an absence of light. Rather, it becomes apparent that the concealed, invisible, and opaque is also part of this flux as soon as we include the 'ethical trace of the failure of communicative engagement with other species, the repudiation of the eco-translator's task' (Cronin, 2017: 153) in the act of geopoetic translation: since the ascent of man, the world has not been a safe place for animals and plants, which have been transplanted, redesigned, combatted and exterminated. Allan Bewell points us towards a plurality of 'natures in translation' and eco-systems in their opacity and their entanglement with cultures (cf. Bewell, 2017: 12–13; 41–44). He shows that, in most parts of this planet, animals and plants were 'not only being renamed but also being remade, transformed, or translated' (Bewell, 2017: 16) and particularly appreciated by the colonial eye in the form of pictorial landscape and botanical garden, since these display the ability of the colonial power to master, transplant and impose natures beyond continents and across oceans. Translated and transformed natures are thus the living evidence of a reclamation, amelioration, and exploitation effort under hegemonic and global terms.

> Beginning with Columbus's second voyage, plants introduced from South America, Europe, Africa, South Asia and [...] the South Pacific steadily displaced the indigenous plants of the Caribbean. Most of the plants that now commonly grow on the islands come from somewhere else, and these transplanted natures were as creole as the people that depended on them. The Caribbean islands can [...] be said to have provided the paradigm for modern natures, where the role of immigration, transplantation, migration, and naturalization in their formation has been dramatic.
> *(Bewell, 2017: 121)*

The translation of natures is not to be mistaken for a fertile intermingling of flora and fauna from different regions, just as the abduction and enslavement of people is not to be mistaken for an easy get-together of people from different cultures. Rather, most of the plants and animals living on the islands, including *homo sapiens sapiens*, are not those that were there before 1492, but were imported or immigrated from many central and marginal places all around the globe. While these translations allowed for the exchange of produce that led to today's regional and national cuisines—just imagine Italian cuisine without the tomato, or most European cuisines without the potato—the ongoing process of creolisation—or 'transculturación', as we could say along with Fernando Ortiz (2002: 414–527)—is based on violence and includes, in the case of the Caribbean islands, the complete cultural annihilation and near complete genocide of Taíno and Carib cultures. This translation is therefore opaque in the sense that it is neither easy to decipher nor easy to retrace, and it is also dark in the deadly sense of unleashing the extinction of species. Indeed, the violence of extinction is not limited to the rapid extermination of the encountered *homo sapiens sapiens*, but includes the 'slow violence' (Nixon, 2011: 2) of ecocide that affected many endemic plants and animals. Interestingly, these creolisations of natures in translation are not accessible to the untrained eye, but rather reserved to the botanist and the amateur: only if one knows about plant history and how to distinguish endemic from imported species do the many layers of extinction become visible on which the translated plants and animals feed while adapting.

The example of natures in translation serves to acknowledge that opacity is indeed available to unknown translation all the time. It further serves to demonstrate that the 'geopoetic' translation of the relation between man and the geosphere into text is often already a translation of a translation. Furthermore, the hidden complicity of translation in ecocide shows a simultaneous presence of the 'Pink Floyd paradigm' and the 'Star Wars paradigm'; this complicity is, however, not restricted to natures in translation.

Eco-translation and another darkness

Indeed, our Earth, the geosphere and its ecologies have never been the same since some forms of hominid started to use fire in order to clear forests and create space for agriculture, but particularly since the colonial triangle provided the financial and material means of the industrial revolution. And translation has a part in this. In his fascinating monograph *Eco-Translation*, Michael Cronin (2017) pinpoints the many problematic aspects of translation to which the title of this volume refers: from complicity in cutting down rain forests, selling unnecessary consumer goods to linguistic communities who were living well without them, to the electric power needed by servers, extraction of rare materials for the production of electronic devices, and pollution, Cronin shows—with the help of Naomi Klein's (2014) *This Changes Everything: Capitalism vs the Climate*—that cultural and linguistic translations have a carbon footprint too, and are aiding the proliferation of extractionism. Nevertheless, Cronin perceives translation as a regenerating force that cross-pollinates contexts with the earlier products of another culture and makes parts of them available again, in another time and context. On a meta-level, he argues that 'translation can be viewed as a *renewable*, a form of cultural and linguistic energy that can be recycled through different forms and that adds to rather than depletes the linguistic and cultural resources that a society has at its disposal' (Cronin, 2017: 38, italics in the original). In this vein, he proposes 'slow translation' as a possible solution to the self-defeating practice of endless growth and acceleration, and closes the book by arguing against uniformity and for translation as a source of regeneration, multiplicity and resistance that allows for a new conviviality after anthropocentrism and within the framework of inter-species dialogue:

> The constant regeneration of materials, peoples, life-forms, ideas, the endless translation, that generates multiple forms of language, textual and cultural practice is the ultimate form of resistance to the extractivist lockdown of toxic uniformity. It is also ultimately the necessary precondition to the transition to 'new ways of living and being'.
>
> *(Cronin, 2017: 153)*

In this sense, then, the myth of monolinguality and of an anthropocentric hierarchy of the species within an extractive and hypercapitalist ideology of exploitation—which, incidentally, also mines translators using poor pay and the threat of computerised translation—can be pinpointed, together with the continued absence of an ecocritical and truly sustainable mode of conviviality of all species, as the contemporary challenges to survival on this planet. In other words, slow translation in darkness, obscurity, opacity and complexity is pivotal to a survival in plurality.

This seems particularly true since 'the dominant conceptions of darkness associated with the primitive, evil and dangerous' might be outdated. Tim Edensor argues that, in the early twenty-first century, 'the real perils that pervaded a pre-illuminated world after nightfall' have largely been erased by infrastructure construction, species extinction and light pollution (Edensor, 2013: 448). It is in this overexposure to light that Edensor reads contemporary reactions to the increasingly rare darkness. In his recollection of a visit to Miroslaw Balka's installation *How It Is*, at London's Tate Modern Gallery in 2009, Edensor recalls two different kinds of visitors: enthralled and troubled. All visitors walk through a 'huge, container-like metal box, with one end open, facing away from the entrance, and inside walls lined with light-absorbing black velvet' (ibid.: 446). Edensor contends 'that both kinds of response were provoked by the absence of darkness in everyday life and its deep unfamiliarity for most people, but also the profound ambivalence that has long surrounded darkness' (ibid.: 447). These negative associations are, however, 'increasingly questioned, particularly in the context of the over-illumination that blights much Western nocturnal space, a condition with which darkness contrasts' (ibid.). Indeed, studies of the psychological and corporeal problems experienced in Arctic winter and summer seem to suggest that the totalitarian presence of one of the two parts of the dialectic is harmful.[10] More specifically, in the words of Gaston, Duffy and Bennie '[a]rtificial night time lighting is increasingly widely recognized as posing a substantial threat to biodiversity through its restructuring of the ecological and evolutionary night' (2015: 1338).[11] The extinction of darkness or, rather, the end of the absence of light in times of electricity, further accelerates the extinction of species—particularly insects and, in consequence, also birds—by confusing their nightly orientation. The reduction of the number of species and the number of exemplars per species is arguably responsible for a new situation: there is less opacity, less density, less variety to translate, and there is less variation in the translation of ecology. We are speaking, in the words of Marcel Robischon, *Vom Verstummen der Welt* (2012), about Earth's falling silence; and we should be asking ourselves how the loss of biodiversity impoverishes us culturally. So, the greater question in our times of ecological crisis no longer seems to be how to evade darkness, but how to stop being blinded by constant brightness. Without a turn away from extractionism and consumerism—exemplified by the light pollution of our metropolises—towards 'slow translation', the non-human voices will diminish and fall silent as the number of species declines.

Conclusion

By accepting my invitation to follow me to the dark side, you were taken on a trajectory that initially distinguished different forms of darkness and paid particular attention to the absence of light, to concealment, and to opacity. I tried to sketch out answers to the question of how to translate these aspects of darkness into language and thought by starting from the idea of *embodiment* as a meaning-making process based on a negotiation between multisensory impressions, memory of experience, and human discourse. I argue that, as a sensory limitation, darkness poses a challenge that amounts to a physical and cognitive provocation, which does not lead solely to the common experience of fear of the dark, but is also used productively as a focus-enhancing quality in meditation and reflection. Such a re-evaluation of darkness leads, within a 'dialectic of light and darkness', to the interplay between all aspects of light and visibility as mutually dependent linguistic and epistemological phenomena, and as a central prerogative for the sense-making process: a differentiation that requires the help of darkness, and is only achievable far from the extremes of total brightness or total darkness. Such a position runs counter to the preference of the Enlightenment and of contemporary scientific discourse for clarity and in-depth understanding, and it is precisely in opposition to this preference that Adorno formulates a critique of positivism and its formal aim of consistency. Similarly, Glissant argues for a right to opacity, a right not to be understood, for everybody, even before oneself, and challenges both 'translation is understanding' and 'understanding is translating' with his notion of opacity as a defence against understanding cognitive and communicative actions. In this line of thought, Singh proposes 'translative' forms of multilingual writing that challenge monolingualism and any unified epistemology while reflecting the inextricable complexity of the world. I argue that such 'geopoetic' translations intertwine the ways human thought and arts shape and inform the perception of ecologies with the ways ecologies and natural disasters inspire human languages and arts, and that 'geopoetics' are actually translations of translations, as our global ecosystem already consists of what Bewell calls 'natures in translation'. The slow violence of ecocide that follows these translations within the physical world is only one of many forms in which, according to Cronin, translation comes to the aid of extractionism. Cronin proposes to counter this tendency with 'slow translation': a renewable source of regeneration, multiplicity and resistance against uniformity that allows for a new conviviality after anthropocentrism and within the framework of inter-species dialogue. In consequence, I argue that darkness, obscurity, and opacity are valuable resources for the 'slow translation' of ecologies into thought, language, and literature and are thus as important as the reduction of light pollution so as to survive in multiplicity in lieu of ending in silence.

Notes

1 Here, lunacy is understood not in the old sense of moon-blindness, but as an 'intermittent insanity such as was formerly supposed to be brought about by the changes of the moon; now applied generally to any form of insanity'. It is also understood in a figurative sense: 'Mad folly. Often in much weakened sense' (OED).
2 Furthermore: the 'quality of being dark in shade or colour', 'blindness', '[t]he want of spiritual or intellectual light', 'death', 'sorrow, trouble, or distress', '[o]bscurity of meaning' and the low phonetic resonance of back vowels (OED).
3 'The Empiricist's declaration of war on obscurity is one of the phenomena of the times. Most revealing, however, from the standpoint of obscurity theories are the learned disputes in which divergent persuasions were polarised and the arguments of the vying parties were made explicit.' (Mehtonen, 2003: 166).
4 'For example, God creates light and declares it good (Gen 1:3–4); God's countenance shines the blessing of light (Ps 4:6, 31:16); light is wisdom and darkness is folly (Eccl 2:13); and, most of all in Christian traditions, Jesus is the light of the world and those who follow Jesus do not walk in darkness, but in light (John 8:12)' (Stone, 2017: 102).
5 'La pensée de l'opacité du monde, à un autre bout de ce déroulé, opacité qui ne se définit ni ne se commente. [/] Acclamer le droit à l'opacité, en tourner un autre humanisme, c'est pourtant renoncer à ramener les vérités de l'étendue à la mesure d'une seule transparence, qui serait mienne, que j'imposerais.' (Glissant, 2009: 69).
6 'Because you have a right to be obscure, firstly to yourself' (my translation).
7 'Opacity is an attribute of the being as being existent which philosophy takes into account without illuminating it.' (My translation). Glissant seems to refer to what Martin Heidegger calls '*the* question of metaphysics': the '"question of being" […] concerning the being of beings [*das Sein des Seienden*], in other words: the question concerning the beingness of beings [*die Seiendheit des Seienden*], in which a being is determined in regard to its being-a-being [*Seiendseins*]' (Heidegger, quoted in Capobianco, 2010: 19).
8 Originally: 'On dit souvent: traduire, c'est comprendre. On pourrait partir, avec profit, de la proposition inverse: comprendre, c'est traduire. C'est *déjà* traduire. C'est déjà se raconter, à propos du texte ou à côté de lui, des histoires dans sa langue à soi, c'est se le raconter' (Pasquier, 1983: 494; italics in the original).
9 During the reading from her novel *Winters Garten* (2015), opening the conference on *The Dark Side of Translation* on the evening of Wednesday October 11, 2017 in the Theatersaal of the Austrian Academy of Sciences, Vienna.
10 'Reduced exposure to natural light appears to increase the perception of obtaining insufficient sleep. Arctic workers were more prone to develop depression than Equatorial workers' (Marqueze, Vasconcelos, Garefelt, Skene & Moreno 2015: 1). '[N]octurnal daylight has a major effect on the human circadian system and can cause insomnia and/or circadian rhythm misalignment' (Paul et al., 2015: 406).
11 'Between 1992 and 2010 there were widespread increases in the average nighttime light in many protected areas […]. Particularly notable are the 32–42% […] of protected areas in Europe, Asia, and South and Central America that have had significant increases.' (Gaston, Duffie & Bennie 2015: 1136)

References

Beecher, D. (2016) *Adapted Brains and Imaginary Worlds: Cognitive Science and the Literature of the Renaissance*, Montreal and Kingston: McGill-Queen's University Press.
Bewell, A. (2017) *Natures in Translation*, Baltimore: John Hopkins University Press.
Britton, C. M. (1999) *Edouard Glissant and Postcolonial Theory: Strategies of Language and Resistance*, Charlottesville, VA: University Press of Virginia.

Capobianco, R. (2010) *Engaging Heidegger*, Toronto et al.: University of Toronto Press.
Cavell, S. (2002) 'Night and Day: Heidegger and Thoreau', in *Revue française d'études américaines* 91(1): 110–125.
Cronin, M. (2017) *Eco-Translation: Translation and Ecology in the Age of the Anthropocene*, New York and London: Routledge.
Demastes, W. (2015) 'That Looney Juney Far Side of the Moon: Tom Stoppard Celebrates Forty Years of The Dark Side of the Moon with Darkside, a Radio Play', *Five Points: A Journal of Literature and Art* 16(3): 146–156.
Eberl, J. T. (2015) 'Know the Dark Side: A Theodicy of the Force', in J. T. Eberl & K. S. Decker (eds.), *The Ultimate Star Wars and Philosophy: You Must Unlearn What You Have Learned*, Chichester: John Wiley & Sons, 100–113.
Edensor, T. (2013) 'Reconnecting with Darkness: Gloomy Landscapes, Lightless Places', *Social & Cultural Geography* 14(4): 446–465.
Finlayson, J. G. (2012) 'On Not Being Silent in the Darkness: Adorno's Singular Apophaticism', *Harvard Theological Review* 105(1): 1–32.
Fritsch, V. (2015) *Winters Garten*, Berlin: Suhrkamp.
Gaston, K. J., J. P. Duffy & J. Bennie (2015) 'Quantifying The Erosion of Natural Darkness in The Global Protected Area System', *Conservation Biology* 29(4): 1132–1141.
Glissant, É. (2009) *Philosophie de la relation: Poésie en étendue*, Paris: Gallimard.
Graziadei, D. (2011) 'Geopoetics of the Island. Strategies against Iconic Isolation', in M. Mastronunzio & F. Italiano (eds.), *Tra paesaggio e geopoetica: Studi di geo-grafia*, Milan: Unicopli, 163–182.
Günzel, S. (2001) *Geophilosophie. Nietzsches philosophische Geographie*, Berlin: Akademie Verlag.
Handley, S. (2016) *Sleep in Early Modern England*, New Haven and London: Yale University Press.
Harman, G. (2005) *Guerrilla Metaphysics: Phenomenology and the Carpentry of Things*, Chicago and La Salle: Open Court.
Iser, W. (1980 [1978/1976]) *The Act of Reading: A Theory of Aesthetic Response*, Baltimore and London: The John Hopkins University Press.
Italiano, F. (2009) *Tra miele e pietra: Aspetti di geopoetica in Montale e Celan*, Milan: Mimesis.
Jakle, J. A. (2001) *City Lights: Illuminating the American Night*, Baltimore: Johns Hopkins University Press.
Jóhannesson, G. T. & K. A. Lund (2017) 'Aurora Borealis: Choreographies of Darkness and Light', *Annals of Tourism Research* 63: 183–190.
Johnson, E. (1988) 'A Phenomenological Investigation of Fear of the Dark', *Journal of Phenomenological Psychology* 19: 179–194.
Klein, N. (2014) *This Changes Everything. Capitalism vs the Climate*, New York: Simon & Schuster.
Marqueze, E. C., S. Vasconcelos, J. Garefelt, D. J. Skene, C. R. Moreno & A. Lowden (2015) 'Natural Light Exposure, Sleep and Depression among Day Workers and Shiftworkers at Arctic and Equatorial Latitudes', *PLoS ONE* 10(4): 1–14.
Marsen, S. (2008) 'The Role of Meaning in Human Thinking', *Journal of Evolution and Technology* 17(1): 45–58.
Maximin, D. (2006) *Les Fruits du Cyclone: Une géopoétique de la Caraïbe*, Paris: Éd. du Seuil.
Mehtonen, P. (2003) *Obscure Language, Unclear Literature. Theory and Practice from Quintilian to the Enlightenment*, Helsinki: Academia Scientiarum Fennica.
Morton, T. (2014) 'Deconstruction and/as Ecology', In G. Garrard (ed.), *The Oxford Handbook of Ecocriticism*, Oxford: Oxford University Press, 291–304.

NASA (2016) 'Earth's Moon – Luna 3', *Catalog of Spaceborne Imaging*: https://nssdc.gsfc.nasa.gov/imgcat/html/object_page/lu3_1.html (viewed 15/ 12/2018).

Nixon, R. (2011) *Slow Violence and the Environmentalism of the Poor*, London: Harvard University Press.

OED (2018) 'darkness, n.', *Oxford English Dictionary*: www.oed.com.emedien.ub.uni-muenchen.de/view/Entry/47317 (viewed 15/ 12/2018).

Ortiz, F. (2002) *Contrapunteo cubano del tabaco y el azúcar. Edición de Enrico Mario Santí*, Madrid: Cátedra.

Pasquier, M.-C. (1983) 'A Propos de Gertrude Stein: la Traduction Rêvées', *Revue Française d'Etudes Américaine* 18: 487–499.

Pasquier, M.-C. (2015) 'Concerning Gertrude Stein: Dreaming Translation', in trans A. Anderson, in S. Posman & L. L. Schultz (eds.), *Gertrude Stein in Europe: Reconfigurations Across Media, Disciplines, and Traditions*, Bloomsbury: London, 187–200.

Paul, M. A., R. J. Love, A. Hawton, K. Brett, D. R. McCreary & J. Arendt (2015) 'Sleep Deficits in the High Arctic Summer in Relation to Light Exposure and Behaviour: Use of Melatonin as a Countermeasure', *Sleep Medicine* 16: 406–413.

Robischon, M. (2012) *Vom Verstummen der Welt: Wie uns der Verlust der Artenvielfalt kulturell verarmen lässt*, München: Oekom.

Rössner, M. & F. Italiano (2012) 'Translatio/n: An Introduction', in F. Italiano & M. Rössner (eds.), *Translatio/n: Narration, media and the staging of differences*, Bielefeld: Transcript Verlag, 9–16.

Singh, K. A. (2014) 'Translative and Opaque: Multilingual Caribbean Writing in Derek Walcott and Monchoachi', *Small Axe* 45: 90–106.

Stone, M. J. (2017) 'The Servant that Brings Light', in *Review and Expositor* 114(1): 101–109.

Tate Modern Exhibition: The Unilever Series: Miroslaw Balka: 'How it is' (2009–2010): www.tate.org.uk/whats-on/tate-modern/exhibition/unilever-series/unilever-series-miroslaw-balka-how-it (viewed 15/ 12/2018).

Tovée, M. J. (1996) *An Introduction to the Visual System*, Cambridge: Cambridge University Press.

Tymieniecka, A. T. (1992) 'Light and Darkness: The Primeval Dialectic of Life', in Anna-Teresa Tymieniecka (ed.), *Analecta Husserliana: The Yearbook of Phenomenological Research*, Volume XXXVIII, vii–viii.

White, K. (1989) 'What is Geopoetics?', *Scottish Centre for Geopoetics: A Relationship to the Earth and the Opening of a World*: www.geopoetics.org.uk/what-is-geopoetics/(viewed 15/12/2018).

PART IV

Translation as zombification

8
ZOMBIE HISTORY
The undead in translation

Gudrun Rath

Entering the passage

When the Harvard-trained ethnobotanist Wade Davis published *Passages of Darkness: The Ethnobiology of the Haitian Zombie* in 1988, he was already well known to the US public. His 1986 study on the same subject, *The Serpent and the Rainbow*, quickly became a bestseller and served as a basis for the Wes Craven horror movie of the same name. Davis' scientific publications on the zombie, especially *Passages of Darkness*, became widely known to a public far beyond academia.

They figure amongst other key twentieth-century publications on the zombie, such as William Seabrook's sensationalist account *The Magic Island*, published in 1929, which in 1932 was adapted into the first zombie movie, *White Zombie*, directed by Victor Halperin. Seabrook, a US author and self-declared cannibal, had published *The Magic Island* during the US occupation of Haiti. Subsequently, his book on Haitian Vodou was used to underpin the stereotype of 'barbarian' Afro-Caribbean cultures.[1] While Seabrook's *The Magic Island* discussed the zombie within the context of a semi-autobiographical horror story, Davis took up Seabrook's 'documentary' narrative and transferred the figure into the realm of academic explanation. Using academic discourse, Davis, like Seabrook before him, fostered the idea that the figure of the zombie is exclusively to be associated with Haiti, once again turning the country into a subject to be explored by US academia. Both publications are still a seminal influence in European and US conceptualisations of the zombie, seen as an undead body deprived of language, will and personality.

However, a look back at the historical space of the Atlantic shows that the zombie can neither be exclusively seen as an undead *body* nor solely associated with Haiti. Rather, historical print culture makes it quite clear that it has to be viewed in a broader, transatlantic frame, including Africa, Europe, the US and the

Greater Caribbean. As J. Lorand Matory (2007) has shown, similar concepts exist all along the shores of the Atlantic, as for example in Cuban Palo Monte. The relevant historical texts, mainly published in France, open up a connection across the Atlantic that reaches beyond Haiti and comprises Guadeloupe, Martinique and French Guiana, amongst others. This shows that the zombie concept, too, circulated between France and the French Caribbean. The extensive use of the concept in historical French texts also indicates that the zombie cannot be seen as a concept derived exclusively from a Caribbean or an African past. Rather, European contributions to this concept have to be taken into account as well.

A broader historical and transatlantic frame also shows how the figure of the zombie has historically been invested with a whole variety of significations. Historical print culture mainly shapes zombies as (invisible) undead souls, referring to a version of the zombie that can still be found in Caribbean cultures today. In Haiti, for example, this understanding of the concept exists alongside the undead body, the *zombi corps cadavre*, and is called *zombi astral* or zombie of the spirit (Ackermann and Gauthier, 1991: 482). This relates to concepts of the multiple soul and its relation to the body as encountered in Afro-Caribbean religions and philosophies. It also shows that the undead body, associated with Haitian Vodou, has only quite recently entered the scene, promoted by publications like Seabrook's *The Magic Island,* Davis' *Passages of Darkness* and successive Hollywood films. The Hollywood zombie (in contrast to other current audiovisual versions, such as Nigerian Nollywood films), can thus be seen not just as an example of the circulation of concepts within the space of the Atlantic, but also as an example of cultural and linguistic translation that, on various levels, has disambiguated complex histories and significations and made the zombie into a simplistic figure.[2] The privileging of either the undead body or the soul in historical textual and current filmic media representations can thus be seen as a consequence of a Eurocentric understanding of body and soul as two separate entities. This is why only an investigation of the historical texts—as opposed to current media representations—can provide insight into the translation and transformation of all of these concepts throughout history.[3]

In this paper, I am particularly interested in how the zombie was used in textual media published in France and Louisiana in the eighteenth and nineteenth centuries, especially scholarly texts, and how these created a variety of significations of the undead. Taking Wade Davis' *Passages of Darkness* as a starting point, I will first discuss some implications of his poison hypothesis. Second, I will refer to the historical texts I mentioned above and examine the use of the zombie as a figure of scholarly discourse. I will then finish with some reflections on how some issues concerning historical zombie figures continue to live on in filmic representation, and conclude with the zombie as a figure of translation.

Toxic discoveries

As recently as 2010, the media platform VICE published a 'documentary' video in quest of the 'truth' about the zombie in Haiti. This sensationalist video is one of the most recent examples of the impact Wade Davis' publications still have. It features a young man's journey to Haiti, accompanied by terrifying music, and is mainly based on interviews with Wade Davis.[4] Davis (1988: 2) himself nurtured this spirit of discovery: *Passages of Darkness* claims to be the first scientific account of 'a folk toxin which had long been rumored to be involved in the process of zombification'. 'Indeed', Davis (1988: 2) states elsewhere in the book, 'though the preparation of the poison is specifically referred to in the Haitian penal code and reports of its existence by both popular and ethnographic literature date well into the nineteenth century, no researcher had managed to discover its ingredients'. Focusing on the discovery of the exact components of the supposed toxin of zombification, the author introduces a '*materialist-pharmacological* argument' (Ingles, 2011: 43), which he claims is a composition of the fish poison Teterodoxin and parts of the poisonous plant Datura, a recipe that other scientists have shown to be physically ineffective.[5] While Davis' texts are still cited uncritically by most academic research on the zombie figure, scholars with more critical views on the matter have cautioned against overhasty conclusions.[6] In his survey of the history of widespread 'white' fears of slave poisoning, which served different ends for planters and for the enslaved, John Savage suggests what can equally be stated for Davis' 'discoveries':

> first of all, that we should avoid taking 'poison' as a known and given object, to be 'discovered' or dismissed according to predetermined definitions. Its cultural meanings were multiple and coexisting, whether for African or Creole slaves, planters or metropolitan physicians.
>
> *(Savage, 2007: 645–646)*

Following this argument, we might say that Davis' 'discovery' of the supposedly 'secret poison' can be seen as a form of cultural translation that narrows down complex discourses and their historical layers to unambiguous meanings. Indeed, the Haitian *Code Pénal* to which Davis refers, which was originally modelled after the Napoleonic Code and implemented in 1835 by President Boyer, was extended in 1864 by President Geffrard. This extension expanded the definition of poisoning and tightened the charges for *les sortilèges* ('superstitious practices').[7] Although the article in question does not mention the term 'zombie', international authors such as Davis, taking up an argument already expressed in Seabrook's *The Magic Island*, have taken it as official 'proof' of the 'existence' of zombification by poisoning in nineteenth-century Haiti (Hurbon, 1988: 113). In so doing, as I would like to argue and emphasise, they have *produced* the zombie as a legal fact and figure.

As Kate Ramsey (2011) has shown, the Haitian *Code Pénal* was embedded within a complex set of circumstances and discourses stemming both from colonial Saint-Domingue and post-independence nineteenth-century Haiti. It was directly related to the official perception and handling of popular religious and healing practices. President Geffrard's extensions can be seen as a reaction to public discourse on the treatment of Vodou stirred up by an alleged case of ritual anthropophagy known as the *affaire de Bizoton* or *affaire Claircine* (Ramsey, 2011: 83–84). Because the group of people accused of, and executed for, the murder of a little girl were alleged practitioners of Vodou, the case attracted international attention and fostered the stereotypical equation of this religious practice with cannibalism and sorcery. The 1864 extensions added by President Geffrard to the *Code Pénal* were explicitly aimed at putting an end to practices that 'dishonoured the nation' (Ramsey, 2011: 90). '[The] expansion of the category of *sortilèges*, and its placement under a harsher regime through these penal revisions,' Kate Ramsey states,

> can be understood, at least in part, as an effort on the part of Geffrard's government to repudiate the barbarism relentlessly attributed to Haiti by foreign detractors. Because *vaudoux* was now figured as the primary sign of that barbarism in such literatures, penal laws and criminal procedures against those identified as its practitioners became an increasingly important space of defense and disavowal for the nineteenth-century Haitian state. Read in a certain way, such laws not only signaled the state's will to 'civilize' and modernize rural Haiti, but, as performatives, seemed to back this authorizing intentions with force.
>
> *(Ramsey, 2011: 90–91)*

In the twentieth century, this association of the zombie figure with the Haitian penal code has additionally been fostered by means of linguistic translation: In 1916, during the US occupation of Haiti, US gendarmerie officers working there were provided with a version of the Haitian *Code Rural* translated into English by Captain R. S. Hooker (Ramsey, 2011: 128). It contained just three of the 413 articles that form the Haitian *Code Pénal*, among them the articles prohibiting *les sortilèges* and the use of poison to produce a state of lethargy. The effects of this selective translation not only influenced the perception of Vodou in Haiti, but also encouraged its stereotypical image abroad, as shown by texts published during the occupation. William Seabrook's *The Magic Island*, for example, cited both the penal code and military reports as undeniable proof of Vodou practices (Ramsey, 2011: 160). The effects of this selective translation can thereby be related to the consequences that followed the introduction of these laws in the nineteenth century:

> The penal pursuit and prosecution of *le vaudoux* by the Geffrard government paradoxically drew more international publicity to such practices (or rather, fantasies thereof) than to the fact of their prohibition and repression. Likewise, during the occupation, the marines' penalization of 'voodoo' was partly driven by and, in turn, further incited foreign fascination with Haitian ritualism. What is more, how such audiences constructed the object of 'voodoo' during and following the occupation was crucially shaped, I would argue, by the penal regime enforced by marines between 1915 and 1934.
>
> *(Ramsey, 2011: 160)*

Wade Davis' 'discovery' of the zombie poison can clearly be situated within a *longue durée* of these constructions. But it's not only discourse regarding the use of 'poison' that has to be situated within the context of its colonial and neo-colonial legacies. We also need to examine neo-colonial structures after the US occupation of Haiti. Although *Passages of Darkness* contains broader explanations of the political and religious history of Haiti, Davis' own role as a US scientist arriving in Haiti can't be delinked from hierarchies that are still operative in unequal geopolitical landscapes on a structural level. In line with this argument, Colin Dayan (1997: 33) has argued that Davis' 'findings' have to be examined in the context of economics:

> If we look at Wade Davis' celebrated discovery of the secret zombi powder, we must keep the economics of the situation in mind. The ethnobotanist arrives in the poorest country in the Western hemisphere loaded with money. When he says he is looking for the zombi drug, the boco [sorcerer, G.R.] will certainly oblige: he not only gives Davis the recipe, but makes sure the requisite skulls, bones, and blood are ready for viewing. [...] And although Davis claims that he wants to rescue Haitian people and their religion from misunderstandings and prejudice, the images that conclude this book tell another story [...].
>
> *(Dayan, 1997: 33)*

While Davis' book clearly promoted the marketability of the zombie, his cultural and conceptual translation of Caribbean zombie narratives into a scientific argument also provided a rational 'behind the scenes' explanation, satisfying US audiences' lust for horror. When Davis states that, '[t]o the Americans in particular, Haiti was like having a little bit of Africa next door—something dark and forboding [sic], sensual and terribly naughty' (Davis, 1988: 73), one cannot deny that the author himself has widely contributed to this stereotypical perception of Haitian Vodou.[8] *Passages of Darkness* has itself walked into the same trap it supposedly tries to avoid.

'Which noir?'[9]

One need only think of Joseph Conrad's African horror story *Heart of Darkness* to be reminded that the usage of the metaphor 'darkness' and its surrounding semantic fields, of which Wade Davis makes such extensive use, can hardly be seen as neutral.[10] Indeed, these figures of speech have been widely criticised by scholars working on the mechanisms of racism and racialisation; first and foremost by the Martinican author Frantz Fanon in his classic study *Black Skin, White Masks*:

> In Europe, evil is symbolized by the black man. [...] The perpetrator is the black man; Satan is black; one talks of darkness; when you are filthy you are dirty—and this goes for physical dirt as well as for moral dirt. If you took the trouble to note them, you would be surprised at the number of

expressions that equate the black man with sin. In Europe, the black man, whether physically or symbolically, represents the dark side of the personality. [...] Darkness, obscurity, shadows, gloom, the labyrinth of the underworld, the murky depths, blackening someone's reputation; and on the other side, the bright look of innocence, the white dove of peace, magical heavenly light.

(Fanon, 2008 [1952]: 165–166)

Of course, these semantics cannot be generalised. In twenty-first-century Haitian *krèyol*, for example, the term for an economically and politically masterful person is *gwo nèg*—literally, a 'big black' (Matory, 2007: 410). Indeed, the term 'black' in Haiti has a different history:

[U]nlike the French *nègre* (in France, Quebec, and even in parts of the French Antilles), the Kreyòl *nèg* and the French *nègre* (in Haiti) not only does not pejoratively connote blackness (as in 'Negro') or less negatively (as in 'black man'), but moreover does not specifically reference race at all, except as a universal. In Haiti *nèg* (in Kreyòl) and *nègre* (in French) have both denoted 'man' or 'human' ever since Jean-Jacques Dessalines—the first ruler of independent Ayiti—tore the white stripe from the French national flag to form Haiti's blue-and-red-striped flag and proclaimed all citizens of the island country *nwa* (noir), and all foreigners *blanc* (blanc), regardless of race. [...] All Polish soldiers, for example, who initially fought under Napoleon Bonaparte to subdue the Haitian slave revolutionaries but later defected and fought alongside the Haitians for the country's independence, were granted citizenship by Dessalines and became *nwa* (in Kreyòl) and *noir* (in French). And to the surprise of many travelling African Americans visiting the country (and even some Haitian diasporics returning home after a long absence), they are *blanc*.

(Braziel, 2008: 5)

However, in the context of representations of the Caribbean nation-state by European or US authors, things look different. The semantic layers that 'blackness' implies in Haitian *krèyol* are scarcely known beyond the island. Historically, 'the Black Republic', as the English diplomat Spenser St. John (1884) called it pejoratively after his visit there, drew international interest because of its revolutionary struggle.[11] While the massive sugar extraction in colonial Saint Domingue made it the French empire's most profitable colony and Europe's largest supplier of sugar, it was the first nation to become independent after a successful slave revolution in 1804 (Mintz, 1986). 'The manner in which independent Haiti appeared upon the world scene inevitably colored everything written about it thereafter; and to some extent this is still true, even today', as Sydney Mintz and Michel-Rolph Trouillot (1995: 125) have argued.

But it isn't only twentieth-century representations that have fostered stereotypical associations with a specific Haitian 'darkness'. Historical print culture about both colonial Saint-Domingue and postcolonial Haiti associated 'darkness' with the political-religious practices of the (formerly) enslaved population. Since colonial times, Haitian Vodou has been equated with 'black magic', while practitioners themselves see their practice as opposed to what is termed 'sorcery'.[12] A closer look at historical texts confirms that the terms 'black', 'black magic' and 'darkness', as used in colonial documents to describe the cultural and religious practices of the enslaved, were often employed in a discriminatory manner to clearly delimit racialised boundaries where, within the cultural dynamics of the Caribbean, no clear boundaries could be drawn.[13]

Historical print culture has predominantly been written by European authors—usually missionaries, ethnologists or members of the French army, merely hiding their political agenda. So while, on the one hand, it is necessary to recognise their active role in the shaping of narratives about the Caribbean, on the other hand it seems equally necessary to suppose that print culture borrowed from oral narratives that were already in circulation, as Laënnec Hurbon (1988: 209) has argued. Hence, while these texts can be seen as a hall of mirrors of Caribbean cultures (rather than as an exact representation), they also affected popular practice in the Caribbean, which, as Lara Putnam has argued, drew on different 'streams of knowledge' (including sensationalist accounts) (Putnam, 2012: 244).

As a handful of researchers have shown, the first traces of the zombie date back as far as the late seventeenth century (Garraway, 2005; Murphy, 2011). But it was particularly in the aftermath of the Haitian Revolution that zombie imaginaries haunted French popular culture and appeared constantly in nineteenth-century print culture. The travelogues, encyclopaedic and literary texts that shaped the zombie in this era were mainly aimed at a French public. Within this context, the zombie was *produced* by colonial and post-independent encyclopaedias and other scholarly texts from both eighteenth and nineteenth centuries as part of a greater narrative tracing stereotypical images of the enslaved non-white population of the French Antilles.

The Enlightenment-era lawyer, author and plantation owner Médéric Louis Élie Moreau de Saint-Méry, for example, who was directly involved both in French and in French Caribbean political events, included a brief zombie episode in his classical proto-ethnographic account of Saint-Domingue.[14] *Description topographique, psychique, civile, politique et historique de la partie française de l'isle de Saint-Domingue* was published in Philadelphia in 1797, shortly after the outbreak of the Haitian Revolution, but had been written in the years preceding the revolutionary events, when the colonial regime was still undisputed. It was intended to detail the French colonies in an encyclopaedic account modelled on Diderot and D'Alembert's *Encylopédie* (Garraway, 2005: 248 and 250). The *Description* is also one of the first known written accounts of Haitian Vodou, referred to by the name *les Vaudoux*, which the text casts as a dangerous 'sect'.

The zombie, however, is not included in this representation of Vodou. Rather, it is situated within the context of one of the main parts of the *Description*, which introduces a hierarchical model of possible racial combinations, subdivided into more than a hundred miscegenation categories. This may be regarded as one of the precursors or models for the spread of 'scientific racism' later encountered, for instance, in the writings of Gobineau.[15] In Moreau de Saint-Méry's text, the figure of the zombie—in this case conceived as an undead spirit without a body—is intrinsically tied to this racialised view of Caribbean society, as it is modelled as a figure in which only the 'superstitious' non-white enslaved believed:

> Enfin elle [cette audace amoureuse] triomphe d'une crainte bien puissante sur les esprits faibles, c'est celle des *revenants*; et ce nègre, courageux d'ailleurs, qui croit aux spectres et aux loups-garous, court la nuit avec empressement, dès que l'espoir du embers le guide. Une jeune beauté au teint d'ébène, qui un conte de *ember* fait trembler de tous ses embers, veille pour l'attendre, lui ouvre une porte qu'elle sait faire mouvoir sans bruit, et n'a qu'une crainte, c'est d'être trompée dans son attente.
> *(Moreau de Saint-Méry, 1875 [1797]: 61–62)*[16]

At the same time, Moreau de Saint-Méry (1875 [1797]: 62) made use of a specific strategy of linguistic translation within this context, stating in a footnote that the word 'zombie' is '[un] mot créole qui signifie *esprit, revenant*'. Although it produces a different signification, Moreau de Saint-Méry's paratextual strategy here has similar effects to those produced by Davis' *Passages of Darkness*: while both authors present themselves as cultural (and, in Moreau de Saint-Méry's case, also linguistic) mediators, the signification they focus on is presented as the only valid one, thereby foreclosing other possible significations. Translation studies scholars have shown how the paratextual strategy employed by Moreau de Saint-Méry produces an 'ideological closure' or 'delimitation of the plurality of possible interpretations' (Kovala, 1996: 121). Drawing on the work of Gerard Genette, Urpo Kovala states that:

> the paratext may either convey work that its writer(s) felt necessary for the reader to comprehend the work properly; or it may strive at appealing to prospective readers. In aiming to fulfil these goals, writers of paratexts are able to rely on the knowledge and expectations of the prospected readers. Thus, the connection of paratext to context cannot properly be described by focusing on explicit references to spheres of knowledge or to readers and their knowledge or expectations. Instead, paratext works together with the entire universe of discourse of a certain society at a certain time.
> *(Kovala, 1996: 135)*

In this sense, Moreau de Saint-Méry's paratextual footnote on the zombie and the subsequent interest in this figure in nineteenth-century France cannot be understood only within a broader contemporary enthusiasm for ghostly, undead figures and the uncanny. Rather, rhetorical strategies like those employed by Moreau de Saint-Méry, which produced racialised knowledge about the Caribbean, were not at all unusual for scholars who are now praised for the achievements of the Enlightenment. They thus reflect a broader frame of societal knowledge production. Indeed, as the Spanish-French philosopher Louis Sala-Molins has argued in his provocative book *Les misères des Lumières*—translated into English as *Dark Side of the Light: Slavery and the French Enlightenment*—such methods were by no means opposed to Enlightenment ideas. On the contrary: while celebrated Enlightenment authors such as Denis Diderot derived income from a shipping company involved in the transatlantic trade in enslaved people, the *Code Noir*, the 1685 decree that defined the treatment of the enslaved in the French empire, still remained valid (Sala-Molins, 2006 [1992]: 11). As Sala-Molins argues, this was not a contradiction: the 'Black Code' had deprived enslaved people of the possibility of being considered as human, and not merely as someone else's property. As the *Code Noir* was still legally binding, philosophers did not face a moral conflict when they promoted Enlightenment values on the one hand, while being directly or indirectly involved in the structures of enslavement on the other (Sala-Molins, 2006 [1992]: 62). The ideas of the Enlightenment, Sala-Molins concludes, were evidently never meant for enslaved people.

This can be seen clearly if we examine the *Encyclopédie* entry for the term *nègre*, the 'Black people of Guinea'. In this case, too, a relative of the zombie comes into play as a figurative way to signal racialised hierarchies. The *Encyclopédie* states:

> *Caractère des* nègres *en général.* Si par hasard on rencontre d'honnêtes gens parmi les *nègres* de la Guinée (le plus grand nombre est toujours vicieux) ils sont pour la plupart enclins au libertinage, à la vengeance, au vol et au mensonge. Leur opiniâtreté est telle qu'ils n'avouent jamais leurs fautes, quelque châtiment qu'on leur fasse subir; la crainte même de la mort ne les émeut point. Malgré cette espèce de fermeté, leur bravoure naturelle ne les garantit pas de la peur des sorciers et des esprits, qu'ils appellent *zambys*.
>
> *(Formey, 1765: 82)*

This observation also holds true for nineteenth-century scholarly texts, such as the *Complément du Dictionnaire de l'Académie française* or the *Dictionnaire universel de la langue française,* which, while they translate the zombie into different meanings, keep employing it as a way to establish racial hierarchies. These texts produce encyclopedic explanations of the concept but while doing so, of course, they also establish their own understanding of the figure. For example, Louis-Nicolas Bescherelle, in his *Dictionnaire national* (1856), defines the zombie as part of a tale used by the non-white population of the Antilles to scare their children. The same explanation is remodelled in other dictionaries of the 1870s and 1880s, amongst others by a complementary dictionary of the Académie française.[17]

Beyond the realm of encyclopaedic knowledge production, there is also a wide number of popular publications featuring zombie figures throughout the nineteenth century, which make use of different textual strategies. On a conceptual level, different meanings are assigned to the figure, depending on the author. While some texts relate the figure of the zombie to Africa, others signal its relation to European spiritism or to European tales about magic (Mismer, 1890). Some insist that it is a creole word for a demon (Corbière 1832), whereas others state that it means 'sorcerer' (Garaud, 1892). Most texts though opt for a meaning in the sense of 'white apparition', 'ghost' or 'revenant' (for example Adam, 1883). The most interesting explanation probably comes from the French doctor Camille Ricque who, in his 1871 text *Haïti et les Haïtiens*, claims that zombies are the bad souls of white people which return after death to continue tormenting non-white people.

Explanations of this kind also come into play when, following the leading example of Moreau de Saint-Méry, paratextual strategies such as footnotes are added to texts, assigning new meanings to the word 'zombie' while at the same time signalling profound knowledge to the readers. This strategy is widely applied across different genres. But zombies don't just appear in footnotes. They also resurface again and again in standardised phrases or formulas in a great variety of texts, within which they mainly function as exoticist ornament. However, the use of zombie narratives in popular print culture cannot be explained solely by exoticism. Some of these texts even take the zombie to places other than the Caribbean, while continuing to inscribe it into the logics of racialisation. When authors like Eugénie Foa (no date) thus put formulas like 'Par le zombi du mon grand-père!' into a black child slave's mouth in a short story for children set in seventeenth-century Seville, this can be seen as an indication of how the figure of the zombie became part of a popular repertoire and was projected onto an imaginary landscape that went far beyond the Caribbean.

The continuity of the mechanisms employed in this context in popular French print culture—the repeated emphasis on the statement that 'zombie' is a Black people's term for undead spirits and the ensuing argument that the enslaved are especially superstitious—poses the question of how much those texts really tell us about the figure of the undead. Rather than taking them as representations of the popular culture of the enslaved or as sources for exploring the origins of the zombie figure, we should examine how these scientific and philosophical agents are involved with a colonial logic that equally structured the realm of knowledge, and highlight that, since its appearance in written texts, the figure of the zombie has always been involved in racialisation. The evident zombie obsession on the part of many of these French authors in fact makes it a *white* figure that has sustained racialisation as an ongoing mechanism since colonial times.

Niemals vergessen?

Naturally, the figure of the zombie continued to live on after its appearance in historical print culture. The popularity and form of the zombie in Hollywood film and other filmic representations has especially been shaped by the films of George A. Romero. In his classic 1968 movie *Night of the Living Dead*, Romero promoted one very specific version of the zombie, converting the figure into an undead cannibal that attacks humans en masse. As in colonial, post- and neocolonial print culture, this version continues to maintain the divide between 'us' and 'them'. Since then, the figure has gradually evolved further with every representation. In the last decades, filmic representations have not only featured the living dead in search of human brains, but also vegetarian zombies, zombies in love and even 'Nazi zombies'. 'Nazi zombies' are especially fruitful as an example to show how certain narrative structures live on within the forms of translation to which the zombie has been subjected throughout its history.

Nazi zombie films have become well known because of the Norwegian splatter movie *Dead Snow*, directed by Tommy Wirkola and presented at Sundance Film Festival in 2009. Yet this zombie subgenre actually has a history that goes back to the early 1940s. Nazi zombie films shape an imaginary of the perpetrators as the ultimate evil. They also confront us with the possibility that fascism and racism might not actually be dead—these are issues that are more relevant than ever today, in the time of the 'refugee crisis' and the alarming increase of anti-Semitism and racism. So what interests me here is how these films, in spite of their role in reproducing violent images, can at the same time be useful in their expression of political critique and in addressing topics of cultural memory.

The rise of fascism in Europe and the outbreak of World War II also had an effect on the film industry. *Confessions of a Nazi Spy*, released in 1938, set the stage for 'the rapid succession of major studio releases with pro-intervention themes' (Miller, 2011: 140). It was in this context that the 1941 Monogram release *The King of the Zombies* emerged, directed by Jean Yarbrough: the first film to link the zombie figure with Nazism. Its plot centres around two white US citizens (played by Dick Purcell and John Archer), and their black servant Jeff (Mantan Moreland), who crash-land their plane on a mysterious Caribbean island. Seeking shelter in a nearby house, they meet Doctor Sangre, an Austrian scientist (played by Henry Victor). Later in the movie, it turns out that Doctor Sangre has not only created numerous zombies to serve him (all of whom are black), but also has captured a European admiral from whom he wants to obtain information for 'his government' by the use of Vodou magic and hypnosis.

As the film continues to reproduce stereotypes about Afro-Caribbean cultures, it also moves in line with the first Hollywood film that staged the Caribbean zombie nine years earlier: *White Zombie,* released in 1932. This line of reference also becomes clear with the fact that originally Bela Lugosi—whose engagement in *White Zombie*, because of his accent in English, has been seen as a form of response to racialised expectations of the audience—was offered the role of the evil Austrian scientist. He turned down the offer, 'owing to previous commitments (or maybe he just read the script)' (Kay, 2008: 16). As *King of the Zombies* not only refers to issues of fascism and the link between Nazism and the occult, but simultaneously produces highly discriminatory images which reduce Afro-Caribbean cultures to supposedly 'black' magic, and black US citizens to the role of clowns, the film has received considerable attention for issues of racism, and very rightly so.

But what is striking about this film is that it is the first in a whole series—followed by *Revenge of the Zombies* in 1943 and *Creature with the Atomic Brain* in 1955—to address control of the masses and totalitarianism through the zombie theme. All of these films centre on the character of a Nazi scientist who has created an army of zombies to serve his will. Rather than Nazi zombies, these films feature zombies in the service of fascism, and by doing so they touch on issues of political critique. In the case of *King of the Zombies*, this critique of fascism is still encoded, as the film was released before the US entry into the war. But even so—and probably unintentionally—it brings up some issues of mass mobilisation and the role of individual responsibility within totalitarian thought systems.

What renders films like *King of the Zombies* (or *Revenge of the Zombies*) uncanny—released while fascism and World War II were still going on—is not the future threat implied in the zombie figures; which, incidentally, are presented quite grotesquely due to the low-cost production. What makes us shiver today is the fact that these films anticipate so much of the actual historical horrors. Present-day knowledge about mass mobilisation and mass murder, experiments on the human body under the pretence of 'science', and the fact that many Nazis fled to Latin America after World War II constitute the actual uncanniness of these films, thereby forming something we could call *retrospective horror*. The threat it presents, however, never dies. Rather, as current political debates show, it moves in circles.

Kobi Kabalek (2014), a Haifa University scholar of Holocaust studies, has referred to the revenge fantasy implied in scenes of fictionalised violence, like in *Dead Snow*, as offering a 'second chance for Norwegians to slay and even get rid of the former Nazi occupiers'. But does this entertaining version of the figure really help in dealing with or even reappropriating a past that still haunts us? *Dead Snow* has been discussed as an example of a film that brings issues of cultural memory back to present-day cultural debates, in the form of the popular and brainless undead. However, the film not only depicts Nazis as zombies and therefore dehumanises them—which additionally releases them from all individual responsibility—but it also glorifies fascist symbols and uniforms. And, since the film foregrounds grotesque and satirical representations, it obscures other issues: namely, that current neo-fascist symbols have taken other shapes. In conclusion, this means that it is not enough simply to slay the old familiar evil undead.

A never-ending story: the zombie in translation

Even before it entered the medium of film, the zombie was a figure of translation, in continuous movement, and attributed with changing signifiers along its way. Nevertheless, Eurocentric conceptions have prevented it from being received as an example of cultural multiplicity. Its supposed 'origins' have usually been identified with the Caribbean, especially Haiti, and have thereby contributed to the underpinning of stereotypical perceptions of Afro-Caribbean cultures. As Ackermann and Gauthier have noted, 'if the Haitian zombi is usually considered a specific Haitian invention, it is probably because of the overexposure of Haiti in the press and a relatively large volume of ethnological research in this country' (Ackermann and Gauthier, 1991: 489).

Indeed, the search for the zombie's origins, as undertaken by scholars such as Wade Davis, has concealed the fact that the history of the figure has always been connected to different spaces across the Atlantic. This becomes especially clear in the first textual mention of the figure, the 1697 novel *Le zombi de Grand Perou*, attributed to the French galley-prisoner Pierre-Corneille Blessebois, which explicitly highlights European attributions to the concept.[18]

That the zombie is a figure of multiplicity also becomes clear when one examines possible etymological explanations: while one source links the term *zombi* to the African *nzambi*, the creator-god of many Bantu cultures, another relates it to the French term for shadows, *sombres* (Ackermann and Gauthier, 1991: 467). These parallels highlight that, while at least parts of the figure trace back to West Africa, they also date back to early modern Europe, from which they crossed to the Caribbean as an effect of the transatlantic slave trade. They were then incorporated into different narratives, and continued to transform themselves on a global level. The zombie can thus look back on a long history within the Caribbean, as well as West Africa, but also and specifically Europe.

The idea that the zombie comes from elsewhere—Africa, the Caribbean, a mysterious, arcane place of the 'other'—or, in other words, that there is an 'original', has been continuously repeated throughout its history. Yet this argument obscures the fact that the zombie has always inhabited different languages and cultures, forms and meanings, at the same time.

Translation studies scholars have repeatedly emphasised the violent aspects that characterise both linguistic and cultural translation processes, especially in colonial and postcolonial contexts.[19] As the texts mentioned above show, such discriminatory methods can also be distinguished in the making of one version of the zombie as a figure of violent translation. Usually, the zombie confronts us with a past by which we are incessantly haunted. As Jennifer Rutherford remarks, 'through the figure of the zombie all that is past, dead and buried looms up in a future time that is upon us' (Rutherford, 2013: 23). The figure of the zombie thus has to be examined in the most critical way to remind us that racism does not belong to the past.

Notes

1 Following Susan Zieger (2012: 737), 'Seabrook's writings and persona' can be situated at 'several cultural transitions: from nineteenth-century travel writing to modern ethnography; from comparative anthropology to the racial desires of primitivism'.
2 For a discussion of the zombie figure in Nollywood films, see Garritano (2012).
3 On translation and transformation of concepts, see Bal (2009).
4 The video is available here: www.vice.com/de/video/nzambi-episode-1 (viewed 25/05/2018).
5 For an account of this controversy of the 'zombi powder', see Ackermann and Gauthier (1991: 466) as well as Ingles (2011). Amongst other things, Davis was also accused of setting back the anthropological study of Haiti by fifty years (Ingles, 2011: 44).
6 One such example of uncritical reference can be found in Lauro (2015).
7 Article 246 states: 'The use of substances that, without leading to death, produce a more or less prolonged lethargic state is also qualified as an attempt on the life of

a person through poisoning [...] If, as a result of this lethargic state, the person was buried, the attempt will be defined an assassination'. (Nau 1909: 265–266 translated by Kate Ramsey; cited in Ramsey, 2011: 89).

8 The spelling 'Vodou' has been chosen here in accordance with current research on the Haitian religion and in opposition to the term 'Voodoo', which has been related to stereotypical and racist views and expressions. For a discussion on the terminological implications, see Ramsey (2012).
9 The Haitian writer and editor Edwidge Danticat (2011: 17) poses this question in the collection *Haiti Noir*.
10 On this matter, see most prominently Chinua Achebe's controversial 1977 essay 'An Image of Africa: Racism in Conrad's "Heart of Darkness"'. For a more recent discussion of the racist mechanisms in the equation of Africa with the 'dark continent', see Mbembe (2013).
11 See Buck Morss (2000).
12 For the equation of Vodou with 'black magic', see Kate Ramsey's excellent study *The Spirits and the Law* (2011: 9); for the self-description of practitioners, Ramsey (2011: 59–60).
13 For an example on the impossibility of drawing boundaries, see Benítez Rojo (1998).
14 For a detailed account of Moreau de Saint-Méry's political engagement before and after the French and Haitian Revolution, see Pierce 2007.
15 See Banton 2000.
16 Kieran Murphy (2011: 49) has shown how Moreau de Saint-Méry applies the then-fashionable vocabularies of mesmerism for this description.
17 For example, the dictionary entry in the *Dictionnaire national* (1856: 1681) states: 'Zombie, s.m. Relat. Espèce de croquemitaine [sic] dont les créoles d'Amérique font peur a leurs enfants. Gare au zombi! Le zombi va venir'. Other dictionaries, such as the *Complément du Dictionnaire de l'Académie française* (1881: 1279), literally reproduce this entry. In a similar manner, the *Dictionnaire des dictionnaires* (n.d.: 1124) defines the zombie as follows: 'Zombi, s.m. Epouvantail dont les créoles d'Amérique menacent les petits enfants.—Après avoir peuplé son ciel de zombis, ces revenants des contrées noires, ces écorchés troublants, munis d'ailes.' (L. Hennique) F.L.
18 On this matter, see Rath (2014) and forthcoming.
19 On this matter, see most prominently Venuti (1996).

Bibliography

Achebe, C. (1977) 'An Image of Africa: Racism in Conrad's "Heart of Darkness"', *Massachusetts Review*, 18(4): 782–794.

Ackermann, H.-W. and J. Gauthier (1991) 'The Ways and Nature of the Zombie', in *The Journal of American Folklore*, 104(414): 466–494.

Adam, L. (1883) *Les idiomes négro-aryen et maléo-aryen. Essai d'hybridologie linguistique*, Paris: Maisonneuve et Compagnie.

Bal, M. (2009) 'Working with Concepts', in *European Journal of English Studies*, 13(1): 3–23.

Banton, M. (2000 [1980]) 'The Idiom of Race. A Critique of Presentism', in L. Back and J. Solomos (eds), *Theories of Race and Racism: A Reader*, London and New York: Routledge, 51–63.

Benítez Rojo, A. (1998) *La isla que se repite*, Barcelona: Casiopea.

Bescherelle, L. (1856) *Dictionnaire national ou Dictionnaire universel de la langue française*, Paris: Dondey Duprey.

Blessebois, P. (no date [1697]) *Le Zombi du Grand Pérou, ou la comtesse de Cocagne*, Brussels: Lacroix.

Braziel, J. (2008) *Artists, Performers, and Black Masculinity in Haitian Diaspora*, Bloomington: Indiana University Press.
Buck-Morss, S. (2000) 'Hegel and Haiti', *Critical Inquiry*, 26(4): 821–865.
Complément du Dictionnaire de l'Académie française, publié sous la direction d'un membre de l'académie française (1881), Paris: Firmin Didot Frères.
Corbière, É. (1855 [1832]) *Le Négrier, aventures de mer* (4th edition), Havre: Brindeau et Compagnie.
Danticat, E. (2011) (ed..) *Haiti Noir*, New York: Akashic Books.
Davis, W. (1988) *Passages of Darkness: The Ethnobiology of the Haitian Zombie*, Chapel Hill and London: University of North Carolina Press.
Dayan, J. (1997) 'Vodoun, or the Voice of the Gods', in M. Fernández Olmos and L. Paravisini-Gebert (eds), *Sacred Possessions: Vodou, Santería, Obeah and the Caribbean*, New Brunswick: Rutgers, 13–36.
Fanon, F. (2008 [1952]) *Black Skin, White Masks*, trans R. Philcox, New York: Grove Press.
Foa, E. (no date) 'Le zombi d'atelier', in E. Foa *Petits artistes. Extrait des* Contes historiques, Paris: Librarie nationale d'éducation et de récréation, 99–115.
Formey, J. (1765) 'Nègre', *L'Encyclopédie*, 11: 82.
Garaud, L. (1892) *Trois Ans à la Martinique. Etudes des mœurs. Paysages et croquis. Profils et portraits*, Paris: Alcide Picard et Kaan.
Garraway, D. (2005) *The Libertine Colony: Creolization in the Early French Caribbean*, Durham: Duke University Press.
Garritano, C. (2012) 'Blood Money, Big Men and Zombies: Understanding Africa's Occult Narratives in the Context of Neoliberal Capitalism', *Manycinemas* (issue3): 50–65.
Guérin, P. (no date) (ed) *Dictionnaire des dictionnaires. Lettres, sciences, arts. Encyclopédie universelle*. Vol. VI, Paris: Librarie des imprimeries réunis.
Hurbon, L. (1988) *Le Barbare imaginaire: Sorciers, zombis et cannibales en Haïti*, Paris: Cerf.
Ingles, D. (2011) 'Putting the Undead to Work: Wade Davis, Haitian Vodou and the Social Uses of the Zombie', in C. Moreman & C. Rushton (eds), *Race, Oppression and the Zombie: Essays on Cross-cultural Appropriations of the Caribbean Tradition*, Jefferson: McFarland, 42–59.
Kay. G. (2008) *Zombie Movies: The Ultimate Guide*, Chicago: Chicago Review Press.
Kovala, U. (1996) 'Translations, Paratextual Mediation and Ideological Closure', in *Target*, 8(1): 119–147.
Lauro, S. J. (2015) *The Transatlantic Zombie: Slavery, Rebellion, and Living Death*, New Brunswick: Rutgers.
Matory, J. (2007) ''Free to Be a Slave: Slavery as Metaphor in the Afro-Atlantic Religions', *Journal of Religion in Africa*, 37: 398–425.
Mbembe, A. (2013) *Critique de la raison nègre*, Paris: La Découverte.
Miller, C. (2011) 'The Rise and Fall—and Rise—of the Nazi Zombie in Film', in C. Moreman & C. Rushton (eds), *Race, Oppression and the Zombie: Essays on Cross-cultural Appropiations of the Caribbean Tradition*, Jefferson: McFarland, 139–148.
Mintz, S. (1986) *Sweetness and Power: The Place of Sugar in Modem History*, London: Penguin.
Mintz, S. and M. Trouillot. (1995) 'The Social History of Haitian Vodou', in D. Cosention (ed), *Sacred Arts of Haitian Vodou*, Los Angeles: University of California Press, 123–147.
Mismer, Ch. (1890) 'A la Martinique', in *Le Figaro. Feuilleton de supplément littéraire de dimanche*, Paris, 12 April 1890, no. 15, 58.

Moreau de Saint-Méry, M. (1875 [1797]) *Description topographique, psychique, civile, politique et historique de la partie française de l'isle de Saint-Domingue*, Vol. 1 (2nd), Paris: Guérin, Morgand.
Murphy, K. (2011) 'White Zombie', *Contemporary French and Francophone Studies*, 15(1): 47–55.
Nau, L. (1909) *Code d'instruction criminelle et pénale*, Paris: Libr. Générale de Droit de Jurisprudence.
Pierce, J. (2007) 'Moreau de Saint-Méry, Médéric Louis', in P. Hinks, J. McKivigan, & R. Owen Williams (eds), *Encyclopedia of Antislavery and Abolition*, Vol. 2. Westport and London: Greenwood Press (Greenwood Milestones in African American History), 480–481.
Putnam, L. (2012) 'Rites of Power and Rumours of Race: The Circulation of Supernatural Knowledge in the Greater Caribbean, 1890-1940' in D. Paton et al. (eds), *Obeah and Other Powers: The Politics of Caribbean Religion and Healing*. Durham NC: Duke University Press, 243–267.
Ramsey, K. (2011) *The Spirits and the Law: Vodou and Power in Haiti*, Chicago and London: University of Chicago Press.
Ramsey, K. (2012) 'From "Voodooism" to "Vodou": Changing a U.S. Library of Congress Subject Heading', in *Journal of Haitian Studies*, 18(2): 14–25.
Rath, G. (2014) 'Zombifizierung als Provokation', in G. Rath (ed), *Zombies. Zeitschrift für Kulturwissenschaft*, Vol. 1/2014. 49–60.
Ricque, C. (1871) 'Haïti et les Haïtiens', in A. Malte-Brun (ed), *Annales des voyages, de la géographie, de l'histoire et de l'archéologie*, Paris: Challamel aîné, 145–170.
Rutherford, J. (2013) *Zombies*, London and New York: Routledge.
Sala-Molins, L. (2006 [1992]) *Dark Side of the Light: Slavery and the French Enlightenment*, trans. J. Conteh-Morgan, Minneapolis and London: University of Minnesota Press.
Savage, J. (2007) '"Black Magic" and White Terror: Slave Poisoning and Colonial Society in Early 19th Century Martinique', in *Journal of Social History*, 40(3): 635–662.
Seabrook, W. (1929) *The Magic Island*, New York: Blue Ribbon Books.
St. John, S. (1889 [1884]) *Hayti or the Black Republic*, London: Smith Elder.
Venuti, L. (1996) 'Translation as a Social Practice or, the Violence of Translation', in M. Rose (ed), *Translation Horizons Beyond the Boundaries of Translation Spectrum*, Translation Perspectives, Vol. IX. New York: State University of New York, 195–213.
Zieger, S. (2012) 'The Case of William Seabrook: *Documents*, Haiti, and the Working Dead', in *Modernism/modernity*, 19(4): 737–754.

Websites

Kabalek K. (2014) 'Who cares about Nazi zombies?': https://haifaholocauststudies.word press.com/2014/10/30/who-cares-about-nazi-zombies/(viewed 25/05/2018).
VICE (2010) Nzambi: www.vice.com/de/video/nzambi-episode-1 (viewed 25/05/2018).

Films

Dead Snow (Norway. 2009/D: Tommy Wirkola)
Night of the Living Dead (U.S. 1968/D: George A. Romero)
The King of the Zombies (U.S. 1941/D: Jean Yarbrough)
The Serpent and the Rainbow (U.S. 1988/D: Wes Craven)
White Zombie (U.S. 1932/D: Victor Halperin)

9

'MmmRRRrr UrrRrRRrr!!'[1]

Translating political anxieties into zombie language in digital games

Eugen Pfister

Translating into zombie video games

The zombie apocalypse in video games has its own perverted beauty. Games like *The Last of Us* (Naughty Dog, US 2013/PS3 et al.), *Left4Dead* (Valve, US 2008/Xbox360 et al.) or *Dying Light* (Techland, PL 2015/PS4 et al.) immerse us in a mesmerising dystopia of gigantic collapsed skyscrapers and picturesquely crumbling government buildings. Once-proud cities are now littered with car wrecks and debris, overrun by emergent vegetation glistening golden in the evening sun. With the continuous technological development of increasingly powerful game engines, these dystopian imaginations of our near future become more and more enthralling. The interactive zombie apocalypse has become photorealistic, with an image quality as close to real life as possible. Rendered in high definition, zombies in these games appear on our computer screens as intricately designed walking corpses. Every inch of their crumbling bodies is exposed to us with exhibitory glee. They are covered with purulent and putrescent wounds, showing the human body in the vibrant colours of its different states of decomposition. Zombie video games are thus a strong aesthetic experience relying on the intricate symbiosis of attraction and repulsion, as described by Noel Carrol: 'In short, there appears to be something paradoxical about the horror genre. It obviously attracts consumers; but it seems to do so by means of the expressly repulsive' and 'horror attracts because anomalies command attention and elicit curiosity' (Carrol, 2002: 33). This aesthetic moment, which Carrol calls 'art-horror' (Carrol, 1989: 13) and which we have learned to appreciate in popular culture via feature films and TV, is potentially replicated ad infinitum by the required interactivity of video games. Here, we are no longer passive spectators but agents of the story, accountable for the actions of the protagonists in a world in disarray. But what if these zombie video games go beyond having a function as entertainment products, and are more than just a global commodity of distraction and amusement? What if they also communicate political statements through the medium of popular culture, contributing to a global discourse?

Lauro (2011: 128) argues that the figure of the zombie first and foremost serves the narrative of crisis, of cultural discomfort. In this sense, the myth of governmental breakdown is central to the narrative of the zombie genre. The failure of modern states to cope with the zombie threat is perceived as a natural component of the genre, and therefore is not usually questioned by the audience. But why should we begin to question the failure of government? Without it there would be no zombie games. A failing society is almost a basic prerequisite of zombie narratives.

There appears to be a correlation between the proliferation of zombie narratives and the rising number of people who believe in the inability of modern western governments to cope with similar large-scale catastrophes today. As Drezner wrote: 'The threats to national security are less grave but provoke more uncertainty than during the Cold War. Zombies are the perfect symbol to represent the threats in popular culture' (Drezner, 2015: 138–139). This growing feeling of unease and uncertainty might explain the increased popularity of the zombie apocalypse theme (Bishop, 2015: 39). In the following chapter, I will therefore attempt to draw some conclusions about the nature of this act of representation/communication.

Representations of the apocalypse in popular culture are not new, and they are definitely not an invention of zombie video games. The modern (post-) apocalypse is an integral trope of dystopian fiction, with a long tradition in science fiction films and literature. Our desire for images of empty cities and ruins appears to be insatiable. The fact that we choose to use the very specific terms 'apocalyptic' and 'post-apocalyptic' to describe these fictional settings indicates, however, that these representations of destruction are not only an aesthetic experience: they also imply a hidden revelation, a message. Not only do the apocalypses of our various religions and mythologies have an educational motif (thus creating good believers), but the same is also true for most of apocalyptic and post-apocalyptic fiction in popular culture. For example, Aldous Huxley's *Ape and Essence* (Huxley, 2005 [1948]) can thus be read as a warning about the politics of mutually assured destruction of the Cold War, and Pixar's *WALL-E* (US 2008/D: Andrew Stanton) as a critique of consumerism and environmental pollution. George R. Romero, best known for reviving the zombie film in the late 1960s, declared: 'If there's something I'd like to criticise, I can bring the zombies out. [...] So I've been able to express my political views through those films' (Romero, 2010).

By this logic, the figure of the zombie ought to be understood not only as an instrument of horror, but also as a means of communication. Zombies in literature, film, television and video games do not always represent the same cultural or political statement; they are not one signifier relating to one concrete meaning (the signified) in the logic of semiotics. Instead, I would argue that the figure of the zombie functions as a 'language', allowing a multitude of different statements to be made. This is, of course, not a singular phenomenon of zombie fiction, but a common—though often neglected—aspect of our popular culture. Philipp Sarasin has established, for instance, that the fictional figure of the mad scientist is a way for our society to negotiate the norms and values of science policies with the general public (Sarasin, 2003: 256–266). This means that the exaggerated figure of the mad scientist also functions as means of communication. It spreads, for example, the message about the dangers of uncontrolled scientific research (Pfister, 2017). The translation of an increasingly hypercomplex scientific discourse into the language of popular culture is a necessary step to enable a public discussion, itself required for democratic political decision-making. This translational moment can also be analysed in video games. This could be understood as an extension of Jürgen Habermas' understanding of mass media as a public sphere of political communication. In Habermas' understanding of public communication, mass media allows the public to develop a critical consensus, which he considers necessary for any public participation in democratic political processes. While Habermas was most certainly thinking of the traditional press, this agreement on common values and norms between a (political) elite and the greater public also happens in popular culture (Habermas, 2008: 136; Pfister, 2018c).

Popular culture—and in this case video games—should thus also be understood as a translational moment. To differentiate here between 'communication' and 'translation' is not mere sophistry. It helps us more effectively to understand some of the mechanisms and problems involved. While the term 'communication' implies a complete transfer of contents, a translation can be neither frictionless nor complete. As every language has its own logic, one-to-one translation is not possible. The process of translation always changes the statements communicated; it has to adapt the content to the 'grammar' and 'syntax' of the host language, as I have shown in the case of the figure of the mad scientist in video games (Pfister, 2017).

To analyse zombie video games as a translational moment of a political discourse first requires a thorough understanding of how to speak Zombie Video Game. To work out its grammar and syntax we have—in a way—to consciously learn a new language. We have to reconstruct its functions based on our knowledge of other similar languages. To this end, I will refer to the iconography of architectural ruin and human decomposition, or to the history of political ideas of dystopia, to establish accepted meanings. At this point, I cannot ascertain whether a complete reconstruction of the 'linguistic' functions of zombie video games is useful or even possible. Understanding the communication of political and cultural statements in zombie video games is a thought experiment. I am, however, positive that this experiment will give us additional insights into the process of (unconscious) political communication in popular culture.

Horror as a language, zombies as a dialect?

While there has been no explicit attempt to study the zombie genre as a language until now, the search for political meaning in the zombie genre is not new per se.

Zombie studies is, fortunately, no longer seen as an obscure scholarly pursuit. Legitimated by a constant supply of zombie content in popular culture (Morrissette, 2014: 1), it has become an emerging field of research (Perron, Leiva and Archibald, 2015; Rath, 2014; Platts, 2013: 547; Drezner, 2015: 137; Bishop, 2015: 38). Zombies have become a 'current cultural currency' (Lauro and Embry, 2008: 86). Fuelled, among other things, by George A. Romero's declaration that he uses 'his zombies' to express his political views through films, scholars have undertaken close readings of some zombie allegories using the theoretical frameworks of Michel Foucault (Pulliam, 2009), Roland Barthes, Gilles Deleuze and Felix Guattari (Carr, 2009), to name only a few.

Consequently, the portrayal of zombies in popular culture has since been recognised as 'politically charged' from its very beginnings (Backe and Aarseth, 2013: 1). While we must assume that all of our popular culture can potentially function as a translation between a political/cultural/social elite and the greater public, horror genres are known to be especially suited to the negotiation of common values and taboos. Relying on the distinction between 'good' and 'evil', horror stories, films and games alike can help us better understand the 'cultural coordinates', the 'symbolic categories and valuations' (Santilli, 2007: 173) of a particular society. Santilli argues, for example, for the relevance of horror to the understanding of moral judgements (ibid.: 178). Horror helps reaffirm the outer borders of our collective identities by focusing on the taboos and the abject (Kristeva, 1980; Santilli, 2007), both aspects which are central to the zombie genre.

According to John S. Nelson, horror might also function as a primer for political action: 'Awaken to evils in our midst. Turn to face those shadows, revealing awful forms more human than we had imagined. Unite to track down those troubles, confronting them at home' (2005: 382). In Nelson's logic, this call to action happens via subtext: '[S]ymbolism that creeps beneath surface meanings to assault and awaken our minds' (ibid.: 382). Zombies are therefore not just an interesting historical source that helps us better to understand specific societies and cultures (Platts, 2013); they also take an active role in creating parts of our societal reality. In the logic of discourse analysis, they are not only a reflection of reality but also a component in the construction of meaning (Landwehr, 2009: 19) and societal reality (Sarasin, 2003: 12).

Similarly, Niklas Luhmann opened his reflections on the reality of mass media as follows: 'Whatever we know about society, or indeed about the world in which we live, we know through the mass media', and: 'Even if all knowledge were to carry a warning that it was open to doubt, it would still have to be used as a foundation, as a starting point' (Luhmann, 2000: 1). All information we acquire through mass media, all information translated by mass media, frames our future cultural, economic, social and political knowledge. This means that we are in fact partly socialised through video games (Fromme and Biermann, 2009: 120). Our collective identities are a result not only of our upbringing and education, but also of our interaction with mass media, especially when related to the more abstract concepts of politics and society. 'It is also in the cultural imagery that significant political battles are fought, "because it is here that coherent narratives are produced, which in turn serves as the basis for any sense of community and political action'" (Grayson et al., 2009: 157).

However, this does not mean that we consciously apply the knowledge gained from zombie games to our everyday life. Zombies are—quite unmistakably—fictional, but they 'comment and respond to the real' (Platts, 2013: 553). Even in fantastical scenarios, we have to accept some details as plausible that potentially relate us to the game world. In the case of zombie games, we might, for instance, find it believable that there is an antisocial monster hidden inside every man, or a tendency to antidemocratic behaviour within all military organisations. We could also come to believe it possible that our modern western governments are no longer fit to respond adequately to certain exterior threats (Pfister, 2019). Such 'knowledge transfers' can function unconsciously because we have been explicitly taught by the game industry not to expect political content in video games (Klimmt, 2009: 68). Particularly in situations of heightened immersion and stress brought about by gameplay, we might lack our usual scepticism towards political content in media. I, however, prefer the term 'knowledge *translation*' to 'knowledge transfer'. Understanding this phenomenon of political communication as an act of translation emphasises the incomplete, and the corruption of the message through its transformation: its 'dark side', so to speak.

I intend to demonstrate that, whereas political myths in zombie video games correlate with some aspects of an actual political discourse (loss of confidence in the democratic system paired with calls for a 'strong politician' to take care of the problems, rising xenophobia and isolationism, etc.), it is the logic of Zombie Video Game—its grammar, so to speak—that partly changes the political statements communicated. This means that zombie video games are not a one-to-one transposition of a 'real' political discourse into 'fiction'. By applying game logic to the message, the message itself changes. But, before we focus on the influence of video games, we must reconstruct the rule of grammar and 'linguistic customs' of the zombie video game genre. To this end, I will focus on the iconography, the narrative traditions and the game mechanics at play.

An iconography of blood and gore

Video games like *Resident Evil 7: Biohazard* (Capcom, J 2017/PS4 et al.) depict the zombies in a hyper-realistic way. Through the game play, the walking corpses become more and more grotesque. The games focus on the abject: the missing limbs and sagging parts of their rotten flesh, as well as broken bones. They are covered with repulsive growths, ooze nauseating fluids and show the human body in different states of decomposition. With the proliferation of ever more explicit images, and to counter our habituation to such repulsive images, the zombies in video games have become increasingly absurd: take the bizarrely bloated 'Boomers' in *Left4Dead* (2008), the 'Floaters' in *Dead Island* (techland, PL 2011/Xbox360 et al.), or the 'Fat Molded' in *Resident Evil 7* (2017). Such images of increasingly dehumanised bodies apparently break all of our traditional cultural taboos concerning the dead.

The visualisation of mutilated bodies and the vivid display of internal organs, blood and bones—in short, gore—is deeply connected to the zombie genre. And while the motif of rotten and corrupted zombie bodies is relatively new, the motif of the decaying human body is not. 'Blood and gore' is not an invention of our modern media society. On the contrary, we find similar imagery of a destroyed human body as early as the fourteenth century in the Christian iconography of Judas Iscariot. There have been gruesome representations of Judas' suicide based on a passage in the Acts of the Apostles: 'his body burst open and all his intestines spilled out' (1:18). One vivid visualisation of this Bible passage was painted by a pupil of Anthony van Dyck in the seventeenth century. It shows Judas hanging from a tree with a distorted face, a blue tongue hanging from his mouth and entrails exploding from his stomach accompanied by gushes of blood (ca. 1620/Stift Göttweig). A similar representation can be found in a fresco by Giovanni Canavesio from 1491 in the Notre Dame des Fontaines shrine, as well as the *Giuda impiccato* by Pietro Lorenzetti in the Basilica San Francesco in Assisi (around 1310).

Apart from depictions of Judas' suicide, there was, of course, also very vivid imagery of hell and purgatory using similar iconographic strategies. A well-known example is the *Garden of Earthly Delights* by Hieronymus Bosch. Here, human bodies are mutilated in every way imaginable: pierced, cut, sewn together, and tortured by perverted creatures. These drastic depictions arguably served a didactic purpose in Christian iconography. They were supposed to attract interest, to frighten, and thus to deter the viewer from committing 'sins'.

From the fifteenth to the sixteenth century, cadaver tombs or *transi* (from Latin trānsīre, to 'pass away') became fashionable, depicting the deceased as realistic rotten corpses in the state of decomposition. A good example of this is the tomb of Archbishop Henry Chichele at Canterbury Cathedral: 'The double representation contrasting the figure of the archbishop in his ecclesiastical robes to the dead body below seems to illustrate the contrast stated in the epitaph between worldly power and the degradation of man in death' (Cohen, 1973: 38). Even more impressive in its explicitness is the *transi* tomb of Cardinal de Lagrange, sculpted in 1403 in Avignon as a 'symbol of the nemesis of worldly glory' (ibid.: 38). The historian Johan Huizinga argues in his monograph that the popularity of such macabre depictions might be explained as a reaction to widespread materialism in the late Middle Ages (Huizinga, 1924: 126). In this sense, they were also meant as a warning, a reminder of the transient nature of human lives. A similar iconographic tradition can be found in *Kusozu,* Japanese watercolour paintings depicting corpses in the process of decomposition: 'The earliest function of the image of the nine stages was for the pious contemplation on human impurity by Buddhist monks who wished to expunge the sensual desires that disturbed their lives of spiritual devotion' (Savage, 2005). I would argue that our contemporary imagery of zombies references these historical antecedents, at least on the surface.

At the same time, the figure of the zombie sits within the realm of terror and the realm of revulsion. The body of the zombie not only symbolises our fear of death but is also abject, tapping into the most basic bodily reflexes that we learned as a species to help defend our health, to recoil from those infected and stay clear of hazardous substances. It is also a symbol of a very atavistic fear of alienation, the loss of control of our body. The human body is invaded and ultimately ruined by nature. The decomposition of the human body foreshadows the decomposition of human society. Representations of ruined cities in zombie games, as well as films and TV series, work on a similar level. Depictions of architectural ruins are an integral trope of dystopian fiction, with a long-standing tradition in science fiction films. Images of political and societal failure communicate the warning to us that even our hometowns are not safe from a similar fate. All that remains of once familiar environments are deserted universities, flooded subways, and decaying offices threatening to collapse at any moment. The key to zombie horror lies not in the spectacular but in the familiar. The prevalence of the 'non-spectacular' is key: a motel and a farm in *The Walking Dead*, a diner and a hospital in *Left4Dead* (2008), a shopping mall in *Dead Rising* (Capcom, J 2006/Xbox360 et al.). The uncanny lies in the alienation of the familiar. Small suburban single-family houses, stereotypical symbols of American domesticity, are no longer the safe haven of the middle class, but are invaded by the other and by nature itself.

Images of ruined cities paradoxically develop an impression of peace. They are a resting place in a game environment normally dominated by conflict and brutality. This becomes particularly obvious in a scene from *The Last of Us* (2008), when the two protagonists meet a wild herd of giraffes in the middle of Salt Lake City. The publishers of these games are well aware of the potency of such images, as shown by a marketing campaign accompanying the release of *The Last of Us* (2008). This consisted of post-apocalyptic visualisations of well-known European cities: Berlin Central Station, Buckingham Palace in London, the Eiffel Tower in Paris, Fredericksberg Palace in Denmark and the medieval city of Avila are all ruins. In *Zombi/ZombiU* (Ubisoft Montpellier, F 2012/WiiU et al.) it is the crumbling Buckingham Palace that symbolises the inevitable demise of the British state.

This fascination with ruins is, of course, not a twentieth-century invention. The ruin was a central theme of Romanticism in the nineteenth century. The interplay between the ruin and nature was central to the way Romanticism functioned, as is evident in the paintings of Caspar David Friedrich. 'Ruin Poetry' was a genre in its own right, as was the ruin landscape from the sixteenth century onwards (Böhme, 1989). The *mis-en-scène* of the ruin was not only a moment of self-reflexive melancholy, but often also a conscious political statement. In German Romanticism, representations of ruins were intended to function as a critique of modernity and the Enlightenment, but were also used to promote German nationalism:

> The German Romantics, in contrast, shifted their gaze from antiquity to the Middle Ages and to such monuments as the castles of Heidelberg, Weibertreu, and Marienburg and the monastic ruins of Eldena and Sankt Wolfgang. Poets from Brentano and Chamisso to Eichendorff and Kerner regarded them not so much as cultural-historical treasures for the cultivated few but, rather, as popular symbols of nationalistic pride and future unification.
>
> (Ziolkowski, 2011)

We can therefore establish that ruins function as a warning within these genres. Depictions of the decomposition of the human body are intended to remind us of our mortality and, in particular, deter us from vanity. The same is true for architectural ruins. They are supposed to remind us of the long-lost glory of former empires. Human decomposition and architectural ruins therefore are used to translate a warning concerning the fragility of our identity.

A narration of societal collapse

Throughout its history, the figure of the zombie has been used as an allegory for slavery, mass-poverty, racism, consumerism (Platts, 2013; Rath, 2014) and xenophobia (especially towards refugees: Comaroff and Comaroff 2017; Mouflard 2016) and more. In early zombie literature, for example, the figure of the zombie was primarily a metaphor for the alienation of man. With Romero's work, it became a critique of racism and consumerism, while modern zombie narratives appear to be a comment on the refugee crisis.

Modern zombie games tell us a gruesome interactive tale of complete political and societal collapse. In these scenarios, political actors are in no position to react appropriately to the threat of a zombie invasion and/or epidemic. However, the moment of actual failure of the state is normally not explained, but presupposed. This is particularly well illustrated by the introductory film sequence in *Left4Dead 2* (Valve, US 2009/Xbox360 et al.), when one protagonist called Coach is reading out an old government leaflet he finds: 'Wait for official instructions', which leads him to sneer: 'Wait, my ass!' This in turn is followed by a remark from the redneck mechanic Ellis: 'Kill all sons of bitches. That's my official instructions'.[2]

Government action, if it is mentioned at all, is ineffectual or downright ridiculed, as exemplified by a short news insert in the intro of *Dead Nation* (Housemarque, FI 2010/PS3 et al.), stating that 'World leaders have again urged the public to remain calm', while showing pictures of destroyed cities. In some games, the player's narrative requirements are satisfied by short text inserts, such as in *Left4Dead* (2009): '2 weeks after first infection'.[3] In others, like *The Last of Us* (2013), the narration is presented in an elaborate expository game sequence. The protagonist, Joel, is fleeing his home together with his daughter in the middle of the night, and later must helplessly watch when a soldier shoots his daughter due to a misunderstood precaution.

This scene foreshadows the later transformation of the military into a dangerous antagonist. If the military is mentioned in the zombie genre, it is only seldom shown as a considerate helping hand. In other games, it is shown to have failed to protect its citizens, and the soldiers themselves have become zombies, as in *Dead Nation* (2010) and *Left4Dead* (2008); or the military has itself become the evil element within the game. In *State of Decay* (Undead Labs, US 2013/Xbox 360 et al.), the army does not intend to evacuate the survivors, and instead seeks to contain the zombie threat and try to find the cause of the outbreak. In *Dying Light* (2015), the Ministry of Defence of an unnamed Middle Eastern government erects a wall around the plague city of Haram and considers whether to totally destroy the city. In *The Last of Us* (2012), the military performs summary executions of presumed infected citizens. Similar military policies are also suggested by the expanded backstory in *Left4Dead* (2008). An impotent government and a fascist military are apparently the narrative conditions of most zombie narratives.

Furthermore, it is of vital importance for these narratives that the executive power breaks down completely. Often, order breaks down worldwide (Drezner 2015: 16), as suggested in *The Last of Us* (2012), *Dead Nation* (2010) and *The Walking Dead* (Telltale Games, US 2012–2017/PS4 et al.). In other cases, it appears to be geographically restricted, as in *State of Decay*, *Dead Island*, *Dead Rising* or *Dying Light*. But inside the game scenario, the collapse of social and political order has to be absolute: a virtual world without government, political parties, NGOs, police, fire rescue, etc. This is even true of the *Resident Evil* series (Capcom, J 1996–2017), exemplified by the first game *Resident Evil* (Capcom, J 1996/PS1 et al. [original title: *Biohazard*]), where the players take the role of Special Forces police officers investigating some unsolved acts of cannibalism. Initially, this could be seen as an effective response of the executive power to a perceived threat. Later, however, it comes to light that the police force cannot contain the threat because it has been corrupted by the same evil corporation responsible for the zombie outbreak: the Umbrella Corporation.

There are, of course, exceptions to the rule: *Atom Zombie Smasher* (Blendo Games, US 2011/Windows et al.) is a small indie game by Brendon Chung where the player deploys military units on a 2D map to save citizens. In *State of Decay* (2013), there are vestiges of governmental authority in the character of Judge Lawton and local law enforcement officers, but the ending of the game suggests that the federal government of the United States itself has failed.

While the zombies are apparently the antagonists of these games, they are not truly evil. They are obeying natural instincts in attacking the remaining survivors. This does not mean, however, that there are no instances of evil in the narrative. True evil is evident in human society in the gameplay. This is also the main theme of the *Walking Dead* narrative universe (graphic novels, TV series and video games), where every attempt to recreate society ends in brutal autocratic tyrannies. Such narratives thus feed us the image of an inherent evil that exists within humankind itself. This is often inaccurately associated with the writings of Thomas Hobbes, in particular, his book *Leviathan* (Hobbes, 2007 [1651]). For

Hobbes, it is not evil that motivates humanity, but the impulse of self-preservation. If everyone pursued their own desires, the consequences would be collectively disastrous, as shown by the narrative of the zombie games: 'The state of nature thus becomes a state of war, savagery and degradation' (Tuck, 2002: 69). But where Hobbes argued for a covenant and strong government, to secure peace and allow civilisation (Hobbes, 2007: 156–166), zombie games propagate a much more pessimistic view of humanity: one in which almost all efforts to recreate society are doomed and only a handful of chosen individuals (among them, of course, the protagonist) show truly ethical behaviour (cf. Pfister, 2019). This naturally undermines the belief in the ability of a democratic society to function, and can in extreme cases even fuel a libertarian individualism as lauded by Ayn Rand (cf. Vizzini, 2011). In 2015, Brian Merchant wrote in the online journal Motherboard (part of vice.com): 'The basic tenets of zombie logic also track with hardline conservative principles (self-sufficiency, individualism, isolationism), which have been increasingly forcefully articulated over the last fifteen years' (Merchant, 2015).

This apocalyptic view of society has become omnipresent in the zombie game genre but has, interestingly enough, not had a very long history. Early zombie games like *Alone in the Dark* (Infogrames, F 1992/DOS et al.) and *House of the Dead* (Sega, J 1996/Arcade) tell quite a different story. Their zombies are still situated in the realm of the supernatural, in the tradition of H. P. Lovecraft and early horror movies, and are confined to single houses and neighbourhoods—*Zombies Ate My Neighbors* (LucasArts, US 1993/SuperNES et al.)—thus staying much truer to the early history of the zombie myth and its roots in vodou.[4] It is therefore important to note that the modern zombie narrative, which originated with Romero's use of the zombie genre as political critique, broke with its origins in the realm of magic. A fear of something extrinsic—the supernatural—was substituted by a fear of something intrinsic: the baseness of human beings.

Press x for zombie apocalypse

One could argue that both the iconography and the narration of zombie games do not greatly diverge from similar films and novels and, for the most part, this would be right. The differences from other media become particularly apparent in terms of game mechanics. For a start, games are an interactive experience. They cannot be consumed passively, but require the active participation of a 'player'. Even linear games require significant effort to progress through the game. This means that we have to actively take part in the action for most of the time. We have to move our avatars, hide from zombies as well as combat them. Thus, in contrast to other media, games provide a sense of agency.

This sense of agency is almost exclusively expressed by the player's ability to run and hide and/or to kill zombies. Human cooperation is not an option. The logic of video games apparently dictates that all possible stories still have to be thought through only in terms of conflict. Armed conflict might at first glance appear the natural choice where zombies are concerned, but this was not always the case. Early zombie myths, in contrast, were much more about hierarchical human interactions and cunning. The majority of zombie games, however, are based on the mechanics of a first-person or third-person shooter. This means the players have to learn how to kill zombies in these games, or learn how to evade them. The focus on stealth mechanics additionally emphasises the vulnerability of the protagonist, which is a central moment within the horror genre. It is when confronted with seemingly endless hordes of zombies that the fragility of the protagonist becomes most apparent. This feeling is intensified by the traditional scarcity of ammunition. Zombie games stress the moment where the player can be overpowered and subject to excessive stress, which culminates, in some cases, in short moments of genuine distress.

> Dead Rising—especially for players weaned on Resident Evil—creates the same deceptive feedback loop. Zombies are so slow, so easy to kill, that beating up on them is a deeply satisfying power trip. Downing one, two, three, even four zombies is fun. It's so fun that the player may fail to notice that, in the time it has taken them to kill four zombies, seven more have appeared to their left, twelve have appeared to their right, and a good thirty or forty may have appeared behind them. The player may turn around, triumphant, only to be staring directly into a vast ocean of the undead. At this moment the player may realize, to their embarrassment, that the 'stupid' character they used to make fun of in the zombie film is, in fact, them
>
> *(Weise, 2009: 258)*

The importance of an overwhelming foe in zombie games means that the actual confrontations are usually programmed in such a way that they can only be mastered after continuous repetition. The 'death screen' is a common experience when playing such games. Often, the last image seen by the player is one of a seemingly endless river of zombies running towards the screen. Thus, the players have to learn the game patterns to avoid confrontation, to hide, to sneak and to flee their foes. And they also learn that they cannot rely on the help of others: in single player zombie games, cooperation with virtual allies is usually not an option. The players can only rely on themselves, and they must always stay alert. For the zombie narrative to work in video games, it has to be translated into the language of game mechanics. And, because the simulation of violent conflict is not only the predominant but apparently the only gameplay imaginable in these games, the story has to be told this way: a narrative that strings together stealth and fighting.

Translating political anxieties into zombie language in digital games

Through a comparison with antecedent or diachronic 'languages', i.e. post-apocalyptic fiction, Christian iconography and action video games, we can conclude that zombie games, their recreational function aside, are particularly adept at communicating collective warnings. Thus, they translate collective anxieties into popular culture. In the last ten years, the breakdown of a democratic executive power has become a natural trope of the zombie genre, in video games but also in other media. We do not normally question this when we encounter it in games. Why should we? It belongs to the genre of the zombie apocalypse. We feel it has always been this way, but this is not the case. The idea of total social and political breakdown is a new quality that zombie games have acquired, disguising itself as something historical and inherent to them. There are two kinds of translation here:

1. The political statement of systemic collapse is not only a translation of a 'rising tone of scepticism about democracy'[5] but potentially also an influencing factor of this scepticism. This process of translation from public anxiety to popular culture goes both ways.
2. Through the translation of the zombie narration into video games, zombies lost much of the original conscious political message that they had in the movies of George Romero, for example, and became a myth in the sense of Roland Barthes (Barthes, 2014: 209–272; Pfister, 2018b). I believe the main problem lies in the fact that, in contrast to all other media, open political themes, political messages and statements are still taboo in video games (Pfister, 2018a). Due to this apolitical paradigm, zombie video games have become an empty discursive shell waiting for content. This void has automatically been filled by the very successful myth of systemic political failure.

I argue that this was never a conscious act. Because zombie narratives have been so successful, we produce more and more of them and try to copy this success. But if we do not invest time in a proper story, we just copy the framework, which then itself increasingly becomes the content. This means that these zombie games increasingly communicate the image of overstrained governments and the futility of all forms of human cooperation or governance, without the previous underlying messages which critiqued racism or capitalism. Without a specific societal target to be critiqued, there is also no longer hope for a solution. And what we learn, by constant repetition, is that in the end we can only trust ourselves. A rampaging individualism is being enabled by traditions of game design, and the heavy reliance by game developers on the simulation of violent conflict in video games.

Notes

1 For the title I used the 'zombie translator' programmed by Jachin Rupe in 2014, to translate the phrase [political anxieties] into 'Zombie'. http://zombietranslator.net
2 www.youtube.com/watch?v=Iqid90JR6BY (30.11.2017).
3 www.youtube.com/watch?v=lVW8MNy82rE (30.11.2017).
4 For an explanation of the term *vodou* (rather than Voodoo), please see infra, page 158, note 8.
5 www.theatlantic.com/international/archive/2017/06/why-do-democracies-fail/530949/

Ludography

Alone in the Dark (Infogrames, F 1992/DOS et al.)
Atom Zombie Smasher (Blendo Games, US 2011/Windows et al.)
Dead Island (techland, PL 2011/Xbox360 et al.)
Dead Nation (Housemarque, FI 2010/PS3 et al.)
Dead Rising (Capcom, J 2006/Xbox360 et al.)
Dying Light (Techland, PL 2015/PS4 et al.)
House of the Dead (Sega, J 1996/Arcade)
The Last of Us (Naughty Dog, US 2013/PS3 et al.)
Left4Dead (Valve, US 2008/Xbox360 et al.)
Left4Dead 2 (Valve, US 2009/Xbox360 et al.)
Resident Evil (Capcom, J 1996/PS1 et al. [original title: *Biohazard*]),
Resident Evil 7: Biohazard (Capcom, J 2017/PS4 et al.)
State of Decay (Undead Labs, US 2013/Xbox 360 et al.)
The Walking Dead (Telltale Games, US 2012–2017/PS4 et al.)
Zombi/ZombiU (Ubisoft Montpellier, F 2012/WiiU et al.)
Zombies ate my Neighbours (LucasArts, US 1993/SuperNES et al.)

Filmography

WALL-E (US 2008/D: Andrew Stanton)

Bibliography

Backe, H.-J. and E. Aarseth (2013) 'Ludic Zombies: An Examination of Zombieism in Games', in *Proceedings of DiGRA 2013: Defragging Game Studies*: www.digra.org/wp-content/uploads/digital-library/paper_405.pdf (viewed 25/ 09/2019).

Barthes, R. (2014) *Mythologies*. Paris: Editions du Seuil.

Bishop, K. W. (2015) 'L'émergence des Zombie Studies: comment les morts-vivants ont envahi le monde universitaire et pourquoi nous devrions nous en soucier', In B. Perron, A. Dominguez Leiva & S. Archibald (eds), *Z pour Zombies*, Montréal: Les Presses de l'Université de Montréal, 31–44.

Böhme, H. (1989) 'Die Ästhetik der Ruinen', In D. Kamper and C. Wolf (eds), *Der Schein des Schönen*, Göttingen: Steidl, 287–304.

Carr, D. (2009) 'Textual Analysis, Digital Games, Zombies', in *Proceedings of DiGRA 2009: Breaking New Ground: Innovation in Games, Play, Practice and Theory*: www.digra.org/wp-content/uploads/digital-library/09287.241711.pdf (viewed 25/ 09/2019).

Carrol, N. (1989) *The Philosophy of Horror*. London: Routledge 1989.

Carrol, N. (2002) 'Why Horror?', In M. Jancovich (ed), *Horror: The Film Reader*, London: Routledge, 33–45.

Cohen, K. R. (1973) *Metamorphosis of a Death Symbol: The Transi Tomb in the late Middle Ages and the Renaissance*. Berkeley: University of California Press.

Comaroff, J. and J. Comaroff (2017) 'Alien-Nations: Zombies, Immigrants and Millennial Capitalism', In S. J. Lauro (ed), *Zombie Theory: A Reader*, Minneapolis: University of Minnesota Press, 137–156.

Drezner, D. W. (2015) *Theories of International Politics and Zombies—Revived Edition*. Princeton and Oxford: Princeton University Press.
Fromme, J. and R. Biermann (2009) 'Identitätsbildung und politische Sozialisation', In T. Bevc & H. Zapf (eds), *Wie wir spielen was wir werden. Computerspiele in unserer Gesellschaft*, Konstanz: UVK, 113–138.
Grayson, K., M. Davies and S. Philpott (2009) 'Pop goes IR? Researching the Popular Culture-World Politics Continuum', *in Politics* 29(3): 155–163.
Habermas, J. (2008) *Ach, Europa*. Frankfurt a. M.: Suhrkamp.
Hobbes, T. (2007) *Leviathan*. Stuttgart: Reclam.
Huizinga, J. (1924) *The Waning of the Middle Ages*. London: Edward Arnold.
Huxley, A. (2005 [1948]) *Ape and Essence*. London: Penguin.
Klimmt, C. (2009) 'Empirische Medienforschung: Kommunikationswissenschaftliche Perspektiven auf Computerspiele', In T. Bevc & H. Zapf (eds), *Wie wir spielen was wir werden. Computerspiele in unserer Gesellschaft*, Konstanz: UVK, 65–74.
Kristeva, J. (1980) *Pouvoirs de l'horreur*. Paris: Editions du Seuil.
Landwehr, A. (2009) *Historische Diskursanalyse*. Frankfurt a.M.: Campus. 2009.
Lauro, S. J. (2011) *The Modern Zombie: Living Death in the Technological Age*. PhD. Thesis University of California.
Lauro, S. J. and K. Embry (2008) 'A Zombie Manifesto: The Nonhuman Condition in the Era of Advanced Capitalism', *Boundary 2: An International Journal of Literature and Culture* 35(1): 85–108.
Luhmann, N. (2000) *Art as Social System*. Stanford: Stanford University Press.
Merchant, B. (2015) 'Why You Really Should Be Afraid of the Zombie Apocalypse', in *motherboard*. vice.com: https://motherboard.vice.com/en_us/article/d73ev7/why-you-really-should-be-afraid-of-the-zombie-apocalypse (viewed 25/ 09/2019).
Morrissette, J. J. (2014) 'Zombies, International Relations and the Production of Danger: Critical Security Studies versus the Living Dead in Studies', *Popular Culture* 36(2): 1–27.
Mouflard, C. (2016) 'Zombies and Refugees: Variations of the "Post-Human" and the "Non-Human" in Robin Campillo's *Les Revenants* (2004) and Fabrice Gobert's *Les Revenants* (2012–2015)', *Humanities* 5(48): www.mdpi.com/2076-0787/5/3/48/htm (viewed 25/ 09/2019).
Nelson, J. S. (2005) 'Horror Films Face Political Evils in Everyday Life', *Political Communication* 22(3): 381–386.
Perron, B., A. Dominguez Leiva & S. Archibald (2015) *Z pour Zombies*. Montréal: Les presses de l'Université de Montreal.
Pfister, E. (2017) '"Doctor not mad. Doctor insane." – Eine kurze Kulturgeschichte der Figur des mad scientist im digitalen Spiel', In A. Görgen & R. Inderst (eds), *PAIDIA-Sonderausgabe: Die Darstellung von Wissenschaft, Forschung und Technologie in digitalen Spielen*, www.paidia.de/?p=10074 (viewed 25/ 09/2019).
Pfister, E. (2018a) 'Keep your Politics out of my Games!' in *Spiel-Kultur-Wissenschaften*: http://spielkult.hypotheses.org/1566 (viewed 25/ 09/2019).
Pfister, E. (2018b) 'Der Politische Mythos als diskursive Aussage im digitalen Spiel. Ein Beitrag aus der Perspektive der Politischen Geschichte', in T. Junge and C. Schumacher (eds), *Digitale Spiele im Diskurs*: www.medien-im-diskurs.de (viewed 25/ 09/2019).
Pfister, E. (2018c) 'Politische Kommunikation in digitalen Horrorspielen', in *Horror-game-Politics*: https://hgp.hypotheses.org/176 (viewed 25/ 09/2019).
Pfister, E. (2019) 'Zombies Ate Democracy: The Myth of a Systemic Political Failure in Video Games', in S. J. Webley and P. Zackariasson (eds), *The Playful Undead and Video Games: Critical Analyses of Zombies and Gameplay*, London: Routledge, 216–231.

Platts, T. K. (2013) 'Locating Zombies in the Sociology of Popular Culture', *Sociology Compass* 7: 547–560.
Pulliam, J. (2009) 'Our Zombies, Ourselves: Exiting the Foucauldian Universe in George A. Romero's "Land of the Dead"', *Journal of the Fantastic in the Arts* 20(1): 42–56.
Rath, G. (2014) 'Zombi/e/s. Zur Einleitung', In G. Rath (ed), *Zombies, Zeitschrift für Kulturwissenschaften*, Vol. 8(1): 11–20.
Romero, G. (2010) '10 Questions for George Romero', in *time.com*, 7 June 2010: http://content.time.com/time/magazine/article/0,9171,1992390,00.html (viewed 25/ 09/2019).
Santilli, P. (2007) 'Culture, Evil and Horror', *American Journal of Economics and Sociology* 66 (1): 173–194.
Sarasin, P. (2003) *Geschichtswissenschaft und Diskursanalyse*. Frankfurt am Main: Suhrkamp.
Savage, S. (2005) 'Behind the Sensationalism: Images of a Decaying Corpse in Japanese Buddhist Art', in *Redorbit.com*: www.redorbit.com/news/health/140943/behind_the_sensationalism_images_of_a_decaying_corpse_in_japanese/(viewed 25/09/2019).
Tuck, R. (2002) *Hobbes: A Very Short Introduction*. Oxford: Oxford University Press.
Vizzini, N. (2011) 'Rick and Rand: The Objectivist Hero in The Walking Dead', in J. Lowder (ed), *Triumph of the Walking Dead: Robert Kirkman's Zombie Epic on Page and Screen*, Dallas: Smart Pop, 127–141.
Weise, M. (2009) 'The Rules of Horror: Procedural Adaptation in Clock Tower, Resident Evil and Dead Rising', in B. Perron (ed), *Horror Video Games*, Jefferson: McFarland, 238–266.
Ziolkowski, T. (2011) 'Ruminations on Ruins: Classical versus Romantic', *German Quarterly* 89(3): 265–281.

INDEX

8 Myths about Public Understanding of Science (2015) 111

Abe, S. 36n6
Abensour, M. 52
Aching, G. 132
Ackermann, H.-W. 156–157
Act for the English Order, Habit and Language (1537) 99
Acts of the Apostles 166
Adorno 132, 138
advents 102
aesthetic humanism 19–21, 24, 27, 29, 34
affaire de Bizoton or *affaire Claircine* (alleged case of ritual anthropophagy) 148 *see also* Haiti
affection 96, 102
Agamben, G. 10
Alexander, Z. 70
Algonquian 4
Alien (1983) 34
Alone in the Dark (1992) 170
Altounian, J. 96
American Scientist 111
An Inconvenient Sequel (2017) 121, 122n9
An Inconvenient Truth (2006) 119, 122n9
Anglo-American: imperialism 3; policy 4
Antelme, R. 65–66
Anthropocene 11, 27, 34–35, 95, 100, 102, 106; from the Holocene to the 102; or Capitalocene 35; post-Sputnik world of the 34

anthropological(ly): coded 21, 26; difference 20–22, 26–27, 29, 31–34; exception 20, 27, 29, 32, 34; superiority 21
anti-colonial struggles 99 *see also* colonial
Ape and Essence (1948) 162
apocalypse 162; interactive zombie 161; zombie 13, 161–162, 170, 172 *see also* zombie
apocalyptic: narrative 117, 120; scenario 113; storytelling 11, 112, 121; view 170; eco-apocalyptic 122n5; post-apocalyptic 13, 119, 162, 167
apories of justice (Derrida) 46
Apparatus of Area (Solomon) 9,19, 26–27, 29, 31–34
applied translation 32
Apter, E. 5, 11, 79, 80–82
Archer, J. 155
architectural ruins 167–168
Arendt, H. 32–35, 39; on conquest of space 34–35; on human rights 39–40; migration 51–52; on Sputnik 31–32
Aristotle 97, 118
Armenian genocide 96
Armstrong, F. 119–120
Arnds, P. 8
art-horror 161
Artaud, A. 25
Asano, T. 22
Aschenberg, H. 66
Ashcroft, B. 3
Assomons les pauvres! (2011) 50
asylum procedure 45, 47–48, 50

Atom Zombie Smasher (2011) 169
Auerbach, E. 81
Austria(n): Corporate Code 46–47; government 45

Babel 9, 28, 82; curse of 63
Baker, M. 5–6
Baldwin, J. 28
Balibar, É. 38, 52
Balka, M. 137
Balkan war 81
Barthes, R. 164
Bassnett, S. 4
Baumgarten, A. G. 131
Before the Flood (2016) 119
Being Ecological (2018) 101
Benjamin, W. 81
Bennett, J. 106
Bennie, J. 137
Berg, M. 108
Bergson, H. 105
Berman, A. 7
Bescherelle, L. 153
Bewell, A. 12, 135
Bhabha, H. 3, 11, 79, 82–84, 86–87
biàntōng 11, 97
Bielsa, E. 6
binocular vision 104
biopolitics 32, 35
biphasic sleep 130
Black Skin, White Masks (2008) 149
Blessebois, P. 157
Blindness and Insight (1979) 24
Boase-Beie, J. 8
Bonanno, G. A. 8
Bosch, H. 166
bourgeoisie 19–20
Boyer, J. P. 147
Braidotti, R. 11, 103, 105
brain 31, 128
Bravo, A. 69
bridges (Levi) 60
British liberators 68
Britton, C. 133
Bruni, L. 7
Burke, E. 131
Burke, K. L. 111–112
Burton, R. 2

Cameron, J. 118
Campbell, G. 131
Campbell, N. 101–102
Campiello prize 60
Can the Subaltern Speak? (2008) 21

Canavesio, G. 166
Capitalist Realism: Is There No Alternative? 108
Caribbean islands 135, 157; cultures 145–146, 151–152, 155–156; French Caribbean 146, 151; religions 146; plants 135
carpal X-ray 42
Carrol, N. 161
Caruth, C. 8, 81
Chakrabarthy, D. 4–5
Chapman, A. 121
Cheyfitz, E. 3–4
Chichele, H., Archbishop of Canterbury 166
Chilton, P. 5
Chinese: art 97; economies 100; market 26; literature 27, 30; studies 10, 27–28
Christian: faith 25; iconography 13, 166, 171; saints 129; relics 7
citizen 10, 38–39, 45, 51–52; non-citizens 10, 38–39, 51
Clausewitz, C. von 5
climate: awareness 104; catastrophe 118; change 9, 11, 95, 98, 100–103, 112–117, 121, 122, 122n9; communication 11, 112–114, 117, 121; disaster 118; fiction 116; meltdown 98; nonfiction 119; science 12, 112, 116–117, 119–121
climatologist 114–119
Clinton, B. 26
Code Noir (1685 decree) 153
Code Pénal (1835) 147–148
Cohen, B. 121
Cohen, U. 69–71
colonial: causality 27, 30; contexts 157; difference 20, 27, 29, 32, 34; documents 151; encyclopaedias 151; expansion 3; exploration 33; eye 135; governmentality 25, 28; imagination 84; Imperial Modernity 8; legacies 149; logic 154; missionary 26; novel 20; practice 1; print culture (neocolonial) 155; project 134; power 135; Saint-Domingue 147, 150–151; science 28, 32; situation 83; struggles (anti-colonial) 99; subject 79, 82; transition (decolonial) 24; triangle 136; violence 27
Columbus, C. 135
Commons 103, 107
Confessions of a Nazi Spy (1938) 155
Confucian 30
Congress of Chapel Hill 31
Conners, N. 119

Conrad, J. 149
conversion: financialised 26; of faith 22, 24–26
Conway, E. 119
cortex 128
Craven, W. 145
Creature with the Atomic Brain (1955) 155
crematorium Esperanto 61
creolisation 135
Cronin, M. 11, 12, 112–113, 120, 136, 138
cultural: annihilation 135; authority 82; capital 43; currency 164; mediators 152; memory 10, 75, 155–156; transfer (cultural studies) 28; translation 3, 5, 10–11, 51, 75, 79, 87, 147, 157
Cunningham, C. D. 44, 46, 49
Curtius, E.R. 98

Dabić, M. 41, 49
D'Alembert, J. B. 151
dark side 1–2, 4–7, 9–11, 21, 32, 59, 67, 69–71, 95, 109, 112, 115, 121, 126–127, 132, 150, 165
Dark Ecology (2016) 115
Dark Side of the Light: Slavery and the French Enlightenment (2006) 153
date of birth 41–42
Datura (plant) 147
Davies, P. 8
Davies, S. 111
Davis, W. 12, 145–147, 149, 152, 157
Dayan, C. 149
De interpretatione recta (1426) 7
Dead Island (2011) 165
Dead Rising (2006) 167, 169, 171
Dead Snow (2009) 155–156
death screen (in video games) 171
Debord, G. 22
decolonial transition 24 *see also* colonial
decomposition: cadaver tombs 166; human body 161, 165, 168; Japanese art (*Kusozu*) 166; of human society 167
Deleuze, G. 105, 164
de Man, P. 24
Demastes, W. 127
democracy 33, 52; scepticism of 172
Derrida, J. 19–21, 27, 29–31, 35, 35n1, 40, 46, 83
Description topographique, psychique, civile, politique et historique de la partie française de l'isle de Saint-Domingue (1797) 151
Dessler, A. 120
Dictionnaire national (1856) 153
Diderot, D. 107, 151, 153

Di Khurbn Eyrope 27
disparation (Simondon) 104–105
Distancing-Embracing Model of the Enjoyment of Negative Emotions in Art Reception (2017) 118
Docherty, T. 100, 107
domesticating and foreignising (Venuti) 7
Doppelgänger 78, 87
Dössekker, B. (Binjamin Wilkomirski) 85
Douglas, M. 62
Drezner, D. W. 162
Duffy, P. 137
Dunne, T. 111, 114
Dutton, M. 28–29, 32
Dying Light (2015) 161, 169

eco-apocalyptic 122n5 *see also* apocalyptic
eco-translation 11–12, 112, 115, 117, 120, 126, 136
Eco-Translation (2017) 11, 136
eco-translator 135
École Polytechnique 99
ecology 1, 11, 169; *Dark Ecology* (2016) 12, 115, 118; planet 11; of knowledge 9; translation of 137
Edensor, T. 129–131, 137
Elemental University (Cronin) 104
Eliot, G. 101
embodiment 11–12, 78, 126, 128, 138; re-embodiment 134
Emmerich, R. 116–118
Encyclopédie (1765) 153
Encyclopedie de la Pleiade 65
Endō, Shûsaku 9, 22
Enlightenment 131, 138, 153, 167
epistemic habits 95; violence 28–29
Espagne, M. 28
Étiemble, R. 19, 29–31
European: authors 150; cuisines 135; spiritism 154; universities 98; zombie conceptualisation 157
Europeanisation of Turkey 8

fabrication 38; uncanny 88
famine 96
Fanon, F. 149
Felman, S. 8
Ferenczi, S. 96
Fieldnotes from a Catastrophe (2006) 119
figure of the third 11, 78, 80, 82; in social philosophy 76; the psychoanalyst as 81; the translator as 77; uncanny 75
film industry World War II 155
fingerprints 42

Fischer, J. 76–77
Fisher, M. 108
Flights (2018) 95
Foa, E. 154
footnotes (paratextual strategy) 154
Force (*Star Wars*) 2, 127
foreign: cultural contents 81; detractors 148; fascination (Haitian ritualism) 148; locus of the 33; policies 3; soil 30; students 100
foreigner 38, 150
Foucault, M. 36n2, 164
Fox, J. 121
Francis I of France (François 1er) 99
Franz, K. 66, 72n10
French Caribbean 146, 151; colony 150–151; monarchy 99; Sino-French literature 27–30; territory 99; zombies in French popular culture 151
Freud, S. 79–83; interpretation of the puppet Olympia 82; theory of the uncanny 82–83
Friedrich, C. D. 167
Friend, S. 119
Fritsch, V. 134
functionaries low-ranking, prisoner 64–65

Galewski, M. 66
game mechanics 165, 170–171
Gansel, M. 108
Garden of Earthly Delights (Bosch) 166
Garfield, A. 22
Gaston, K. 137
Gauthier, J. 156–157
Gawalewicz, A. 61, 71n1
Geffrard, F. 147–148
Genette, G. 152
geo-constructivism 34–35
geo-ontology 106
geopoetics 126, 134–136; geopoetic translation 12, 138
Giuliani, M. 71n8
Glissant, É. 12, 132–133, 138
global: commodity 162; discourse 13; economic concerns 103; ecosystem 138; financial market 26; warming 113, 116–117; world 33
globalisation 11, 99–100
globality 33–34
Globalization, Political Violence and Translation (2009) 6
glossary 4
Goldschmidt, G.-A. 80

Gombrich, E. H. 97
Goodell, J. 119
Gore, A. 122n9
governmental breakdown 162
Grabowski, L. 86
Gray Zones: Ambiguity and Compromise in the Holocaust and its Aftermath (2005) 71n6
Graziadei, D. 12
Green Campus initiatives 103
grey zone (Levi) 10, 59, 63–65, 68–71
Griffiths, G. 3
Guattari, F. 105, 164
Guggenheim, D. 119
Günzel, S. 134
Gyllenhaal, J. 118

Habermas, J. 13, 163
Haifa University 156
Haiti: *krèyol* 150; Penal Code (*Code Pénal*) 147–148; postcolonial 151 *see also* postcolonial; revolution 151; U.S. Occupation 145, 148–149; voodoo 145–146, 148–149, 151; zombie 12, 145–148, 156
Haïti et les Haïtiens (1871) 154
Halperin, V. 145
Hammel, A. 8
Hansen, J. 119
Hardach, S. 41–42
Harding, S. 6
hardware 98
harsh language 62
Hatoyama, I. 36n6
Heart of Darkness (Conrad) 149
hegemon 10, 41–44, 48, 51; language of the 44
hegemony, hegemonic: aesthetic humanism 21 *see also* aesthetic humanism; clerical 99; counter-hegemonic 9; modern science 29, 32; postwar American leadership 25; of logistic 32; *Pax Americana* 25–26; practice 9; rationality 46; species 103; transnational ideological 26 *see also* transnational
Heidegger, M. 80
Heine, H. 62
Heinzelmann 7–8
Henry VIII, 99
Hirakawa, S. 21
Hobbes, T. 169–170
Hollywood cinema 25–26; climate change block-buster 116; film 118; zombie films 146, 155
Holocene 102 *see also* Anthropocene

Homo economicus 20; *faber* 20; *sapiens* 20, 134–136
Hooker, R. S. 148
horror: art horror 161; genre paradox 161; moral judgements 164; 'primer for political action' 164; retrospective 156
Horst, M. 111
House of the Dead (1996) 170
How It Is (installation 2009) 137
How to Let Go of the World (2016) 121, 122n9
Howell, R. 120–121
Hughes, C. W. 6
Huizinga, J. 166
human body 7, 42, 105, 128–129, 146, 161, 165–168; body language 67; undead body 145–146, 152; undead spirit without a 152; dead body 166
human eye 104, 128
human rights 39–40, 43, 50; Universal Declaration of Human Rights (1948) 45, 39
Humboldtian university (Readings) 99
Hume, D. 116–118
Hurbon, L. 151
Huxley, A. 162
hylomorphic model of creation 104
hyperobject (Morton) 101, 103, 113
Hyperobjects: Philosophy and Ecology after the End of the World (2013) 122n1

If Not Now, When? (1985) 60
If This is a Man (1959) 60, 62, 64
indication (linguistics) 23
indigenous: knowledge 29; people 106; plants 135
individuation 104, 105; cultural 28
Inghilleri, M. 6
Inherit the Truth (1996) 68
Insana, L. N. 9
Institutio Oratoria (Quintilian) 131
interpreter: in Silence (2006 Scorsese) 22–23, 25; in asylum seeking procedures 41, 48–51; as moral obligation (Levi) 63; in the *grey zone* concept (Levi) 64–65, 68–69; in concentration camps 64–69; in *L'espèce humaine* (Antelme) 65–66; in *Treblinka* (Steiner) 66; in *If This is a Man* (Levi) 67; in *Sonderkommando: dans l'enfer des chambres à gaz* (Venezia) 68; in *Inherit the Truth* (Lasker-Wallfisch) 68–69; in *Interpreters and Translators in the War Zone* (2010) 5
ironic speech-act 75–76

Italiano, F. 112, 113, 126
interpreting: in asylum procedures 48, 50; in concentration camps 59, 67, 70; *grey zone* (Levi) 64–70; *ex officio* interpreters 65
Interpreting in Nazi Concentration Camps (2016) 9
inter-semiotic 3
Interstellar (2014) 35

Jakle, J. 130–131
Japanese imperialism 24
Jedi 2, 22
Jóhannesson, G. T. 130
Johnson, E. 129
Joon-Ho, B. 116
Judas Iscariot 166
Jullien, F. 11, 97–98

Kabalek, K. 156
Kaplan, E. A. 8
Kapo 63–65, 68
Kingdom of Heaven (2005) 22
Kipling, R. 62
Kishi, N. 36n6
Klein, N. 105, 136
Knowledge and Taste (1958) 31
knowledge: communication 82; cultural 83; encyclopaedic production 153; indigenous 29; infrastructure 106; indigenisation of 105; knowledge production-as-translation 30; nativity, language and 26; natural 26; of German 61; of translation 62; of languages 65, 67; organisation 11, 98–103, 108; power-knowledge argument 6; racialised 152; regime of knowledge production 31; scientific 11, 114, 122n8; societal production 153; streams of 151; transfer 165; translation 165
Kolbert, E. 119
Koschorke, A. 76
Kosinski, J. 85
Kovala, U. 152
krèyol 150
Kundera, M. 107
Kunze, R. 108
Kurzweil, R. 34
Kusozu 166

labour 19, 25–28; division of 20, 26
Lacan, J. 82–84
LaCapra, D. 8
lagerszpracha 61–62
Lagrange, Cardinal de 166

language: Arabic 80; Catalan 64; Czech 64; Dutch 68; English 64, 78; French 64, 68; German 64, 68, 80; Irish 95–96; Italian 64, 67; Middle English 2; Old English 2; Old High German 2; Middle High German 2; Polish 64, 68; Russian 64; Spanish 49; Turkish 80–81
Language and Conquest in Early Modern Ireland (2001) 95
Languages of the Night (2015) 96
La philosophie de la relation (Glissant) 132
Lasker-Wallfisch, A. 68–69
Laub, D. 8, 78
Lauro, S. J. 13, 162
lawyer 19, 25–28; as translator 44
L'espèce humaine (1947) 66
les sortilèges (superstitious practices) 147
Lefevere, A. 4, 7
Left4Dead (2008) 161, 165, 167–169
legal: language 10, 39, 43–45; judge 48; counselling 44–45
Leiserowitz, A. 116–117, 121
Leitgeb, C. 10
Leopardi, G. 71n5
Lertzman, R. 121–122
Lesch, T. 42
Leviathan (Hobbes) 169–170
Levi, P. 10
Levi-Strauss, C. 62
Le zombi de Grand Perou (1697) 157
liberalism 20, 35; neo-liberalism 26, 35
Li Jinjia 30
L'Inexistence divine (2011) 102
logistical: capitalism 35, extremism 35; logistics 33, 35
Longinus 131
Lorenzetti, P. 166
Lovecraft, H.P. 170
Lubling, Y. 66
Lugosi, B. 155
Luhmann, N. 164
Luna 3 Spacecraft 127
Lund, K. A. 130
Lyotard, J. 10, 46

Mächler, S. 85
McCrea, B. 96
Mad Max: Fury Road (2015) 116
mad scientist 163
Magellan, F. 33
Mahfouz, N. 80
Manchu Qing Dynasty 29
Mann, M. 114–115
Mann, T. 84

Marsen, S. 12, 128
mass media 163–164
materialist-pharmacological argument (Ingles) 147 *see also* zombification
Matory, J. L. 146
matter-realist 103
Maximin, D. 134
Mehtonen, P. 12, 130–131
Meillassoux, Q. 102
memories: forged 87–88; authentic 87; traumatic 8, 78
Meng Hua 29–30
Menninghaus, W. 118–119
Merchant, B. 170
Mignolo, W. D. 3
Miller, G. 116
Milton, J. 7
mimesis 134
mimicry (Bhabha) 83–84, 86 *see also* post-colonial
Minority Treaties (1920s) 52
Mintz, S. 150
missionaries 22–23, 26, 151
Mokre, M. 10
monarchical university 99–100
Moreau de Saint-Méry, M. L. É. 151–152, 154, 158n16
Moreland, M. 155
Morocco, Y. 86
Morton, T. 12, 101, 105, 113, 115, 118, 121, 130
Motherboard (VICE) 170
mother tongue 39, 44, 48
Motherless Tongues (2016) 6
Mouaz, M. 54n14
mueki 24–25
Muselmann 70, 87

national, nationality: aesthetics 19; cultures 34; cuisines 135; *Dictionnaire National* (Bescherelle) 153; German 167; humanism 21–22, 28; 'Humboldtian University' 99; identity 26–27, 99; Japanese 26; language 99; minorities 40; nationalism 21, 25, 132; naturalisation of th schema of 33; order 38; representation 25; security 162; sentiment of 24; socialism 10, 59, 75; socialist crimes 86–87; sovereignty 22, 24, 40; Turkish 81; university 99–100; US Imperial nationalism 25; vs. transnationaliy 33 *see also* transnationality
Nature Geoscience (scientific journal) 114
Nazi Zombie 155–156
Neeson, L. 22–24

Nelson, J. S. 164
neocolonial print culture 155 *see also* colonial
New York Magazine 113–114
New York 2140 (2017) 121
Neyrat, F. 34
Nietzsche, F. 24
Night of the Living Dead (1968) 154
night time 129–130
nihilism (Morton) 115
Nolan, C. 35
non-human 11, 103, 106, 112–113, 138
nyctophobia 12, 129
nzambi 157

OED (Oxford English Dictionary) 127
Oder (river) 95
Of Tragedy (1965) 117
Ogata, I. 22
Olson, C. 107
On Translating and Being Translated (2016) 62
opacity 12, 112–113, 126, 131–138; right to 12, 132, 134, 138; Glissant's notion of 133; as strategy 134
orality 96
Ordonnance de Villers-Cottêrets (1539) 99
Oreskes, N. 119

Palmer, P. 95
paradox of tragedy (Hume) 118
Paramount Pictures 26
paranoia 82
paratextual strategy 152, 154
Pascal, B. 96, 98
Pasquier, M. C. 133
Passages of Darkness (1988) 12, 145
patriarchal 23
Pax Americana 9, 22–26, 31
Pensées (1670) 96
Petersen, L. C. 119
Pfaller, R. 76
Pfister, E. 13
Pink Floyd 2, 7, 9, 127
Plantinga, C. 118
Platts, T. K. 13
Plumwood, V. 105
poiesis 130, 134
police 40–42, 46, 50, 52, 169
pollution 136, 162; light 137–138
Portuguese Jesuit Priests 22
post-apocalyptic 13, 119, 162, 167 *see also* apocalyptic

post-colonial 2, 7, 12, 21–22, 24, 83–84, 87, 151, 157; argument 82; context 59, 157; criticism 3; culture 83; Haiti 151; literatures 2–3; mimicry 84; post-imperial world 34; post-*Khurbn* world 21–22; sovereignty 24–25; theories 3, 79
post-Khurbn 21, 22
Postel, P. 27–28
Postlethwaite, P. 119
Povinelli, E. 106
Powhatan 4
Probert, W. 43
projective geometry 107
Provincializing Europe (2000) 4
Purcell, D. 155
Putnam, L. 151

Quaid, D. 118
Quintilian 131

Rafael, V.L. 6
Rahmstorf, S. 117
Ramsey, K. 147–148
Rand, A. 170
Rath, G. 12–13
Readings, B. 99
Real Climate (science blog) 114
Redfield, M. 27
Renaissance 3, 97
Repression, Accessibility and the Translation of Private Experience (1990) 8
Resident Evil (1996) 169, 171
Resident Evil 7: Biohazard (2017) 165
Resonanz: Eine Soziologie der Weltbeziehung (2016) 107
resource extraction 105; fixation on 108
Rethinking Comparativism (2009) 29
re-traumatisation 47 *see also* trauma
retrospective horror 156 *see also* horror
Revenge of the Zombies (1943) 155
Ricque, C. 154
Roberts, D. 121
Robinson Crusoe 29
Robinson, K. S. 121
Robischon, M. 137
Romanticism 24, 27 167; German 167–168
Romero G. A. 154, 162, 164, 168
Rosa, H. 107
Rosen, A. 8
Rössner, M. 6, 53n10, 126
rough translations 4–5
Rubinstein, R. 71–72n8
Rundle, C. 6
Rupe, J. 172n1

Rushdie, S. 2
Rutherford, J. 157
Ruyer, R. 105

Said, E. 80
Saint-Domingue 147, 150–151
Sakai, N. 33–34, 36n2
Sala-Molins, L. 153
Santilli, P. 164
Sarasin, P. 163
Savage, J. 147
Sayad, A. 38
Schindler's List (1993) 22
Schleiermacher, F. 7, 49
science: communication 111; translation 112, 115–116; language 114
Scorsese, M. 9, 22, 24–26
Scott R. 22, 34
Seabrook, W. 145–148
Seeber, B. 108
selective translation 148
Sensible Wege (Kunze) 108
Shenk, J. 121
signification (linguistics) 23–24
Silence (2016) 9, 22, 24–26
Simmel, G. 11, 77
Simon, S. 6
Simondon, G. 104–105
Singh, K. A. 12, 133–134, 138
Singularity (Kurzweil) 34–35
Sinha, S. 50
Sino-French 27, 29
sleep 129–130
Smith, N. (Time.com) 26
Snowpiercer (2012) 116
societal collapse 168–169
Solomon, J. 9–10
Sonderkommandos 68, 71, 72n9
Soziologie (1908) 77
speaking cure 85
species-faculty 20
speech act theory of irony 75–76; languages 80; fabrication 88; dark-uncanny 115
Spinoza, B. 105
Spitzer, L. 80
Spivak, G. 11, 21, 29, 79
Sputnik: crisis (1958) 31–33; post-Sputnik world 35 *see also* Anthropocene; space exploration after 34
Stahuljak, Z. 6
Stanton, A. 162
Star Wars 2–7, 9, 127, 136; *Episode I - The Phantom Menace* 22
State of Decay (2013) 169

St. John, S. 150
Steiner, G. 133
Steiner, J.-F. 66, 72n9
Stempel, W. 10–11
Stevens, F. 119
Storms of my Grandchildren (2009) 119
Stratford, L. 86
Stumm, B. 8–9
Sturge, K. 6
sub-altern 10, 21, 48
Suhrkamp 85
Svoboda, M. 117

Taken (2008) 23
Tell, W. 76
testimony 78, 87
Teterodoxin 147
Tetsuro, W. 23
Texas A&M 120
Theatre of Cruelty 25
The Age of Stupid (2009) 119
The Darker Side of the Renaissance: Literacy, Territoriality, Colonalization (1995) 3
The Dark Side of the Moon (1973) 2, 127
The Day After Tomorrow (2004) 116–118
The Difference Between Words Esteemed Synonymous (1766) 1
The Drowned and the Saved (1988) 59–60, 63, 67, 70
The 11th Hour (2007) 119
The Empire Writes Back: Theory and Practice in Post-Colonial Literature (1989) 2
'The Empire Writes Back with a Vengeance' (1982) 2
The Flooded Earth (2010) 119
The Future of Life (2003) 103
The King of the Zombies (1941) 155–156
The Last of Us (2008/2013) 161, 167–169
The Location of Culture (1994) 3, 82
The Magic Island (Seabrook) 145–148
The Origins of Totalitarianism (1958) 32
The Painted Bird (1965) 85
The Poetics of Imperialism (1997) 3–4
The Serpent and the Rainbow (1986) 145
The Severed Head and the Grafted Tongue (2011) 95
The Slow Professor (2016) 108
The Translation Zone (2006) 5, 81
The Trial (1925) 62
The Truce (1965) 60
The Uninhabitable Earth (2017) 113–116, 119–120
The Walking Dead 167
The Water Will Come (2017) 119

The Wrench (1986) 60
third space (Bhabha) 83
This Changes Everything (2014) 105, 136
Thoureau, H. D. 129
Tiffin, H. 3
Titanic (1997) 118
Tokarczuk, O. 95
Tokugawa 22; shogunate 23; official 23, 25
transitional university 101, 105, 107
translandum 7, 9, 12
Translating Holocaust Literature (2015) 8
Translating Holocaust Lives (2017) 8
translation: act(s) of 81–82, 111–112, 134, 165; and conflict 5, 6, 59; and voicelessness 47; and the uncanny 79–82, 86; as ambiguous activity 59; as both a hegemonic and a counter-hegemonic practice 9 *see also* hegemony, hegemonic; as cultural activity/practice 1, 62, 107–108; as disparation 105; as logistical operation 28; as manipulation 4; as negotiation 3; as practice of relation 21; as process 126; as regenerating force 136; as social practice 29, 33; as survival 60; as zombification 9, 12; burden of 43, 45; computerised 137; cultural 3, 5, 10–11, 51, 75, 79, 87, 147, 157; culturalist representation of 26; devious side of 4; difference between logistics and 33, 35; doomist 119; dystopian 121; ethics of 7; experiences of 70; geopoetic 135–136; industry 108; impossibility of 51–52; (in)humanity of 11, 103; internal dynamic of 96; in the *grey zone* 69–71; kinetics 107–108; literary 7, 33; mistranslation 5–6; modern regime of 19, 21–22, 24–25, 27, 29, 31, 33; natures in 138; necessity of 51; of ecology 137; of natures 135; of the saints' relics 8; of the unconscious into the conscious 81; of the zombie narration into video games 172; of trauma 8; ontological status of 98; popular culture as translational moment 163; relationship between armed conflict and 5; shady corners of 3; slow 12, 126, 136–138; structural proximity between war and 6; unsuccessful 45; violent 157; zombie video games as translational moment 163; zone 82
translational: dynamic 21, 95; ethics 29; moment 13, 163; scene 25; regime 26; theory 30
Translation and Violent Conflict (2010) 6

Translation, History & Culture (1990) 4
Translation under Fascism (2010) 6
translationes (reliquary cult) 8
translator 4–5, 22, 27, 40–41, 49–50, 59, 62, 64, 78, 80–81, 86–87, 108, 113; prisoner-translator 9; lawyer as 44; as a figure of the third 77; eco-translator 135; ideal 78; as ferryman 79; witness and 87; zombie translator 172n1
Translator's Invisibility (1995) 7
transnational: ideological hegemony 26 *see also* hegemony, hegemonic; business enterprise 100
transnationality (Sakai) 33 *see also* national, nationality
trauma 1, 8–10, 47–48, 78, 81, 96; childhood 85–86; post-traumatic 47; re-traumatisation 10, 47, 49; traumatisation 10, 47, 75, 78; transgenerational 96
Trauma Culture: The Politics of Terror and Loss in Media and Literature (2005) 8
Treblinka (1966) 66
Trouillot, M. R. 150
Trusler, Rev. J. 1
Tudor period 95
Turin 60
Tymieniecka, A. T. 130

uncanny 1, 10–12, 75–88, 152, 156–167; in psychoanalysis 10, 75, 79, 81, 83, 85
Unclaimed Experience: Trauma, Narrative and History (2016) 81
unconscious 81, 82
universal metalanguage (Derrida) 21
Universities at War (2014) 100
untranslatability 6, 70, 80; the experience of 6; untranslatable(s) 63, 70, 79, 81; non-translatability 5; non-translation 95
Urry, J. 102

Vanity Fair 22
Venezia, S. 67–68
Venuti, L. 7
Viareggio Prize 60
Vibrant Matter: A Political Ecology of Things (2010) 106
VICE 146
Victor, H. 155
vital materiality (Bennett) 106
Vom Verstummen der Welt (2012) 137

Walden (1854) 129
Waldron, J. 45
Wallace-Wells, D. 113–119, 121

WALL-E (2008) 162
Walser, M. 84
Walser, R. 84
Wanda's List (Israeli documentary film) 86
Ward, P. 119
Watanabe, K. 22
Waterhouse, P. 40–41
Watsuji, Tetsuro 23
Weber, S. 84
Weik von Mossner, A. 11–12
Weisberg, D. S. 119
Wellek, R. 19
Western: art 97; Christendom 98–99; culture 131; hemisphere 149; ontology 11, 95, 97–98; governments 162, 165; nocturnal space 137; thought systems 12, 131
wetware 98
White, K. 134
White Zombie (1932) 155
Wiesel, E. 21, 85
Wilson, E. O. 103
Winters, M. 8
Winters Garten (2015) 139n9
Wirkola, T. 155
Witness Between Languages: The Translation of Holocaust Testimonies in Context (2018) 8
Wolcott, J. 22–23
Wolf, M. 9–10
Women's Orchestra of Auschwitz 68

Writing and Rewriting the Holocaust (1997) 78
Wynne, F. 108–109

Yale Climate Connections 117
Yarbrough, J. 155
Yokota-Murakami, T. 21
Young, J. E. 78

Zimetbaum, M. 68–69
Zombi astral 146
zombie: apocalypse 13, 161–162, 170, 172 *see also* apocalypse; as undead body 146; in the context of economics 149; as figure of translation; as figure of multiplicity 167; Hollywood film 154–155; as means of communication 163; nazi 155–156; as political critique 156; poison 147, 149; 'proof' of 'existence' 147; in French popular culture 151; print culture 151, 153–154; racialised 152–154; Ricque definition 154; video games 161–164
zombification 9; as thematic trope of the narrative 12; materialist-pharmacological argument (Ingles) 147; through poisoning 147
Zombi/ZombiU (2012) 167
Zombies Ate My Neighbours (1993) 170

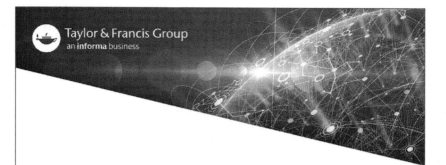